Common Terms to Be Familiar with so You Don't Sound Like a Dummy

Term	What it Means
Articles	The title of the document filed in many states to create a corporation. Also known as the *certificate of incorporation* or *corporate charter*.
Bylaws	The regulations of a corporation that, subject to statutory law and the articles of incorporation, provide the basic rules for the conduct of the corporation's business and affairs.
Certificate of authority	Formal evidence of qualification issued by a state to a foreign corporation.
Certificate of good standing	A certificate issued by a state official as evidence that a corporation is in existence or authorized to transact business in the state. Also known as a *certificate of existence* or *certificate of authorization*.
Domestic corporation	A term applied to a corporation doing business in its state of incorporation.
Foreign corporation	A term applied to a corporation doing business in a state other than its state of incorporation.
Franchise taxes	A tax or fee usually levied annually upon a corporation, limited liability company, or similar business entity for the right to exist or do business in a particular state.
LLC (limited liability company)	An artificial entity created under and governed by the laws of the jurisdiction in which it was formed. Limited liability companies are generally able to provide the limited personal liability of corporations and the pass-through taxation of partnerships or S corporations.
Minutes	A written record of meetings of or actions by the board of directors or shareholders.
Par value	A minimum price of a share below which the share cannot be issued, as designated in the articles of incorporation.
Registered agent	A person or entity designated to receive important tax and legal documents on behalf of the corporation. The registered agent must be located and available at a legal address within the specified jurisdiction at all times. Also known as a *resident agent*.
SubChapter S corporation	A corporation granted a special tax status as specified under the Internal Revenue Code (IRC). Since this type of corporation pays no income tax, all gains and losses of the corporation pass through to the individual shareholders in proportion to their holdings.

Incorporating Your Business For Dummies®

Cheat Sheet

Incorporation Worksheet

State of Incorporation _____

State(s) of Qualification (1)_____

(2)_____

Type of Entity (circle one):

General   Close   Professional

SubChapter S   LLC   Non-stock/non-profit

Desired Corporate Name _____

Alternate Corporate Name _____

Desired Domain Name _____

Alternate Domain Name _____

Number of Shares of Stock _____

Par Value of Shares of Stock _____

Names/Addresses of Directors or Members

(1)_____ (2)_____

_____ _____

_____ _____

_____ _____

Name/Address of Registered Agent

_____

_____

_____

It's Time to Incorporate When . . .

- ✔ You want to protect your company name.
- ✔ You want greater protection of your personal assets.
- ✔ You have been told by your financial advisor that your business is no longer a hobby.
- ✔ You're just starting up.
- ✔ You want to open a company bank account.
- ✔ You have a "great" idea.
- ✔ You hire employees.
- ✔ You want to take tax deductions on medical, life, and disability insurance you provide for yourself and your employees.
- ✔ You plan to go public.
- ✔ You're looking for investors.
- ✔ You want to grow your company.
- ✔ You want to impress your friends and business associates by adding "Inc." to the end of your company name.
- ✔ You're running a home-based business.
- ✔ You want your business to continue operating after your or a partner's death.
- ✔ You want to raise capital through the sale of stock.
- ✔ You plan to open another business.
- ✔ You plan to expand your business to another state.

For Dummies: Bestselling Book Series for Beginners

Incorporating Your Business For Dummies Endorsements

"Before you incorporate, first be sure to read this 'how-to' book. One of the most comprehensive resource tools of its kind, this step-by-step manual provides small business owners and entrepreneurs with state-of-the-art guidance on the 'best practices' to use in forming and maintaining a corporation — from beginning to end."

> — Mark Shultz, Research Institute for Small
> and Emerging Business

"As an entrepreneur, one of the key decisions you will make is how to incorporate your business. This book is an invaluable tool to help you make the proper decision on how to incorporate, and in what form."

> — Larry Kesslin, Let's Talk Business Network, New York

"In the new millennium, the trend toward business ownership is changing the face of the American workplace (or the American economy), with more than 9.1 million women already discovering the benefits of being a business owner. *Incorporating Your Business For Dummies* provides a valuable resource with clear and informative directions for anyone who has caught the entrepreneurial bug.

"*Incorporating Your Business For Dummies* provides a tool kit in a single volume, with step-by-step instructions for everything you'll need to get your business up and running. Whether you are a do-it-all-yourself type of person or someone who prefers to delegate to legal and financial experts, you'll obtain a clear working knowledge of the incorporation process."

> — Melissa Wahl, Executive Director, National Association
> for Female Executives

Incorporating Your Business

FOR

DUMMIES®

by The Company Corporation®

Wiley Publishing, Inc.

Incorporating Your Business For Dummies®

Published by
Wiley Publishing, Inc.
111 River St.
Hoboken, NJ 07030
www.wiley.com

Copyright © 2001 by Wiley Publishing, Inc., Indianapolis, Indiana

Published simultaneously in Canada

For general information on our other products and services or to obtain technical support, please contact our Customer Care Department within the U.S. at 800-762-2974, outside the U.S. at 317-572-3993, or fax 317-572-4002.

Wiley also publishes its books in a variety of electronic formats. Some content that appears in print may not be available in electronic books.

Library of Congress Control Number: 00-110787

ISBN: 0-7645-5341-0

Manufactured in the United States of America

10 9 8

1O/SR/QV/QS/IN

About the Authors

The Company Corporation was founded to provide entrepreneurs and small business owners the opportunity to get the same savings and legal benefits enjoyed by the largest corporations in America at a reasonable and affordable cost. Today, The Company Corporation is the largest direct incorporating company in the United States. The company has more than 20 offices strategically located throughout the United States and files corporations, limited liability companies, and other business entities in all 50 states.

According to Dun & Bradstreet Information Services, over 800,000 new corporations were formed in the United States last year. The Company Corporation and its affiliated companies formed over 125,000 of these, which equates to 1 out of every 7 new corporations established in the United States.

The Company Corporation is a subsidiary of the privately held Corporation Service Company (CSC). CSC is an industry leader serving the major corporate law firms and the corporations they represent with public record document filing, retrieval, and registered agent services.

Since 1899, CSC and its affiliated companies have provided incorporation and business services to the entrepreneurial, legal, and corporate communities. In fact, the founders of the company were instrumental in preparing the corporate laws of the State of Delaware, the world-renowned standard for corporate governance.

The Company Corporation was the first incorporation service company to provide easy access to online incorporations. In fact, 60 percent of business formations conducted with the help of The Company Corporation are completed online at www.incorporate.com. The company is the designated incorporation services provider on many prominent small business sites.

The Company Corporation maintains a staff of highly trained personnel skilled in the incorporation process who assist the hundreds of entrepreneurs who call toll-free (888-811-0111) every day to form their companies. These Incorporation Specialists answer state-specific questions as well as numerous calls from business owners abroad in countries all over the world.

In addition to filing corporation and limited liability company formation documents with each state, The Company Corporation services thousands of clients daily, providing a wide range of corporate services including registered agent services, corporate kits, publications, document retrieval, plus many other small business and corporate services. These services include domain name registration; Web site development tools; mail forwarding in Delaware and Nevada; Tax-on-Time® Service in Delaware; and Compliance Watch ℠ at www.compliancewatch.com. Compliance Watch is an online state-specific corporate compliance service designed to help business owners keep track of required corporate formalities.

Carl R. J. Sniffen: With a degree in journalism from the University of Kansas and a law degree from the University of Missouri–Kansas City, Carl has been actively engaged in the practice of business law, arbitration, and mediation for more than 20 years. His areas of emphasis include working with small business clients on a variety of business-related issues, nonprofit and tax-exempt entities, and community service organizations.

Carl has written or co-authored a number of business-related books, including *A Company Policy and Personnel Workbook, Developing Company Policies, The Essential Corporation Handbook,* and *Starting and Operating a Business in Oregon.*

Carl has also written articles for various publications pertaining to tax and legal implications of special events. He has contributed subject matter expertise to The Company Corporation in the development of its Compliance Watch service.

Carl lives, works, and plays in Grants Pass, Oregon, along with spouse Barb, sons Neil and Brian, and wayward dogs Bert and Bailey. Since 1995, Carl has served as the head cross-country coach and assistant track and field coach at Grants Pass High School.

> THE COMPANY CORPORATION IS AN INCORPORATION SERVICE COMPANY AND DOES NOT OFFER LEGAL OR FINANCIAL ADVICE.

About the Technical Reviewer

Matthew J. O'Toole: Matthew is a partner of Morris, James, Hitchens & Williams LLP in Wilmington, Delaware. Mr. O'Toole concentrates his practice on corporate and business law, focusing particularly on the organization and operation of Delaware corporations, limited liability companies, general partnerships, limited partnerships, and business trusts. He also advises clients on intellectual property matters, including trademark registration applications and licensing issues. Mr. O'Toole recently served on the Technology Update Committee established by the Council of the Corporation Law Section of the Delaware State Bar Association, which comprehensively reviewed Delaware's General Corporation Law to study and recommend changes to that statute to accommodate current technology. He is a regular speaker at seminars and an author of articles regarding Delaware business entities.

Dedication

To all the visionary entrepreneurs and business owners in the world who have the "great ideas" and the determination to bring them to the marketplace.

Authors' Acknowledgments

The Company Corporation: In preparing *Incorporating Your Business For Dummies,* The Company Corporation relied on the advice and assistance of a number of talented individuals whose contributions made this book possible. First and foremost, we'd like to thank Carl R. J. Sniffen for contributing his valuable legal expertise in writing this book. Special recognition is also due to Lori Goldman from The Company Corporation for her ongoing insight and editorial contributions and suggestions, and to Stephen Demarest, Associate General Counsel for The Company Corporation and CSC for his thoughtful and professional review of the manuscript. A special thank-you goes to our Chairman Dan Butler and CEO Bruce Winn for guiding our company into its second 100 years of service to the business community.

In addition, we are indebted to Mark Butler, Senior Acquisitions Editor, who saw the need for a book on this important subject, and to editor Colleen Esterline, whose efforts carried it through to completion.

Our sincere thanks also go to attorney Matthew J. O'Toole of Morris, James, Hitchens & Williams LLP, who served as technical reviewer for the project.

A final acknowledgment goes to the staff of Incorporation Specialists at The Company Corporation who respond to thousands of queries each month from entrepreneurs all over the United States and abroad who need help starting their companies. Equipped with knowledge and confidence, they are dedicated to providing exceptional customer service and exceeding customer expectations.

Carl R. J. Sniffen: Writing is a challenge. Thanks to my wife Barb and sons Neil and Brian for putting up with me for so many years and for their never-ending love, encouragement, and support. Thanks also to my many business clients who never hesitated to tell me, "Explain it in a way that I can understand." I need to thank Ali Rapose who helped me survive a few computer crashes during this project and traveled the Internet to retrieve articles of incorporation from every state. Finally, thanks to the Grants Pass High School cross-country and track athletes who provide a wonderful respite from business law and always manage to keep me on my toes.

Publisher's Acknowledgments

We're proud of this book; please send us your comments through our Dummies online registration form located at www.dummies.com/register/.

Some of the people who helped bring this book to market include the following:

Acquisitions, Editorial, and Media Development

Project Editor: Colleen Williams Esterline

Acquisitions Editor: Jonathan Malsyiak

Acquisitions Coordinator: Lauren Cundiff

Technical Editor: Matthew J. O'Toole of Morris, James, Hitchens & Williams LLP

Senior Permissions Editor: Carmen Krikorian

Editorial Administrator: Michelle Hacker

Media Development Manager: Laura Carpenter

Editorial Assistant: Carol Strickland

Cover Photos: © 1998 Ken Reid / FPG International LLC

Composition

Project Coordinator: Nancee Reeves

Layout and Graphics: Amy Adrian, Joe Bucki, Jackie Nicholas, Jacque Schneider, Julie Trippetti, Jeremey Unger

Proofreaders: David Faust, Andy Hollandbeck, Nancy Price, York Production Services, Inc.

Indexer: York Production Services, Inc.

Publishing and Editorial for Consumer Dummies

Diane Graves Steele, Vice President and Publisher, Consumer Dummies

Joyce Pepple, Acquisitions Director, Consumer Dummies

Kristin A. Cocks, Product Development Director, Consumer Dummies

Michael Spring, Vice President and Publisher, Travel

Brice Gosnell, Associate Publisher, Travel

Suzanne Jannetta, Editorial Director, Travel

Publishing for Technology Dummies

Andy Cummings, Vice President and Publisher, Dummies Technology/General User

Composition Services

Gerry Fahey, Vice President of Production Services

Debbie Stailey, Director of Composition Services

Contents at a Glance

Cartoons at a Glance

By Rich Tennant

page 97

page 199

page 9

page 49

page 169

Cartoon Information:
Fax: 978-546-7747
E-Mail: richtennant@the5thwave.com
World Wide Web: www.the5thwave.com

Table of Contents

Introduction

● ●

*I*ncorporating Your Business For Dummies is for anyone planning to start a business, anyone already in a start-up, or anyone who has been operating a successful business for some time.

For incorporation, the benefits are many, and here are just a few:

- Enhanced protection of your personal assets
- The possibility of tax breaks that may mean the difference between success and failure of a small business
- The image of your business with "Incorporated" in your name, creating a sense of permanence

But incorporation may not be for everyone. We recommend you discuss the pros and cons with your legal and financial advisors.

What You Shouldn't Expect

Imagine standing on top of Oregon's Mount Thielsen. At more than 9,000 feet in elevation, you can see for miles and miles. You observe all of the surrounding peaks. You can also see well enough to know that there are hundreds of valleys, ravines, and ridges that lie below the peaks. While you can make out the peaks in some detail, it's harder to see what's in the valleys. In fact, the only way to find out for sure would be to climb down from the mountain and walk through and explore the valleys.

In this book, time and space only allow us to observe the peaks of corporate law. We are limited in our ability to cover the depths. For example, we touch upon securities law, but make no attempt to take you through the complex web of state and federal laws and regulations.

Many other laws and regulations have an impact on corporations and their activities. These include laws and regulations in the areas of criminal law, tax law, environmental law, employee benefits and employment law, international law, and more.

The information contained in this book is general. There is no way to tailor it to meet all of your personal and business needs and interests. We provide basic information — don't hesitate to use your professional team to provide you with information specific to your situation. The information contained in this book isn't intended to provide you with legal advice. Only your lawyer can do that.

Each state has its own corporation law. You would be well served to familiarize yourself generally with the corporation law of your state. Many states now publish their corporation laws on the Internet. Each state also has a court system that has been employed to interpret that state's corporation law. Even if two states have the same statute, it's possible that courts in each state have interpreted those laws differently.

Each state has its own laws regarding professional corporations, limited liability companies, limited liability partnerships, limited partnerships, general partnerships, and a variety of other available entities. Other than a few references to most of these entities, this book will not address these business entities in any detail. You also won't find any discussion about non-profit corporations, another creation of state law, or tax-exempt entities.

About This Book

This book will serve as a valuable resource. Refer to it often as you trek the hills and valleys of the incorporation trail. With *Incorporating Your Business For Dummies* you'll:

- ✔ **Get value.** You will learn what you need to know to form a corporation and keep it in compliance. Expect to gain a good understanding of the essential basics without the fluff or legal mumbo jumbo.

- ✔ **Save time.** This book gets to the point. It is organized so that you can go directly to where you think you need to go. Where sections overlap, you will be directed to earlier or later chapters to fill in the missing information. You'll find sample forms to help you as you go forward. Use as much as you like; skip as much as you like.

- ✔ **Save money.** Whether you do it yourself or use a service company or an attorney, you'll be better informed about the choices available to you. If you hire out part of the work, you'll know what questions to ask.

- ✔ **Have fun.** Creating a new corporation can be a challenge, but it's not brain surgery. Don't take it too seriously, and you'll do fine. We've included enough anecdotes, stories, and quotes to help lighten the journey.

What You're Not to Read

Whenever you see the Technical Stuff icon, the information that follows is for your convenience. It's not essential for your understanding of the subject at hand. In fact, you may skip it if you like. You'll still get the main ideas presented in the book with a little less detail. Can you incorporate yourself and understand what you need to do to keep your corporation in good standing without the Technical Stuff material? Yes!

Foolish Assumptions

At the outset, we make certain assumptions about you and the things you find important. How dare we? Let us count the ways:

- You aren't a lawyer. If you are, where were you in law school? As you'll see, you may want a lawyer or other professional from time to time to assist you with such things as securities law, mergers or acquisitions, and maintaining or defending against lawsuits.

- Simplicity is a virtue. The KISS (keep it simple, stupid) principle sits right below the Golden Rule (do unto others as you would have them do unto you). Corporations can be simple and straightforward or they can be complex. We'll focus on simpler models with guidance and direction for those who seek a more complex structure.

- You have a life. Your priorities include family and your business. Learning everything there is to know about corporations may not be high on your list. Running a business is an exhausting, time-consuming task. Focus on it. After all, there are only so many hours in a day (24, if you did not already know).

- You are comfortable with a certain amount of risk in your life. Consider the risk spectrum, which is set forth below. It looks like this:

No Risk_____High Risk

Very few folks are at the No Risk level. You can't possibly contemplate beginning a family or your own business without being somewhere to the right on this spectrum.

Other folks like to throw caution to the wind in everything that they do. Evel Knievel comes to mind. Put them on the High Risk side of the spectrum. Most people, however, fall somewhere in the middle. For these individuals, measured risks are acceptable. They make decisions after they carefully consider the potential plusses and minuses of a particular action. This book will help you make an informed, risk-reducing decision about the pros and cons of incorporation and whether it's right for you. It's important to know where you fall on this spectrum, recognizing that you may find yourself at different places depending upon the activity involved.

How This Book Is Organized

Effort has been made to provide useful, straightforward information in a logical order. Like most subjects, corporations can't be put into isolated boxes. There is much overlap. You will be referred from time to time to earlier or later chapters to help fill in important information. Feel free to go directly to chapters that are most important to you. We won't mind.

Part 1: Is a Corporation Really for Me?

It would be presumptuous of us to presume that a corporation is for everyone. In this part, we provide a brief history of corporations and introduce you to the key benefits of incorporation. We also give you an introduction to corporate basics: corporate statutes, articles of incorporation, and bylaws. You'll meet the key players: shareholders, the board of directors, and officers. You'll discover the differences between a C corporation and an S corporation, and decide which one is right for you.

You'll meet other forms of business entities, one of which may be better suited to you than a corporation. We also highlight the key differences between corporations and other business entities.

If you're going to incorporate, you need to know where. In this part, you'll discover what you need to know about picking your state of incorporation. What factors should be considered in choosing your place of business? What impact do modern corporation laws have on this decision? What does it mean to "do business," especially in today's economy? We also give you some information about the leading state for incorporating: Delaware.

Finally, this part leaves you with a checklist that identifies key components to the incorporation process and can serve as your personal springboard into other chapters of interest.

Part II: How Do I Incorporate?

Once you decide that a corporation is for you, you need to know what happens next. In this part, we explore real nuts and bolts issues — the information you'll need to know to form your corporation.

Need help? Relief is on the way. Here's where you can learn who can help you. Don't try to do it all — do what you can, and let the professionals do the rest. You'll also discover a valuable and often free assistant in the office of your state's secretary of state. You may never have realized what a friend you have in government.

In Chapter 7 we cover articles of incorporation. You'll discover what information they must contain, what potential pitfalls exist, and when it's good to be wordy.

Let's not forget the bylaws. Bylaws set forth the process and procedure by which a corporation regulates the relationships among its board of directors, officers, and shareholders. In Chapter 8 you'll see what information must be included in bylaws.

This part will also help you capitalize your corporation and explain why it is important. It's good to know how to get money in and out of a corporation. Learn about concepts of debt, equity, and corporate stock.

What if your corporation does business in more than one state? In this part, you'll learn the step-by-step approach to qualify your business in those states where you do business and the ramifications for failing to qualify.

Part III: I've Incorporated My Business, Now What?

You can't identify the players without numbers on their jerseys. The same could be true of corporations. In this part, we introduce you to a number of important concepts needed to keep your corporation running smoothly. One of those concepts relates to corporate identification numbers. What are they? How do you obtain them?

What is an S corporation? Should your corporation elect to become an S corporation? We discuss what you need to know about making this election in a timely and effective way.

Another integral component is a discussion of the roles, responsibilities, and duties of corporate directors, shareholders, and officers. Although a corporation has a separate legal existence, the corporation is entirely dependent upon its directors, officers, shareholders, and others to act in its behalf. In this part, we answer these questions for you. You will also be introduced to basic agency concepts to help you understand your role when acting on behalf of your corporation.

You'll learn the ins and outs of conducting board and shareholder meetings, indemnifying officers and directors, and obtaining directors' and officers' insurance to protect your corporation.

Once you're up and running, you need to know how to get money out of the corporation and what types of documentation you will need in order to be able to move money in and out of the corporation. This section should be valuable for everyone.

Part IV: Compliance Issues — The Paper Trail Continues

While Parts II and III get you up and running, there's much more you need to know if you want to continue to conduct business as a corporation.

You may have heard of corporate compliance and corporate formalities. This section highlights important areas of compliance and formality. Adherence to these concepts goes a long way to ensure that you retain the limited liability benefit of incorporating. Failing to adhere — well, that's just not a good idea.

Most states require that corporations file annual reports. Some also require documents referred to as franchise tax reports. This part tells you where you can get these forms and tells you what types of information should be included.

You'll discover in this section what types of corporate records you must keep and for what purposes. In some instances, shareholders have a right to inspect these records. You'll discover what inspection rights exist and what types of documents they cover.

How do you document corporate activity? From your written minutes of corporate meetings to business cards and letterhead, understand why it's important for you to document your corporate activities and how you do it.

Finally, you'll read about the death of a corporation. Technically, a corporation dissolves, but any way you cut it, it's the end of the road. Learn about corporate dissolution and bankruptcy, both voluntary and involuntary.

Part V: The Part of Tens

In this part, you'll receive valuable information that will serve you well whether you incorporate or not. The information presented will help you incorporate, maintain, and sustain your corporation for years to come.

How do you select the professionals who can best meet your needs and expectations? What questions should you ask? What professionals will you need? What things can you do without professional help? Chapter 23 offers ten ways to find and keep a quality professional team.

What things should my corporation never do? Some matters are pretty obvious, and good common sense should be your guide. Other areas aren't as clear. Chapter 24 offers ten tips to set you off on the right track.

Finally, we offer you a bonus — ten common-sense principles to help you in your business and personal life. Follow these principles, and you'll be a happier, healthier person. Your corporation will be in good shape as well.

Icons Used in This Book

This book uses a number of little pictures, called icons, to note special information. This is what each of the icons means:

We use the Tip icon to show solid and practical advice.

If you see this icon, heed its warning. Ignoring it can get you into trouble.

This icon flags information that's nice to know, but not necessary to know, in your understanding of incorporation.

When we run across something really important you should put to memory, we offer the Remember icon.

Keep your eyes peeled for compliance issues when you see this icon.

Where to Go from Here

Whew! It's hard to catch your breath. There's so much information. Don't worry. We take our time in presenting this information to you in a logical and orderly fashion. Hopefully, you'll find answers to your questions where you would expect to find them. If you find yourself scratching your head for more than a few minutes, try some "dandruff-be-gone" shampoo. No, seriously, head back to the table of contents or index and see if another chapter might provide the answer you need.

Incorporating your business may have legal ramifications. Attorney Carl R.J. Sniffen wrote much of the information contained here. But again, don't be your own lawyer. Review your decisions with your professional team. You'll be glad you did it now versus later.

It's time to move forward. Good luck!

Part I
Is a Corporation Really for Me?

The 5th Wave   By Rich Tennant

"It's an interesting idea, Mr. Gizzard, but there's just no way you can incorporate your marriage in order to afford you limited liability for forgotton birthdays, anniversaries and the like."

In this part . . .

More entrepreneurs and business owners than ever before are researching their options and choosing to structure their companies as corporations or the relatively newer limited liability companies. How do you decide whether a corporation is for you? In this part, we help you answer this important question. You learn the benefits of incorporation so that you are able to compare corporations to other forms of business entities. This part gets you started on the right path with a comprehensive pre-incorporation checklist.

Chapter 1

What's a Corporation?

For most, a corporation is simply a business entity. But what does that tell us? How do you know whether a corporation makes sense for you if you don't understand what a corporation is? In this chapter, you'll gain a greater understanding of what a corporation is, and why that is important for you. Let's get started.

Defining Corporations

Before you get into the thick of this incorporation business, you probably want to know what a corporation is and what makes it special? This section breaks down a few of the defining characteristics of corporations.

The corporation as an individual

A corporation is a separate legal entity that is distinct from its creators. It's not your corporation, and it has its own attributes and qualities, such as perpetual existence and the ability to do things in its own name. Of course, a corporation can't do anything unless people like you (the board and officers) do those things for it. Nonetheless, such individuals are acting on behalf of the corporation and not on behalf of themselves. When you create a corporation, you have created a legal person — it's not an extension of its individual officers, directors, or shareholders.

Corporations are creatures of statute, requiring a corporation law in each state in order to exist at all. Fortunately, all states have corporation statutes.

State of incorporation

Where do you live? You have a legal residence — one that determines where you vote, obtain a driver's license, and pay taxes. This is true even if you spend parts of a year in some other state. The same is true for corporations. Even though your corporation may do business in a number of states, it has only one home. A corporation is considered to be a *domestic corporation* of that state where it incorporates. If it qualifies to do business in other states (a concept we consider in Chapter 10), it's a *foreign corporation* in those other states.

Confused? Assume you incorporate your business in Delaware. Delaware becomes the state of incorporation. For purposes of Delaware law, you are a domestic corporation. What if your Delaware corporation does business in Oregon? It must comply with Oregon law and qualify to do business there as well, so your corporation is considered a domestic corporation in Delaware and a foreign corporation in Oregon.

We discuss these topics in greater detail in Chapters 3 and 10. But for now, understand that you incorporate in one state (domestic corporation) and qualify to do business in other states (foreign corporation).

Limited liability

You may have many reasons why you would want to incorporate your business, perhaps none more important than *limited liability*. With limited liability, the personal assets of corporate shareholders are protected from the claims of corporate creditors. A shareholder's liability exposure is limited to the capital the shareholder has invested in the corporation, usually the amount the shareholder has paid for his stock. So, for example, you may own personal assets worth more than one million dollars, but, in general, if your total investment in ABC, Corporation is the $200 you paid for your stock, $200 is the total extent of your liability exposure to ABC, Corporation creditors.

Here's some more food for thought. Let's say you are now in business as a sole proprietor. You like the informality, low cost, and simplicity. Generally, you have no state filing fees, no record-keeping requirements, and no administrative fees. One of the few things you are responsible for is filing a Schedule C with your personal tax return. But, you have no protection from personal liability because you and your business are the same entity. If a supplier sues your business, it applies to you personally, as well. You can buy insurance, but it doesn't cover every situation.

When you opt for informality, you may have to pay the piper in the future. Suppose you didn't listen to your attorney who recommended you incorporate your antique and collectible business because in her words, "it isn't a hobby anymore." Your business grew exponentially and you now have staff helping you canvass every yard sale in a tri-state region for treasure masquerading as junk. What if one of your employees gets into a horrible accident during one of these junkets? You may be facing many months of litigation, further aggravated by tremendous stress because you could possibly lose your house, boat, and lifetime savings. If you had incorporated your business, you would have greatly reduced the risk of losing your hard-won personal assets. (We discuss limited liability further in Chapter 2.)

In the 1980s and 1990s, new forms of doing business emerged, all focused on extending limited liability protection to a new type of business entity. Limited liability companies and limited liability partnerships are perhaps the best known from this period. Suddenly, business enterprises existed that could provide the limited liability benefit of corporations and the pass-through taxation of partnerships. Thus the choice of business entity became more difficult, as you'll see in Chapter 2.

The Structure of Corporations

Corporations are creatures of statute. Corporate existence depends upon state corporation laws; laws that impose requirements on how corporations are organized and maintained. In effect, corporation laws provide the framework for the corporate structure described in the following sections.

A simple model, a more complex model

While some might say, "The more the merrier," with corporations and other business entities, a more fitting phrase might be, "The less the merrier." Here's a simple corporate model: A single individual serves as sole shareholder and sole director, and holds all of the corporate offices. As you will learn, this is a pretty straightforward model without a great deal of complexity. Contrast this model with an example from the opposite side of the spectrum: Imagine a publicly traded corporation with millions of shareholders, offices throughout the world, a 20-person board of directors, and separate corporate officers. As you can see, a continuum of complexity exists. A good starting question is, "How complex do you want your corporate structure to be?" but a better question may be, "How much complexity can you handle?"

Do you anticipate a complex corporate model? Consider forming your professional team early and seeking advice from them. You may require legal and financial help from the beginning.

Fortunately for most small businesses, the more common corporate model tends to be less complex rather than more. A single individual often owns and controls the corporation. Still other corporations may be owned and controlled by fewer than a dozen individuals. A common model would look something like this: Joe, Jane, and John go into business together. After reading this book, they decide to incorporate. Among the decisions made, each will own one third of the corporation's shares of stock; Jane will serve as president, Joe as vice president, and John will serve as secretary/treasurer. Each will serve as one of three directors for the corporation. While more complex than the single shareholder model, this common pattern is certainly manageable and within the grasp of most business owners.

The players

The corporate structure has three key "teams" of players. Some players may spend most of their time on the field, playing one position. Others may ride the bench (often shareholders) and cheer on the team. Still others may play many positions, including captain. Here's a brief introduction:

- **Shareholders:** Each corporation typically issues shares of stock that represent ownership interests in the corporation. Shareholders own the stock, so they own the corporation. As you'll see in Chapter 9, different types of stock exist, and different rights may be associated with the different types.

- **Board of directors:** The shareholders elect the corporate board to govern the activities of the corporation by setting policy, appointing officers, and authorizing or approving significant corporate acts.

- **Officers:** Corporate officers, appointed by the corporate board, conduct the day-to-day business activities of the corporation in accordance with the board's directions.

Puzzle Pieces for Incorporation: Statutes, Articles, and Bylaws

Corporation statutes and regulations are just one piece of the legal and regulatory puzzle. These laws regulate such things as how corporations are formed, dissolved, merged, or reorganized. They regulate the role and duties of officers and directors, and the rights and responsibilities of shareholders. Because corporations are separate legal entities, they are also subject to other state and federal laws and regulations including criminal, tax, environmental, occupational safety, and other laws.

Corporation statutes

A corporation owes its entire existence, authority, and power to statutes passed by various state legislatures. If the statute doesn't permit it, the corporation can't do it. If the articles of incorporation or bylaws are inconsistent with the statute, the statute prevails over the articles and bylaws.

Each state, plus the District of Columbia and Puerto Rico, has its own set of corporation codes, which makes 52 sets of statutes. The good news is that despite the existence of 52 separate sets of statutes, many of the codes overlap tremendously from state to state. While you always need to check the law in your state of incorporation, it's a good bet that most of the corporate principles we describe in this book will apply to corporations formed in your state.

The Revised Model Business Corporation Act

One important reason for the overlap is the Revised Model Business Corporation Act (RMBCA). The RMBCA is a product of the Corporation, Banking, and Business Law Section of the American Bar Association (no, not the tavern owners, the lawyers). Early corporation laws were cumbersome. They varied widely from state to state. Businesses seeking to engage in business in more than one state were forced to wade through a complex and burdensome maze of corporate laws and regulations, so the American Bar Association created the RMBCA to make things more uniform.

Adopted by nearly half of the states, the RMBCA has, to a large extent, helped organize corporate statutes in the United States. It addresses subjects commonly found in all state corporation laws and reflects the ongoing trend to simplify and streamline corporation laws. Throughout this book, we use the provisions of the RMBCA as a guide to help you understand the how's and why's of incorporation.

Close corporation statutes

Close corporation statutes are specialized laws that exist in a number of states. In fact, one part of the RMBCA is its Close Corporation Supplement.

You may be thinking to yourself "What in the world is a close corporation?" Generally, close corporations are corporations with 50 or fewer shareholders that have elected to be governed by the close corporation provisions of state law. To elect close corporation status, your state must have a corporation law that permits it, and your articles of incorporation must state that the corporation is subject to the close corporation statute.

Why would you want to be a close corporation? Shareholders can eliminate the board of directors or limit board powers. They can also restrict the ability of shareholders to transfer shares to outsiders without prior consent and approval of the corporation and its remaining shareholders.

Unless otherwise provided . . .

Talk about an open invitation — many of the provisions found in modern corporation statutes begin with this phrase, "unless otherwise provided . . ." Effectively, the statute says, "You must do it this way, unless otherwise provided in your articles of incorporation or bylaws to do it some other way."

Many people fail to realize the flexibility that corporations afford. It's this "unless otherwise provided" language that creates this flexibility. Not every provision of the corporation statutes includes this permissive language, so don't get carried away.

A good business lawyer or accountant will ask you, "What do you want to do?" He will recognize the myriad possibilities that are available in structuring your corporation. He will also gain an understanding of your ability to manage various levels of complexity. Don't let someone tell you, "You must do it this way."

Corporations can be flexible vehicles within which to conduct business. Expect a range of choices and possibilities, and select the choices that best meet your needs.

It's important to distinguish a close corporation from a closely held corporation, two similar sounding, but different meaning terms. A close corporation is a corporation that affirmatively elects to be treated as a close corporation, usually to limit the ability of shareholders to transfer their shares to outsiders. A closely held corporation is a corporation where the shares of the corporation's stock aren't publicly traded on a national stock exchange. It's possible for a corporation to be a close corporation and closely held. It's equally possible for a corporation to be closely held and not a close corporation.

Articles of incorporation

Another piece of the puzzle is the articles. Articles of incorporation tell the world about the key elements of the corporation. A corporation springs into existence when you file the articles of incorporation on behalf of the corporation with the local secretary of state or other government office. You then have to wait to see if the office approves your articles before you become a full-fledged member of the corporation gang.

Years ago, preparing articles could be a complex process. Today, thanks to modern corporate statutes, the process is simple and straightforward. In fact, nearly every state will provide you with copies of the articles you need to file to incorporate your business, and state laws tell you what you have to include in the articles (see Chapter 7). Common subjects addressed in articles of incorporation include:

- ✔ The name of the corporation
- ✔ The principle office address
- ✔ The registered agent's name and address
- ✔ The number of authorized shares of stock and their par value
- ✔ The name and mailing address of the incorporator
- ✔ The purpose of the corporation

In the past, creating and maintaining a corporation in good standing had long been a process of rigid adherence to corporate formalities and compliance. Early corporations could only be formed for certain designated purposes. Officers, directors, and incorporators had to meet certain qualifications. The corporations themselves had a limited period of existence. Corporate powers had to be set forth in the articles of incorporation. If a particular power wasn't set forth, it could be argued that the corporation lacked the power to perform that act. If you stated in your powers clause that a corporation had the power to sell, but not the power to buy, a corporation might be unable to purchase a related line of business without going through a formal process to amend its articles of incorporation. Articles of incorporation often required detailed information including the names and addresses of corporate officers. Corporate documents could be rendered ineffective merely because they failed to contain an impression from a corporate seal. Plainly, form was elevated over substance.

Bylaws

The third piece of the puzzle is bylaws. Corporate bylaws provide rules and procedures that the corporation, its officers, directors, and shareholders must follow. These are the marching orders. Common subject matters include:

- ✔ Shareholder and director meeting requirements
- ✔ Quorum issues
- ✔ Supermajority voting requirements
- ✔ Indemnification provisions for officers and directors

Confused by these terms? Don't be. Chapter 8 will clear up any questions you might have.

The Past Paves the Way for the Present

Why do we even have corporation laws? Bet you have been dying to ask this. Up until the early 1800s, the government was very leery about business formations. So much so that the only way to form a corporation back then was to convince the legislature to pass a bill granting your business a corporate charter. Imagine Bill Gates putting up with that!

New York, in 1811, was the first state to pass a general corporation code. This code was very restrictive, setting limits on the types of business that could incorporate, the duration of a corporation, and the amount of capital that could be raised or retained by a corporation. The public didn't warmly embrace the concept of a collective person for a business operation.

In 1896, New Jersey adopted what was considered at the time to be a "permissive" corporation code. New Jersey's law granted broad powers to corporations, directors, and officers, and afforded protection against liability for actions by corporate officers and directors. In 1913, Delaware expanded on this permissive code in an effort to attract incorporation business and the tax revenues and fees such business could attract to the state. While other states have copied Delaware's model, few have been as aggressive in creating a pro-business and pro-corporation climate. We talk more about Delaware in Chapter 3.

Eventually, government leaders recognized the need to promote business growth and innovation. Capital was required to fuel the growing economy. The ability to attract capital by selling shares and limiting the personal liability of shareholders attracted business owners and fueled the efforts of legislators to create corporate laws.

In more recent history, states began to recognize the value of cultivating a positive, business-friendly climate. This extends to the adoption of corporate laws that simplify the process of incorporating; permit corporate indemnification of officers and directors; and protect minority shareholder interests through such things as appraisal and repurchase rights. Delaware led the way by being among the first states to produce a comprehensive, business-friendly corporation statute. Other states were often slow to follow. Eventually, most states understood the message. Congress even helped by creating special incentives for small business corporations including pass-through, partnership-like taxation, and ordinary loss deduction for corporate shares for qualifying small business corporations. (See Chapter 2 for more about these special incentives.)

In addition, many states have adopted as their corporation statute all or parts of a uniform law known as *The Revised Model Business Corporation Act (RMBCA)*. We presented a fuller introduction to the RMBCA earlier in this chapter and refer to the RMBCA throughout this book. This law revolutionized the way states viewed corporations.

The last 50 years have seen too many changes occur to describe them all here, but among the more significant are:

- ✔ The presumption that a corporation has perpetual existence unless its articles of incorporation provide otherwise

- ✔ Statutes that permit corporations to engage in any lawful activity, eliminating the need for detailed descriptions of corporate powers and purposes

- ✔ The ability of corporate directors and shareholders to conduct meetings using telephone conference calls (and perhaps, in the future, e-mail) or to not conduct in person meetings at all if all board members or shareholders consent

- ✔ The ability of a corporation to indemnify its officers and directors from liability for many acts

- ✔ The recognition that a corporation could consist of a single shareholder, officer, and director with the same individual occupying all of these roles

- ✔ The introduction of shareholder appraisal rights permitting dissatisfied shareholders to compel the corporation to purchase their shares in the event of a corporate merger or similar transaction

- ✔ The widespread addition of expanded securities law exemptions that made it easier for corporations to raise money through the sale of stock and securities without the complexity and expense of the securities registration process

- ✔ The adoption of close corporation statutes by a number of states that allow shareholders of qualifying corporations to act in place of the board of directors, effectively eliminating the board, and to restrict the ability of shareholders to transfer shares to outsiders without prior consent and approval of the corporation and remaining shareholders

In the 1980s and 1990s, significant new forms of doing business emerged. Limited liability companies and limited liability partnerships are perhaps the best known from this period. Suddenly, business enterprises existed that could provide the limited liability benefit of corporations and the pass-through taxation of partnerships. Flexibility became a key component to legislative changes during this period.

Looking to the Future of Corporations

As business needs and business technology change, the past 20 years suggest that state corporation laws and federal income tax laws will be modified to embrace these changes. This doesn't mean that corporate formality and compliance are no longer important. Enhanced flexibility suggests that attention to detail is still important. It remains as important as ever that corporations comply with state corporation laws, articles of incorporation, and bylaws. You must still file annual reports and tax returns in a timely fashion. You still must document the activities of corporate boards and shareholders. You must segregate personal and business assets. And corporations must continue to hold themselves out to customers, suppliers, and the public at large as distinct legal entities, not just extensions of their individual owners. Failure to do these things can result in personal liability, dissolution of the corporation, or some other unintended consequence.

Corporations have evolved from a highly regulated and restricted form of business entity to extremely flexible vehicles in which to conduct business. Remnants of this more restrictive past do continue to exist, sometimes in corporate statutes and sometimes through the actions of long-time corporate lawyers who remain wedded to the older, more restrictive models of corporate law. A consequence of this evolution is that it's now easier for anyone to incorporate his or her business quickly and relatively easily without incurring the legal and accounting fees that you might have incurred in the past. An entire do-it-yourself industry has been spawned to do some or all of the incorporating and compliance work for you.

Over time, public resistance to corporations as separate legal entities has waned. Initial concerns about things such as size, concentrations of capital and power, perpetual duration, and the separation of ownership (shareholders) from management (directors and officers) proved unfounded. Legislative restrictions in such areas as securities laws, antitrust laws, employee rights, and other areas have also added protections and reduced public concerns. As a result, the clear trend among corporation codes has been to simplify and streamline requirements and restrictions.

The world's earliest corporations

The earliest corporations were not business corporations as we know them today. Rather, the earliest corporations were municipal corporations in England and Rome. The first business corporations may have been the large English trading companies that existed in the late 1500s and 1600s.

In the United States, the earliest corporations could be formed solely by legislative act. These corporations were formed in the late 1700s and early 1800s. (Imagine having to rely on your state legislator to champion a bill through the legislative process to allow you to conduct business as a corporation! In today's political climate, that process could take years if it were ever completed at all.) Most of these early corporations involved banks, insurance companies, and bridge and road builders.

Chapter 2

Choosing an Entity That Works for Your Business

In This Chapter

▶ Understanding why businesses incorporate

▶ Choosing between corporations and other forms of business entity

▶ Converting to a corporation

*H*ave you already made up your mind about incorporating your business? Congratulations, you've taken your first big step. You may want to skip to Chapter 3. If you're still uncertain, this chapter will describe some advantages and disadvantages to incorporating. You'll also learn about other common forms of business entities, helping you make an informed choice about what type of entity makes the most sense for your business.

Over the last few years, state legislatures and the U.S. Treasury Department, acting through its Internal Revenue Service (IRS), have worked hard to level the playing field in choosing business entities. Many formalistic requirements and technical rules regarding business entity selection have been eliminated. With the removal of these requirements and rules, it's easier than ever to choose the business entity that works best for you.

Reaping the Benefits of Incorporation

Plainly, corporations aren't for everyone. You need to know the good and the bad to make an informed choice. In following sections, we describe common benefits of incorporation. You may be interested in some more than others. We also describe some of the disadvantages of incorporation.

Protecting yourself with limited liability

"I'll take *Reasons for Business Incorporation* for $100, Alex." And the *Jeopardy* board lights up its answer: limited liability. That's one you know the answer to! You hit your button just in time to beat out Nancy the librarian from Kenosha, Wisconsin. "What is the number-one reason for incorporating?" That's right!

A fundamental reason for the existence of corporations is a recognized desire to shield business investors from personal liability. Would you invest money in a business if you knew that you would be exposing yourself to personal liability for the corporation's actions? State legislators knew early on that capital required to fund new industries, machines, and products would be slow in coming without some measure of protection for shareholders.

Limited liability protects shareholders from claims by others for corporate acts. Just like people, corporations make mistakes, get involved in accidents, and otherwise generate claims against the corporation. You can often read about corporate misdeeds in the newspaper. Consider the manufacturer who produces and distributes a defective product that injures people. Automobile, chemical, pharmaceutical, and tobacco industries are frequently involved in product liability claims. Without question, the corporation is liable for its actions. Occasionally, officers and directors share in this personal liability, for example, if they perform illegal activities. Shareholders, on the other hand, are generally shielded from personal liability due to the concept of limited liability. Incorporation can act as an extra layer of protection beyond insurance.

People who invest in large, publicly traded corporations won't be subject to personal liability, as shareholders, for corporate actions. Shareholders of closely held corporations with a small number of shareholders can also enjoy limited liability if the corporation is properly formed and performs its ongoing compliance functions, which we describe in Parts III and IV. You'll also want to check out Chapter 24 to minimize your chances of being personally liable for corporate actions.

Tax brackets

Several years ago, corporate income was taxed at a rate that was significantly lower than the income tax rate assessed against individuals. At that time, many individuals formed corporations as a tax-savings device, allowing dollars to accumulate in the corporation and be taxed at the corporation level, producing a lower tax. When those corporate dollars were distributed to shareholders, they would be subject to tax once again at the shareholder level. Because of this, wealthier taxpayers would let dollars accumulate in the corporation, hoping to withdraw them at a time when their individual tax rates were less. Tax rates have since been changed, and limits have been imposed on corporations to restrict the corporation's ability to accumulate income without a legitimate business purpose.

Today, the corporate tax rate generally ranges from 15 to 38 percent of the corporation's taxable income. This compares to an individual tax rate that ranges from 15 percent to 39.6 percent of taxable income.

S corporations, which we discuss in the next section, also change this equation. S corporations are a creature of tax law. They are *pass-through* entities, which means that they have no corporate income tax. Corporate income, credits, deductions, and the like pass through to the corporate shareholders in proportion to their share ownership. So, for example, assume that you own 50 percent of all the issued and outstanding stock of Best Bicycles, Inc., an S corporation. If the corporation has taxable income of $1,000, you would have to report one half of that income (you own 50 percent of the shares) or $500 on your tax return — that's pass-through taxation. The most common pass-through tax entity is a partnership.

Here's how pass-through taxation works: Shareholders report on their individual tax returns items of corporate income, loss, deduction, or credit. When it comes to items of income, the shareholders are deemed to have received items of income whether the income is actually distributed to the shareholder or member. Assume, for example, that you own 50 percent of all the issued and outstanding stock of Best Bicycles, Inc. And also assume that Best Bicycles has an income of $10,000 after all credits, losses, and other deductions have been applied. You'll be deemed to have income of $5,000, which you will have to pay tax on whether or not this money is actually distributed to you. The corporation may want to keep your $5,000 rather than distribute it to you for a number of reasons. Often it's to preserve working capital, pay debts, accumulate funds to purchase a new piece of equipment, and so on.

Still confused? Let's simplify the pass-through concept. All businesses generate revenue, often the result of sales of business products or services. Businesses also incur expenses. Some expenses are directly related to the production of revenue. For example, if your corporation sells hammers, you generate revenue each time you sell a hammer. You also incur expenses when you purchase or make the hammers that you sell.

Accounting and tax principles and laws determine which expenses can be deducted from your total revenue. Generally, business expenses incurred in the ordinary course of your business can be deducted. When you deduct these expenses from revenue, you're left with a net income figure. For some businesses, especially new start-up businesses, expenses may exceed income, resulting in a net loss rather than net income. Whether you have a positive income figure or a loss, these numbers generally pass through to the shareholders of an S corporation in proportion to the shareholder's ownership interest in the corporation. The shareholders, not the corporation, pay the tax or report the loss.

Unfortunately, accounting and tax principles and laws are more complex, and many more variables such as depreciation, amortization, special credits, and others may come into play. Work with your accountant to help these concepts make sense to you.

S corporations

S corporation election is a popular choice for many small businesses when they form a corporation. In fact, many businesses that choose to incorporate decide that S corporation status is the best choice.

S corporations (sometimes referred to as SubChapter S corporations) are a tax concept. You create your corporation under state law. At this level, a corporation is a corporation is a corporation. Federal income tax laws permit you to make an election to become an S corporation. Corporations that choose not to make this election are described for tax purposes as C corporations. Here's the difference:

- ✔ C corporations must file tax returns and pay tax on corporate taxable income. Items of loss, gain, and credit are all taken into account at the corporate level.

- ✔ S corporations have no corporate income tax return. Items of income, gain, loss, credit, or deduction are taken into account or passed through at the shareholder level in proportion to a shareholder's ownership interest.

Not just any ol' corporation can become an S corporation. Technical rules must be met in order to qualify. These include:

- ✔ The corporation is formed in the United States.
- ✔ The corporation can have no more than 75 shareholders.
- ✔ All shareholders are individuals (with certain exceptions for trusts or estates).
- ✔ None of the shareholders can be non-resident aliens.
- ✔ The corporation issues only one class of stock (distinctions involving voting rights may be permissible, but differences in dividend rights or liquidation distributions will cause a second class of stock to exist).
- ✔ The corporation isn't an insurance company or a domestic international sales corporation.

For purposes of applying these eligibility standards, husbands and wives owning shares jointly count as a single shareholder. Joint owners other than husbands and wives are counted separately. Partnerships and corporations can't be shareholders of an S corporation. In contrast, partnerships, C corporations, and limited liability companies (LLCs) don't have restrictions on who can be a partner, shareholder, or member.

These eligibility standards must exist at the time the S corporation election is made and exist continuously throughout its corporate existence. If an eligibility standard ceases to exist, the S corporation status is terminated immediately. If this happens, the corporation would be taxed as a C corporation with no pass through of tax attributes to shareholders.

Because S corporation status terminates automatically, it's very likely that when a termination occurs, neither the corporation nor its officers, directors, or shareholders know about it. Tax planning goes haywire, as the corporation now must be taxed at the corporation level without passing through tax items to the shareholders.

Eligibility standards most likely to be missed relate to the requirements that there be no second class of stock and that shareholders be individuals. The second class of stock issue often comes up when shareholders loan money to the corporation. You can find a discussion of the problems presented by shareholder loans in Chapter 9.

S corporation status requires a written election signed by all shareholders at the time of election and submitted on Form 2553 to the IRS. The election must be made within 12 months prior to the tax year for which it is to be effective. If you want the corporation to be treated as an S corporation starting January 1, 2002, you should file your election after January 1, 2001. Similarly, you can file your election on or before the fifteenth day of the third month of the beginning of the corporation's tax year. Using the preceding example, an election could be filed on or before March 15, 2002, to be effective for the tax year beginning January 1, 2002.

S corporations ordinarily must use a calendar year as the tax year unless you convince the IRS that significant business reasons exist that support an alternative tax year.

Each S corporation shareholder is deemed to receive his or her pro rata share of S corporation income, loss, deduction, or credit. With our S corporation shareholder, *pro rata* means in proportion to his or her stock ownership interest. If you own 50 percent of the stock of an S corporation, your pro rata share of pass-through items will be 50 percent. Many technical rules and requirements may limit loss deductions and basis calculations. Check with your tax advisor.

An S corporation election can be terminated at any time by agreement of the shareholders. Shareholders owning more than 50 percent of the issued and outstanding common stock must sign and submit a written consent revoking an earlier S corporation election.

Tax-free incorporation

Here's more good news. Individuals seeking to form a corporation can generally do so tax free. This is generally true for persons seeking to create partnerships, limited liability companies, and other business entities. To receive tax-free treatment on incorporation, individuals forming the corporation must transfer money or assets to the corporation solely in exchange for stock or securities of the corporation. Immediately after the exchange, the individuals forming the corporation must own at least 80 percent of the total combined voting power of all classes of stock entitled to vote and at least 80 percent of the total number of issued and outstanding shares of each class of stock.

Here's an example: John, Jane, and Joan want to incorporate their floral business. Each transfers certain assets and cash to the business. The value of property and money each contributes is $5,000. In exchange for this contribution, each receives 100 shares of stock of Three J's, Inc. John, Jane, and Joan are the only shareholders. Since they contributed assets and cash to the corporation solely in exchange for corporate stock, and since they are in total control of the corporation after the exchange, the incorporation is tax free.

Tax issues are complex. There may be reasons why you won't want a tax-free incorporation. You will want to visit with your tax advisor.

Other tax benefits for corporations

The Internal Revenue Code (IRC) contains additional benefits for corporations and their shareholders. It's hard to believe, I know. Take, for example, IRC Section 1244. This section allows individual shareholders to take advantage of ordinary loss treatment if their stock should become worthless. Assume that you have invested $5,000 in Three J's, Inc., the floral business. You received 100 shares of stock for your contribution. Despite the best efforts of its owners, the business fails and your stock is worthless. You may be entitled to an ordinary loss deduction on your tax return.

To qualify for this ordinary loss treatment:

- ✔ Only individual shareholders are eligible; trusts, estates, corporations, and so on aren't eligible.

- ✔ At the time shares are issued, the corporation qualifies as a small business corporation, defined as any corporation that has $1,000,000 or less of money or other property contributed to it.

- ✔ The corporation issues stock in exchange for cash or property; shares issued in exchange for services don't qualify.

- ✔ The corporation doesn't receive more than 50 percent of its aggregate gross receipts from passive income sources such as royalties, rents, dividends, interests, and so on.

IRC section 1202 also benefits corporate shareholders by allowing qualifying shareholders to exclude up to 50 percent of the gain realized on sale or disposition of the shares. Like most tax-related matters, this benefit has eligibility requirements and other limitations. Consult with your tax advisor to see if IRC Sections 1244 and 1202 can help you.

Because the IRS taxes S corporation shareholders similarly to partners in a partnership or members of a limited liability company, certain fringe benefits available to C corporations may not be available to S corporations. These benefits include the ability to exclude from income items such as: group term-life insurance, accident and health benefits, meals and lodging for the convenience of the employer, and group legal services. If these benefits are important to your business, talk with your tax advisor. You may still have these benefits; however, you could be required to treat a portion of these benefits as income on your personal tax return.

S corporations may have a key tax advantage over limited liability companies. Experts disagree on whether this advantage exists. It's a complex matter involving the applicability of self-employment taxes. The general thinking is that all items of income distributed or deemed to be distributed to members of a limited liability company who are actively engaged in the business are subject to self-employment tax. S corporation shareholders, on the other hand, may be able to treat a certain amount of income as salary subject to self-employment tax and the balance as a corporate dividend, subject to income tax, but not the additional self-employment tax. This difference affects the dollars you will have left in your pocket.

Over the last several years, the IRS has worked to level the playing field among its pass-through entities like S corporations, limited liability companies, and partnerships. It's reasonable to expect that the IRS will eliminate or equalize this advantage at some point in time. Remember, it hasn't happened yet.

Going public

Do you dream that someday your business will be publicly traded on a national stock exchange? Why not? Many corporations have successfully taken the plunge. Although this may change in time as limited liability companies gain greater acceptance, most publicly traded businesses are corporations. Stock exchanges understand corporations; they are used to dealing in the purchase and sale of corporate stock. If you want to go public someday, you might as well start the process by forming a corporation now.

It probably goes without saying, but nobody goes public without a lot of professional advice. If you think this is a path for you, find yourself a good professional team early on and discover all that is involved. Chapter 23 will help you put together a professional team that will meet your needs.

Boosting your image in the eyes of the public

Some will argue that doing business in a corporate form helps attract customers. By adding *Inc., Ltd.,* or a related ending to your name you may add credibility. Prospective customers may believe that you are in business to stay. It may suggest that by incorporating your business, you are serious about your business — you've made that extra commitment to the business and its customers. And it may make you appear to be bigger and more professional.

Certainly, to the extent that you have taken the steps to form your corporation and continue to undertake required corporate compliance, you have made an extra commitment not made by sole proprietors. By incorporating your business, you're announcing to the world that you are here to stay.

Protecting your name

You probably spent more time choosing a name for your corporation or company than you did pondering the name of your first born. In fact, you most likely left a paper napkin trail of names and every variation you, your friends, and your relatives could dream up in every restaurant in your hometown. When you're ready to incorporate, the number-one thing on your to-do list is to *check corporate name availability*. We can't stress this enough.

Many of our customers order company stationery or print business cards before they receive confirmation from us that their name isn't available. Many service companies automatically do this for you as a part of your incorporation service. You can find out whether your dream name is available in Delaware, and in most other states in just seconds while you are on the phone with an incorporation specialist or online at `www.corporate.com/dummies`. Checks in some states can take 24 hours or more.

It's a good idea to come up with an alternate name as well. With thousands of corporations formed daily nationwide, you run the chance of having your preferred name already registered.

If you're serious about business, you need to protect your name. Corporations have perpetual existence — unless you elect to have a shorter duration — and perpetual is a mighty long time. Although you can always change your name, it's a good idea to get a name that will pass the test of time.

When the secretary of state or other state office accepts your articles of incorporation, usually no other person or business entity can form a business entity under that name. The mere fact of filing provides a measure of name protection. If you expect that your business name will also be closely identified with your business product or service, you may also consider obtaining trademark protection for your name or logo. You can apply these protections at the state or national levels. If this is important to you, contact an intellectual property attorney in your area. Also, you can contact the U.S. Patent and Trademark Office at `www.uspto.gov` or call 800-786-9199. You can also see The Company Corporation for patent and trademark services online at `www.corporate.com/dummies`. (See Chapter 6 for more information about corporate names.)

If you're not ready to incorporate, but you have a name in mind, all states permit you to reserve a corporate name for a certain period of time, usually 30 to 60 days. Contact your secretary of state or visit your lawyer to get the necessary paperwork. You can also contact a service company to do this work for you. However, remember that if you are the do-it-yourselfer and reserve your preferred name with your secretary of state, no one else — attorney, service company, or other individual — can complete the filing of the formation documents for you until you release the name. Often you'll run across paperwork and annoying delays if you change gears midstream.

Securing your domain name now

In this electronic age, corporations and other businesses are also registering domain names, which can be used not only now but also in the future for business Web sites. Large corporations invest significant time determining which domain names to register, anticipating that additional product or business lines in the future might create a need for these additional names. In fact, demand for Web addresses has been so great, seven new Top Level Domains are slated to be added in 2001. See Chapter 6 for more information about registering Internet domain names.

Even if you are in the earliest planning stages, it's a good idea to reserve your domain name along with your company name — and do it as soon as possible. Ideally, your company name and domain name should be the same or closely related. This will make it easier for customers to locate you on the Web. The number of dot.coms being registered grows exponentially each year. By waiting to reserve your domain name, you run the risk that your preferred Web address will be unavailable when you launch your Web site.

Do you have a name you'd like to protect on the World Wide Web? You can start by doing a simple Web search under the terms **domain name registration** to find a domain name provider. Some incorporation service companies offer domain name registration and Web site start-up and maintenance along with their incorporating services. If you're the do-it-yourself type, check out *Domain Names For Dummies,* by Susan Wels and GreatDomains.com (IDG Books Worldwide, Inc.).

Transferring corporate shares for free

Historically, one of the hallmarks of corporate status is the free transferability of corporate stock. As you'll see in Chapter 14, shareholder agreements greatly restrict the ability of shareholders to sell or transfer their stock. In addition, unless the corporation's shares are traded publicly on a stock exchange, the small corporation stock generally has no recognized market.

Transferability of shares remains a corporate benefit, however. Here's why: You own all of the stock of Big Business Books, Inc., a corporation that has entered into a number of important contracts and agreements with others. You want to sell the business with all of the important contracts and agreements in place. If you sell the assets of Big Business Books, the other parties to those contracts might refuse to contract with the new buyer. If you sell the stock of Big Business Books, the contracts could remain in full effect because Big Business Books, Inc. continues to exist and be in business. The only thing that has changed is the identity of the shareholder.

This benefit may be short-circuited by contract language found in those important contract and agreements. Transfers of more than a specified percentage of stock (often 50 percent) may give rise to a contract right to void the contract.

Partners in a partnership may not freely transfer their ownership interests. Tax law treats the transfer of more than 50 percent of ownership interest as a termination of the partnership. This is a taxable event that may require the filing of tax returns. In addition, many state partnership laws state that persons who acquire a partnership ownership interest from a partner may not be considered partners or allowed voting rights in the partnership until the partnership votes to accept the new partner.

Incorporation Might Not Be for Me If...

Incorporation isn't for everybody. You might not have the temperament or discipline to deal with corporate formality or compliance issues. There could be many reasons, and here are a few:

> ✔ Your business isn't operating in the black yet. It may be just getting by, and the possibility of incurring incorporation fees and expenses simply can't be justified. It's generally less expensive to operate as a sole proprietorship although your exposure to personal liability is greater.

✔ Limited liability won't help you or your business. Many lawyers and doctors are sole proprietors because state laws refuse to limit the liability of professionals, especially when the matter involves professional negligence or malpractice. Perhaps your business is relatively small and the product or service you provide is unlikely to create harm or damage. If so, limited liability would be unimportant to you.

✔ You're a lousy record keeper. Being incorporated means dotting *I*'s and crossing *T*'s. Corporations must prepare and file reports in a timely fashion, must maintain records, and keep business bank accounts and assets separate from personal accounts and assets. Some people are simply not capable of doing these things. Perhaps, they're so busy they don't have time. Maybe they don't have the energy or organizational skills. Or perhaps the business lacks the funds to hire individuals to perform these tasks so that all eyes can be focused on running the business.

What Other Types of Business Entities Are There?

Corporations aren't your only choice. You can choose from corporations (both S and C), limited liability companies, limited liability partnerships, general partnerships, limited partnerships, sole proprietorships, business trusts, and an assortment of lesser-used forms of business. This section focuses on the more commonly used models: sole proprietorships, partnerships, and LLCs. Talk to your lawyer or accountant if you have more specific questions.

No one choice is necessarily better than another. Each has strengths and weaknesses. Each needs to be evaluated in terms of what goals you are trying to achieve and how simple or complex a business structure you wish to have. What works for you and your company may not work for the guy next door.

Table 2-1 offers a quick view of the types of entities and their advantages and disadvantages.

Table 2-1   Advantages and Disadvantages of Each Business Type

	C Corporation	S Corporation	Close Corporation	LLC	Partnership	Sole Proprietor
Advantages						
Personal limited liability	*	*	*	*		
Fewer formalities				*	*	*
Attracts investors	*		*	*		
Anonymity of ownership	*	*	*	*		
Tax-deductible benefits for employees	*	*	*	*		
Allows foreign investors	*			*		
Flexibility in management and organization				*	*	*
Allows more than one class of stock	*					
Disadvantages						
Profits and losses pass through to personal income tax returns of owners		*		*	*	*
Record keeping is less formal				*	*	*
File one tax return (each member)		*		*	*	*
Illness or death may threaten end of business					*	*
Personal liability					*	*
All stockholders must be U.S. citizens		*				
No stock ownership				*	*	*
File two tax returns	*		*	*		
Maintaining corporate records may be time-consuming	*	*	*	*		
Tax deductions for employee benefits not available					*	*

Sole proprietorships

If you are in business by yourself and you do nothing further, your business is a sole proprietorship. It's that simple. Because you are the business, you don't have limited liability for any of your actions. From an administrative standpoint, you'll have less paperwork to file and your compliance obligations are minimal. Any taxable income generated will be based on individual tax rates.

Here are a few examples of folks who should be sole proprietors:

- Individuals engaged in occupations that involve little exposure to people or limited opportunities to damage people or property. These individuals can probably protect against most claims through good business insurance.
- Professionals engaged in practice by themselves. Professionals are always liable to their clients, so a limited liability shield really provides no benefit.
- Individuals who are incapable of doing the compliance things necessary to maintain a corporation in good standing. Many people simply lack the organizational aptitude to prepare corporate minutes and complete annual filings. You've seen these folks — piles of files spread all over their office.

Partnerships

Different types of partnerships exist. A common thread is that partnerships are pass-through entities. That is, no income tax is assessed at the partnership level; it's assessed at the partner level. Partnerships are the original pass-through tax entity. Today, other pass-through tax entities exist, including S corporations and limited liability companies.

By definition, a *partnership* is any association of two or more persons that carries on a business for profit. While you don't need a written agreement, experts strongly encourage a written partnership agreement. Your lawyer can help you with this.

A joint venture is a form of partnership. Joint ventures are generally considered to be partnerships formed to accomplish a specific business objective, whereas partnerships may have more than one business objective.

Partnerships are highly flexible and creative business entities. The partners have great latitude to operate the partnership however they choose. Unlike S corporations, partnerships can allocate income, loss, deductions, and credits among partners however they choose if, in general, there is a rational and business basis for the allocation. S corporation allocations must be made in proportion to stock ownership. The partners can also delegate management responsibilities to specifically named partners.

Corporate formalities are nonexistent. A board of directors, requirements for annual meetings (unless the partnership agreement requires one), or other compliance requirements aren't needed.

Unlike S corporations, you don't have any restrictions on how many partners you can have (although state and federal securities laws could limit you) and you don't have any restrictions on who can be a partner. Partners can be individuals, corporations, trusts, other partnerships, and just about any other form of recognized legal entity. You can't have a corporation as an S corporation shareholder, but a partnership can.

General partnerships

The owners of a general partnership are partners. Generally, each partner is equally liable with all other partners for partnership liabilities, a status commonly referred to as joint and several liability. Many general partnerships form without regard to the type of business entity. Two or more people get together to develop and promote a product, service, or idea; things move forward quickly, and a partnership is sprung into existence. Lots of general partnerships are out there, but it's hard to imagine a good candidate for a general partnership in light of the availability of S corporations or limited liability companies.

Although you don't need a written agreement to form a general partnership, it's a good idea. Disagreements between partners occur. A written agreement can stop disagreements before they occur. Well-drafted written agreements should consider a range of possibilities, including the death of a partner, the selling of partnership interests, and deciding how partnership decisions are made. Flexibility and creativity are good phrases to describe the potential of a partnership agreement. Many of the same issues found in shareholder agreements will be contained in a written partnership agreement. For a discussion of those matters, see Chapter 14.

General partnerships should register their name with the secretary of state's office or their county recorder. See Chapter 6 for the process of registering assumed or fictitious names.

Limited partnerships

The two classes of partners in each limited partnership are general partners and limited partners. Each limited partnership must have at least one general partner. General partners are jointly and severally liable for all of the partnership's debts and liabilities. Limited partners are more akin to corporate shareholders. To the extent that a limited partner is not active in the business or management of the limited partnership, the limited partner's potential liability exposure is restricted to the amounts that he has contributed to the limited partnership. Another way to put it is that the general partner runs the business, and the limited partners are simply the investors.

Years ago, limited partnerships were the vehicle of choice for tax shelters. Investors would contribute monies to the limited partnership. In exchange, most of the limited partnership's taxable income, losses, deductions, or credits would be creatively allocated in whatever manner was most beneficial to the limited partners. The IRS clamped down on tax shelters, and limited partnerships are much less common today.

Limited liability partnerships

The limited liability partnership is the new kid on the partnership block. These partnerships look and act like other partnerships with a couple of notable exceptions:

- Only certain categories of professionals may form them (for example, lawyers, doctors, accountants, architects, engineers, and so on). Check your state statute to see which professionals are eligible to form a limited liability partnership.

- Limited liability partnerships have a modified limited liability, the extent of which varies from state to state.

  For contract claims (claims that are based on a contract) limited liability partners are treated like corporate shareholders. So long as formalities are complied with, there won't be personal liability for partners.

  For tort claims (professional malpractice, negligence) the limited liability treatment is different. If a partner is involved in the professional malpractice or negligence, he or she is likely to have unlimited liability for the actions.

  Partners not involved in the malpractice or negligence may have limited liability in some states. In others, your liability may be limited above a certain dollar amount. In either case, if you're involved in the professional malpractice or negligence, you remain fully liable to the injured party.

The use of limited liability partnerships is fairly restricted. Talk with your lawyer or accountant if you need more information.

Limited liability companies

If corporations have a rival for king of the limited liability world, it's the limited liability company. Plain and simple, limited liability companies seek to provide the flexibility and pass-through taxation of partnerships with the limited liability benefit of corporations.

A limited liability company's owners are its members. Members form a limited liability company by filing articles of organization with the secretary of state just as a corporation files its articles of incorporation. Limited liability companies require few formalities; they don't require a board of directors, annual meetings, or similar requirements.

While some states don't require limited liability company members to execute a written operating agreement, it's a good idea. The agreement can be flexible, like a partnership agreement. You can delegate management tasks to members or nonmembers alike who serve as managers of the limited liability company. An operating agreement serves many of the same purposes as a shareholder agreement. Take a look at Chapter 14 to see the types of provisions you might wish to include in your operating agreement.

Like partnerships (and unlike S corporations) anyone or anything can be a member of a limited liability company, and limits to the number of members don't exist. Fewer administrative and compliance requirements exist for limited liability companies.

When limited liability companies burst on the scene in the late 1980s and 1990s, many experts predicted that they would replace corporations and other forms of business entities. This hasn't happened yet. Will it happen in the future? People are more comfortable with corporations. They've been around longer, and plenty of statutes and court cases exist involving corporations. In a sense, corporations have been battle tested and are more predictable.

Corporate income tax issues are more clearly understood than limited liability company tax issues. While efforts have been made to level the playing field among all pass-through entities like limited liability companies and S corporations, the field still tilts toward the corporation end. For example, it's widely believed that all distributions from a limited liability company to members active in its business are subject to self-employment tax. S corporations have historically been able to treat a certain amount of the distributions as corporate dividends that aren't subject to the self-employment tax.

Converting to a Corporation

Usually you can convert from a partnership or limited liability company to a corporation, and often this can be done tax free. The decision to convert to a corporation from an existing partnership or limited liability company should be made carefully to avoid unintended tax consequences. You'll want to visit with your lawyer or accountant before making this decision. Incorporation specialists at service companies can do the filing once you've made a decision.

Converting your partnership or limited liability company to a corporation simply requires that you follow the steps outlined in this book. If you choose to do it yourself, prepare and file your articles of incorporation, prepare bylaws, and track organizational minutes. Keep the other compliance and formality issues discussed in this book in mind, and you should be fine.

If you're presently doing business as a partnership, limited liability company, or other noncorporate entity, check with your tax advisor before you convert. Chances are you can convert tax free. However, you're better off being safe than sorry. Your tax advisor can also discuss whether there are any other benefits or disadvantages to converting.

When limited liability companies first appeared, many S corporation owners wondered if they should become limited liability companies. It appears that very few converted in the beginning. Why? S corporations already provided the benefit of limited liability, and the owners had adapted to doing business as an S corporation. There was no real benefit in converting. But over the years, conversions have taken off. Now there are more than ever before.

Partnerships present a different challenge. Without the benefit of limited liability, it's often a good idea to incorporate solely to gain this benefit. For partnerships thinking about a conversion, consider both LLCs and corporations before finalizing your decision.

With the addition of LLCs, LLPs, and other new entities, and with states' growing awareness that business growth is good for states, many state legislatures are making it easier than ever to convert from one form of business entity to another. Check with your state to see if one of these so-called *cross conversions* may be available to you.

Chapter 3

Getting My Ducks in a Row — A Pre-incorporation Checklist

. . . .

In This Chapter

▶ Things to consider as you begin the process of incorporating

▶ A cross-reference guide to assist you

▶ A pre-incorporation checklist

. . . .

*W*riting articles of incorporation, choosing a name, selecting S corporation status — all these activities might cloud your head with confusion. Incorporating can be overwhelming . . . if you don't know what to expect or where to start. This chapter tells you what you need to know before you start incorporating. If you can answer all the questions we raise in this checklist before you file your articles of incorporation, you'll be light years ahead. Plus, you'll probably save yourself some dough if you take the lawyer or professional team route.

Choosing a Name

You must have a name, more likely two or three choices since your first choice might be unavailable. Any name you choose must usually end with a term like *Incorporated*, *Company*, or *Limited*. Abbreviations of these terms are usually acceptable. You can find out more about corporate names in Chapters 2 and 6.

What process might you use to help choose your name? Here are some questions you might want to ask yourself:

✔ Do I need a name that describes the products or services I provide to make it easier for customers to know what the corporation does?

✔ Do I want a name that conveys technical or professional expertise or one that might catch the public's attention and be easy to remember?

✔ How long or short should my name be, especially if I want customers to recall it?

✔ Should the name include Incorporated, Company, Limited, or an abbreviation of one of these terms?

✔ Do I want to name the corporation after myself?

✔ What alternatives are acceptable if my first choice isn't available?

✔ Do I want a name that will appear toward the front of the phone book? (Now you know why there are so many corporations that begin with AAA!)

Deciding Where to Incorporate

For small corporations that do business in a single state, you might incorporate in the state where you do business. If you do business in more than one state, you could consider choosing one of those states or Delaware. Plan to grow really big and do business everywhere? Think about Delaware as a place to incorporate. Take a look at Chapters 5 and 10.

Your decision can save paperwork, time, and money if you do your homework first. Different states charge different fees and require you to fill out different forms. Ask yourself these questions to help you decide where to incorporate:

✔ Where do I do business? If you do business in only one state, consider incorporating in that state.

✔ If I do business in more than one state, which state requires the least amount of paperwork or has the least expensive incorporation fees?

Keep in mind that you may still be required to do business in the other state, which will require paying that state's fees and completing that state's paperwork.

✔ Will my corporation go public one day? If so, Delaware may be your best bet. It's business friendly and a favorite of publicly traded corporations.

Chapter 5 provides more information to help you choose your state of incorporation.

Picking Directors and Assigning Duties

Directors are the head honchos for your corporation. In a sense, unless your articles of incorporation provide to the contrary, all corporate authority begins and ends with the board of directors. While the board may delegate tasks to its officers and other employees, it's still ultimately responsible for all corporate actions. If something doesn't get done, the blame lands on the board. Chapters 15 and 16 provide greater insight on board of directors.

While the board may delegate tasks to officers and employees, it's responsible to set policy for the corporation and oversee all corporate activity. Directors have well-defined legal duties and responsibilities, which we discuss in Chapter 15, that they are obligated to follow in dealing with corporate shareholders and others.

Who do you select to serve on your board? Many states allow corporations to have one director. If that's true in your state, you might be it. For smaller corporations, three or five board members are common. Notice the odd number — an odd number helps avoid deadlock that can occur whenever an even number board of directors is unable to agree on an important matter.

Directors of small corporations are often the same as the corporation's shareholders. It's not unusual for the same individual or individuals to wear separate hats as officer, director, and shareholder.

Assigning Officers and Their Duties

The board of directors appoints officers to manage the day-to-day business operations. Most corporations will have a president, treasurer, and secretary whose duties are spelled out in general terms in the corporate bylaws. Corporate officers do whatever the directors tell them to do. Officers have a great deal of authority to act on behalf of the corporation. You'll discover more about officers in Chapters 15 and 16.

You'll need to know who your corporate officers will be early on in the process. Corporate officers need to be identified so the corporation can open bank accounts, sign leases for office space, buy equipment and supplies, and otherwise carry out the business of the corporation.

Just like your directors, your officers are probably corporate shareholders, especially in small corporations. If not, you'll want to find officers who have prior experience with businesses like yours and who have knowledge and skill to operate the day-to-day corporate activities.

Things to Know about Shareholders

Shareholders own the corporation, but they don't manage it unless they also serve as directors and officers, which is common for smaller corporations. Shareholders elect directors and vote on matters of importance, such as a proposed sale or merger of the corporation. They have a number of rights, largely intended to protect their interests. We review shareholders' rights and responsibilities in Chapters 13 and 16.

Many corporations have a single shareholder. This individual may also be the only officer and director of the corporation. At other times, the only shareholders are husband and wife.

It's common for a corporation to be formed by a group of individuals who have a common dream or vision to start their own business. When this occurs, the individuals forming the corporation usually become its shareholders, officers, and directors. Corporations can be family affairs with several family members owning corporate stock, as well.

Who should be a shareholder of your corporation? Here are some things to consider:

✔ Will the prospective shareholder be active in the operation of the business? In some cases this is a must, but not always.

✔ Am I willing to share control of corporate decision making with this prospective shareholder?

✔ Does the prospective shareholder bring experience, contacts, influence, or other skills needed by the corporation?

✔ Is the prospective shareholder willing to pay money for his or her shares, money needed by the corporation to fund its activities?

If your corporation has more than one shareholder, consider a shareholder agreement to address what happens if a shareholder dies or becomes disabled, retires, or seeks to sell or give away his or her shares. Controlling who your shareholders are at any point in time may be critical for the corporation, especially if you depend on the skill or expertise of a particular shareholder. Take a look at Chapter 14 to gain greater insight into shareholder agreements.

What do shareholders pay for their shares?

It depends. Shareholders can pay cash, contribute property, or in some instances receive shares in exchange for services. Income tax ramifications may differ depending on what is paid. Chapters 13 and 16 will increase your understanding of these issues.

Do securities laws apply to me?

Yes! Many corporation owners incorrectly assume that state and federal securities laws don't apply to them. Generally stated, laws prohibit the offer and sale of securities (including corporate stock) without compliance with registration requirements. The good news is that many exemptions exist, especially for small start-up corporations. A corporation that has a single shareholder who also serves as officer and director is unlikely to run afoul of securities laws. Add more shareholders to the mix and you may want to seek legal advice. See Chapter 9 for more.

Capitalizing the Corporation

Before you can start your corporation, you need to figure out where you're going to get the money or assets to get started. Here are a few questions to ask yourself:

- ✔ How much money will I need to get the business up and running?
- ✔ Where will the money come from?
- ✔ Will the corporation be obligated to repay amounts it receives?
- ✔ Should I sell stock, borrow money, or both?
- ✔ Who will loan me money?

Chapter 9 is a treasure trove of useful information and answers on raising the capital you need for your corporation.

Deciding What to Include in the Articles of Incorporation

Here's another good question to consider: What do I put in the articles of incorporation? Corporate *articles* is the document you file with the secretary of state in the state where you plan to incorporate. Once filed and approved, your corporation springs into existence. You have many choices about what to include or exclude in your articles. For certain matters, the articles are the only place where you can make these choices. Here are a few sample questions to ask yourself:

✔ Will the corporation have cumulative voting for directors?

✔ What about preemptive rights for shareholders?

✔ If our corporation qualifies, will we elect to be treated as a close corporation?

✔ Will we have different classes of stock or different rights for our shareholders?

That's a lot to consider, and it may just be the tip of the iceberg. Take a look at Chapters 1, 7, and 16 for suggestions of other areas to consider, and review the sample articles of incorporation in Appendix A.

Putting Together the Bylaws

So many choices, so little time! Like the articles of incorporation, corporate bylaws afford opportunities for flexibility and creativity. Typically, bylaws deal with process issues such as meeting, quorum, and voting requirements. Chapters 8 and 16 provide more detail. If you are creating custom bylaws, here are some sample questions to consider:

✔ How many board members or shareholders must be present in order to constitute a quorum?

Without a quorum, the board and shareholders are unable to act at meetings.

✔ Will decisions be made on the basis of majority vote or some greater vote or supermajority?

Without a supermajority-voting requirement in the bylaws, board and shareholder decisions are made on the basis of majority vote.

✔ Do I want to specify a date for the annual meeting of shareholders?

✔ Is it important to specify where board or shareholder meetings will take place?

See the sample bylaws in Appendix A for more information.

Selecting a Registered Agent and Office

Every corporation must have a registered agent and office located within the state of incorporation. Registered agents receive information, including annual report and franchise tax forms from the state. They also may be served with legal process when a lawsuit is filed against the corporation.

As corporate president, you may serve as your own registered agent, and your principal office may be designated as the registered office. However, many business owners choose to designate a registered agent other than themselves for various reasons. Among the reasons:

✓ Businesses don't like process servers to show up at and potentially disrupt the workplace.

✓ Many business owners travel a lot and run the risk of not being made aware of a potential claim.

✓ Because the registered agent is usually the one served with lawsuits, many business owners prefer that lawyers serve as registered agents so that they can begin providing appropriate responses to the lawsuits.

You do have some alternatives. Service companies routinely provide registered agent services and are especially useful for corporations with business operations in many states. Check out Chapter 4 for more information.

Deciding upon Cumulative Voting for Directors

Cumulative voting is when shareholders multiply their number of votes by the number of directors and apply the product for one candidate, or distribute it among two or more candidates. Minority shareholders can increase their voting strength when electing directors if the corporation allows cumulative voting. In some states, cumulative voting exists unless the articles of incorporation preclude it. In other states, it's just the opposite; the articles must expressly include it. Is it the right choice for your corporation? See Chapters 7 and 16 for more information.

Including or Excluding Preemptive Rights

Preemptive rights is a device intended to safeguard against the dilution of stock ownership. Assume that Richard owns 180 shares or 30 percent of the issued and outstanding stock of ABC Corporation. ABC Corporation plans to issue another 600 shares of stock. With preemptive rights, Richard has the option to purchase up to 180 shares (or 30 percent) of the new 600 shares. If he does so, he can preserve his ownership interest at 30 percent. If he chooses not to, his ownership interest will be diluted, decreasing from 30 percent to 15 percent.

Like cumulative voting, some states grant preemptive rights automatically. In these states, the articles of incorporation must expressly exclude preemptive rights. In other states, preemptive rights exist only if the articles provide for them. How do you decide what to do? Sneak a peek at Chapter 7.

Deciding Whether S Corporation Status Works for You

You should decide whether you want S corporation status before you incorporate your business because an S corporation election form is date sensitive. Failure to file your S corporation election in a timely fashion prevents you from attaining S corporation status for the first year of operations. This means you may miss the opportunity to pass all gains and losses of the corporation through to the individual shareholders.

In addition to being filed in a timely manner, the S corporation election form must be signed by all shareholders. Knowing these things in advance will increase the likelihood that your S corporation election will be effective when filed. Chapter 2 describes S corporations.

Carrying Out Pre-incorporation Activities

Here's the dilemma: You haven't filed articles of incorporation even though you are talking to lenders, investors, landlords, equipment dealers, lawyers, and accountants. Here are a few questions to keep in mind:

- ✔ Who's responsible for pre-incorporation activities such as negotiating leases, purchasing equipment or supplies, or hiring professionals?
- ✔ Can anyone act on behalf of the corporation before it is formed?
- ✔ What happens if, before the corporation is formed, I'm involved in an accident for which I'm at fault?

For start-up corporations, *promoters* are individuals who carry out pre-incorporation activities and are personally liable for their activities. If a promoter signs a contract, he is bound by it, unless the contract includes language stating that the contract isn't binding until the corporation has been formed. The language should also indicate that the corporation — not the promoter — is liable.

For preexisting businesses converting to corporation status, these businesses will continue to be liable for their actions until the articles are filed and the conversion is complete.

Here's a good idea for corporations: Include language in your organizational meeting minutes ratifying the acts of promoters and agreeing to have the corporation indemnify the promoters for any liabilities directly connected with any pre-incorporation activity.

Pre-incorporation Checklist

Corporate name _____

Alternate corporate name _____

State of incorporation _____

Type of corporation _____

Election of SubChapter S status _____

Names of directors _____

Number of shares of stock and their par value _____

What to include in the articles of incorporation _____

What to include in the bylaws _____

Registered agent _____

Part II
How Do I Incorporate?

The 5th Wave   By Rich Tennant

"I'm writing the corporate bylaws. How do you spell, 'guillotine'?"

In this part . . .

You've decided to incorporate. What do you do next? In this part, we discuss how to incorporate and where to go if you need help. Selecting a name, preparing articles of incorporation and filing them, drafting corporate bylaws, capitalizing your corporation, and doing business in other states — it's all here to get your corporation up and running quickly and correctly. We also tell you how to find help if you need it.

Chapter 4

Who Can Help Me Incorporate?

In This Chapter

▶ Finding available resources to help you incorporate your business

▶ Understanding how to incorporate in a cost-effective, time-efficient way

You might want help for any number of reasons. Business owners value cost-effective and time-efficient solutions. For some owners, the most effective and efficient means is to do everything themselves. Others choose to delegate all of the incorporation tasks to a third party. Still others choose a middle ground, performing certain tasks themselves while hiring professionals or service companies to complete other tasks.

There's no right way or wrong way to approach this issue. Do what fits your style and preferences. In this chapter, we outline your options and then give you some help to discover what works best for you.

Doing It Yourself

Before 1974, there wasn't an incorporate yourself economy. Business owners were more dependent upon lawyers to incorporate the business. Weeks (and perhaps a few thousand dollars) later, you'd leave your lawyer's office with your corporate paperwork. It would consist of page after page of articles of incorporation, bylaws, and organizational minutes. You'd probably have a nice leather-bound minute book in which to put your corporate documents and your very own corporate seal. Many clients thought they must have been charged by the page. The entire process, including the fee structure, was a complete mystery to the client.

Today, by contrast, hundreds of publications provide information about how to incorporate your business. Web sites abound seeking to help you incorporate. Interested in knowing more about what help is available for you? Check out Chapters 9, 20, and 23.

Incorporation isn't rocket science. In fact, an individual can incorporate his or her business in almost every state without the services of a lawyer. You're reading this book and discovering the basics of how to incorporate your business. We list additional resources throughout to help answer any additional questions you may have or to obtain state-specific information. Checklists and sample forms are easy to find, within this book and through a wide variety of other resources. Many states provide online resources, which will guide you through the process of incorporating as well as advise you of other state requirements. Appendix A provides you with sample forms to assist you, and Appendix B provides a detailed list of other resources that you may wish to call upon for assistance.

By doing it yourself, you will save money on professional or service company fees. Don't diminish the value of a professional team or the speed and efficiency of a service company, however. You want talented professionals on your team when you need help, and many service companies offer small business services that, when bundled with incorporation services, can provide the tools that a start-up needs to get up and running.

Forming the corporation or LLC is the easy part. The hard part is maintaining it. Don't forget the compliance issues.

Below are step-by-step instructions for incorporating if you are a first-time do-it-yourselfer. If you have some time, let's say a few weeks or so before you absolutely need to incorporate your business, or if you don't have the funds to hire a professional or pay a service company, then this is the way to go. The instructions that follow assume a fairly simple, straightforward incorporation. If you anticipate a large number of shareholders, different classes of stock, or a complex corporate structure, you may want to visit your lawyer or tax professional before you move forward.

1. **Contact the secretary of state or appropriate agency in the state in which you wish to incorporate.**

   They will send you order forms or guidelines or refer you to a Web site if they have one. Many states have Web sites where you can access state-specific forms. Look for these Web addresses in Appendix B.

2. **When you receive the information, spend time carefully reviewing it.**

   If you prepare the documents incorrectly, the state may send them back for revision, causing a delay in the processing. Ask! Ask! Ask! Don't hesitate to call the state with all your questions.

3. **Prepare the forms, or in some states, such as New York, "draft" the documents from scratch.**

   To complete the preparation you will need to select a registered agent and include the agent's address if you aren't going to use your own.

4. **Submit the completed forms to the state for filing. Be sure to include appropriate state filing fees.**

   Filing fees range from as low as $74 in Delaware to $300 in Texas. All states have their own time frames for processing incorporation documents. These may range from seven to ten days or three to four weeks. Many states will charge an expediting fee (ranging from $10 to $100), which will dramatically speed the review and approval of your articles.

   How do you know your business is incorporated? Watch your incoming mail. You will receive the articles of incorporation from the state. Some states will give you a fancy certificate, while others will date-stamp the articles that you prepared and sent in.

5. **Once approved by the state, you may be required to pay a county recording fee (New York, for example, has one) or meet a publishing requirement, such as in Arizona and Georgia. Check your state corporation statute.**

6. **Order your corporate kit.**

   Corporate kits are customized with your company name on the corporate seal and stock certificates. You may order them from an office supply store or from a service company such as The Company Corporation, 2711 Centerville Road, Wilmington, DE 19808; www.incorporate.com; toll-free 888-811-0111; fax 302-636-5454.

7. **Get a current Federal Tax ID Application (IRS Form SS-4) from the IRS.**

   You may download this form by going to Internal Revenue Service's Web site at www.irs.gov. The form includes preparation and filing instructions.

8. **If you are filing for SubChapter S status, you will need to complete IRS Form 2553.**

   The form, also available at www.irs.gov, includes preparation and filing instructions. We describe S corporations in Chapter 2.

Even if you haven't consulted a professional at this point, you may want to consider it. Not only can a professional assist you in the incorporation process, he or she can advise about other matters you will encounter. Take a look at Chapter 23 for help in selecting a professional.

Calling an Incorporation Service Company

Service companies are one-stop shops for incorporation services. Although they cannot give legal or financial advice, they are experts at helping individuals incorporate their businesses. That's what they are in business to do, unlike lawyers or accountants who may be generalists or specialize in other legal and financial services.

It's common for start-up business owners to choose a service company because their early corporate requirements are usually simple, and service companies have experienced staff available during regular business hours to answer questions. Filings completed by service companies are as legal and official as those completed by you directly or by an attorney.

In many cases, a service company can complete the incorporation in less time than if you were to take care of it yourself or hire an attorney. If you're in a rush and time is of the essence, a service company may be your best option. Many entrepreneurs turn to a service company because they have an urgency that can't wait for free time or an appointment with a busy attorney. For example, incorporation is frequently required when it's time to open a business bank account. If you're expecting a payment for your new corporation or LLC, you will need to have a separate account in which to deposit the funds. (Check out Chapter 24 for more on risking the piercing of your corporate veil by commingling funds.) Other common circumstances that require speed include leasing space or equipment, signing business contracts, following bid deadlines, and engaging the services of a utility — all of which must be completed under the corporate name.

Just like all professionals are not alike, not all service companies are alike either. Some offer incorporation services only in Delaware and Nevada and will market those states as the best choice regardless of where you're operating your business. Many have just one office nationwide or offices only in a state or two. Many now have online incorporation functions that will tend to level the playing field but may still have only one office. In this case, it may take longer to get the documents filed on your behalf. The Company Corporation, for example, has offices nationwide and hand delivers the documents directly to the secretary of state or other state agency. Some service companies may have a direct online connection to the secretary of state and can instantly transmit the information electronically. Electronic filing is the wave of the future, and most states are heading in this direction. Some service companies bundle or package registered agent service, corporate kits, and federal application forms with the incorporation. These packages may save you money the first year, but look at what annual renewal services will cost you the second year and what services are included. Select your incorporation company carefully. You may want to compare price and service to make sure you are comparing "apples to apples."

Besides finding local service companies in your Yellow Pages directory, a selection may be located easily on the Internet. On any major search engine, type in key words such as **incorporate, LLC,** or **incorporate online.** Some service companies have toll-free numbers and Web sites where you may incorporate directly online. Besides having an e-mail response mechanism in place for inquiries, a few sites offer specific content that will answer many of your questions about the incorporation process and a glossary of terms frequently used. Being able to incorporate online 24/7 is a valuable feature for busy entrepreneurs who may be working full time at day jobs and are pursuing their "dreams" after hours and on weekends.

Talk to your other small business associates. Word of mouth and referrals are another great way to find reliable incorporation service companies.

What can a service company do? A service company may:

- ✔ Help prepare and file articles of incorporation in any state
- ✔ Help qualify you to do business in any state
- ✔ Check on availability and reserve your corporate name
- ✔ Provide registered agent services
- ✔ Help you complete and file your federal identification number and SubChapter S corporation forms
- ✔ Supply you with customized corporate kits, which include stock certificates, a stock transfer ledger, corporate seal, and sample forms for minutes and bylaws

In addition to incorporation services, some service companies will provide related or ancillary services to help you maintain your entity. These include offering shelf corporations and obtaining certificates of amendments, certified copies of your articles of incorporation, and certificates of good standing.

Also, a few service companies provide support services to help small businesses take off. They may include trademark searches and filings, mail forwarding, franchise tax payment solutions, domain name registration, Web site hosting, and development tools and books.

Partnerships with other small business suppliers are now the norm. By taking advantage of incorporation services with leading service companies, you may have the opportunity to take advantage of discounts offered by preferred vendors for things like credit card services, telecommunications, office supplies, and so on.

One company's tool for success

The Company Corporation (www.incorporate.com) has extended its service menu to include an exclusive compliance-based program known as Compliance Watch. It's included free with its standard registered agent service. This new service assists the business owner with ongoing compliance matters after the incorporation process has been completed. It's simple, easy to manage, and designed to use in conjunction with your corporate kit. With Compliance Watch you can

✔ Access year-end review audit trail reports.

✔ Access a customized calendaring system that can automatically notify you when it's time to hold your annual stockholders' meeting, file annual reports, pay franchise taxes, and perform other duties to meet important deadlines.

✔ Access sample documents and templates you can use to guide you through the preparation of minutes, bylaws, and resolutions.

✔ Alerts you to important deadlines for you domestic state of incorporation as well as for other states in which you are qualified to do business.

✔ Compile reports that may be viewed, printed, and stored with other legal documents in your corporate kit.

✔ Record the official activities of your company or corporation. This includes keeping a stock ledger and recording minutes of annual meetings.

✔ Coordinate activities simultaneously for complex companies comprised of multiple corporations.

Hiring a Professional

Most lawyers and accountants who work with corporate clients will incorporate your business and prepare bylaws, stock certificates, and organizational minutes for a flat fee (ranging from $500 to $2,500). Filing expenses are extra. You know exactly what you get and how much you have to pay. Business owners like the peace of mind that comes from working with competent professionals.

Many lawyers work with their clients to divide up the incorporation work. This allows clients to allocate work between the professional and the client. It's a good way to reduce costs, yet have the confidence that comes from working with professionals.

Business owners often require professional services that go beyond corporate formation and compliance. For these they usually charge an hourly rate. Among the matters that go hand in hand with incorporation are:

- Preparing shareholder agreements, regulating the ability of shareholders to sell corporate shares or elect directors, and providing a market for the sale of shares in the event of a shareholder's death, disability, retirement or termination of employment with the corporation

- Estate planning and business succession issues, which affect key shareholders

- Developing business plans

- Preparing loan agreements, notes, and other documents

- Settling licensing and permit issues

- Dealing with employment-related matters

- Raising capital through stock sales or shareholder loans

- Buying, selling, or leasing real estate or other property

These are just a few examples. Each business owner will have issues unique to him or her that could require professional assistance. Your professional team can be invaluable to you in these areas. Your team understands your needs and aspirations as well as the legal and tax implications of decisions you'll be required to make. As you can tell, we refer you to your professional team in several places in this book, especially when matters can be complex.

Choosing What's Best for You

Take a look inside. Are you a take charge, do-it-all type of person? If so, try to incorporate yourself. Do you prefer to delegate tasks to individuals with legal or financial expertise? You sound like someone who should establish a good working relationship with a professional team and work closely with them. Or you may want a middle ground. If this is the case, a good service company could be your best bet. Service companies are in the incorporation business. While they can't provide the related services like estate planning or business succession, you can always work with professionals on those issues.

How much should you do on your own? That's a hard question to answer. If you're a one-person operation and you have time, chances are you can do most of the incorporation work yourself. If you anticipate additional shareholders, do-it-yourself incorporation gets a little more complicated. The more shareholders, the more the competing needs and interests of each of the shareholders. It doesn't mean you can't do it. You just need to consider a wider range of needs, interests, and possibilities to ensure that you get the results you intend.

The choices we describe in this chapter aren't mutually exclusive. Depending on your time and budget, there's a good chance you will do some of the work on your own while delegating other tasks to professionals or service companies. By reading this book and availing yourself of some of the resources we describe in Appendix B, you'll have a good working knowledge of the incorporation process, enabling you to ask good questions and make informed choices at every step along the way. Happy hunting!

Chapter 5

Where, Oh Where Should I Incorporate?

In This Chapter

▶ Deciding where to incorporate

▶ Discovering the Delaware difference

▶ Trying Nevada on for size

*O*kay, so you're ready to incorporate. Where are you going to do it? Like many things involving corporations, the answer doesn't require a great deal of soul searching. Some fairly straightforward advice should help you choose. Keep in mind, however, that special circumstances may dictate a different choice, as you'll discover in this chapter.

Deciding Where to Do Business

For most corporations, the place to incorporate is the state where you will do most of your business. State legislatures have adopted provisions of the Revised Model Business Corporation Law or otherwise streamlined their corporation statutes to the point where the differences between state law may not be significant for your purposes.

Wherever you incorporate, your corporation becomes subject to that state's corporation laws. Expect to file reports and tax returns in any state where you have incorporated or are qualified to do business. If you do business only in Oregon, you wouldn't want to incorporate in Washington and be subject to Oregon and Washington laws and filing requirements. Most business owners gravitate to the place that requires the least amount of paperwork and compliance headaches.

You have to comply with paperwork and compliance requirements in the state where you incorporate and in each state where you may be required to qualify to do business. See Chapter 10 for more on qualifying to do business.

In today's economy, many corporations do business in two or more states. The concept of "doing business" is a complicated one. A good rule to follow suggests incorporating in the state where most of your business activity occurs. If you incorporate in State A and do business in States B and C, you will need to qualify to do business in States B and C. Qualifying to do business in another state is a process similar to filing articles of incorporation (Chapter 10 deals with this qualification process).

If you still want to shop around, consider these possibilities:

- ✔ Locate a state with little or no corporate or personal income tax.

- ✔ Find a state capable of offering tax breaks or employment incentives for new businesses.

- ✔ If anonymity is important, look for a state that doesn't require you to disclose the names of shareholders or initial directors.

Checking Out the Buzz on Delaware

How can such a small state generate so much corporate activity? Delaware is the undisputed champion when it comes to progressive corporate laws. Its leaders recognized early on that being pro-corporation was good business for the state. Here are a few of Delaware's offerings that give it its reputation:

- ✔ You don't need to disclose or list names and addresses of initial directors in public records.

- ✔ Delaware offers low-cost fees to incorporate.

- ✔ Statutes allow a single person to hold all corporate offices.

- ✔ There is no state corporation income tax on Delaware corporations that don't operate in Delaware.

- ✔ There is no Delaware inheritance tax imposed on stock held outside of Delaware by nonresidents.

- ✔ A special court is available to hear claims brought under the Delaware corporation code.

- ✔ You're not required to have a business office in Delaware, just a registered agent.

Delaware's Court of Chancery provides corporations with judicial expertise in business matters not available in any other state. Delaware's corporate law has been time tested, as well, providing greater certainty and predictability that, if challenged, courts will uphold corporate actions you might engage in.

In other states, criminal and domestic cases often backlog their courts. Business-related lawsuits may take years to get to court. Once there, you have no guarantee that the judge will have any expertise in business- or corporate-related matters. In Delaware, the Court of Chancery hears only business- and corporate-related matters, and its judges are well trained in business and corporate legal issues.

You say your state corporation law has most of these things too? Most state laws have followed Delaware's example and offer comparable provisions, although none has replicated a business-oriented Court of Chancery. If your state has it, chances are that Delaware had it first.

If you plan to do business in more than one state, it's probably a good choice to incorporate in Delaware. Nearly half the corporations listed on the New York Stock Exchange are Delaware corporations. If you anticipate taking your corporation public someday, remember that the stock market knows and respects Delaware, and Delaware has a well-established body of law dealing with shareholder rights and protections. If you worry about fending off hostile takeover offers from other businesses, Delaware leads the way in this area too. And, don't discount the utility of the Court of Chancery to provide expedited and informed relief if needed.

Betting on Nevada

Nevada has opted to follow Delaware's lead by enacting laws that are increasingly friendly to corporations. Because of this, Nevada is winning the attention of businesses by:

- Requiring no state corporate tax on profits
- Requiring no state annual franchise tax
- Requiring no personal income tax
- Allowing stockholders to avoid having their names become part of public record, which permits complete anonymity
- Allowing that just one person can hold all the offices of the corporation: president, vice president, secretary, and treasurer
- Letting stockholders, directors, and officers be nonresidents of Nevada

Consider sunny California!

California legislators passed a bill that lends a helping hand to start-up corporations. Since January 1, 2000, companies that incorporate or qualify to do business in California are exempt from paying the state's minimum franchise tax for the first two taxable years. Depending on the size of your company, this law could save your new company up to $1,900 over a two-year period!

Chapter 6

Winning the Name Game

- -

- -

*I*s a business name important? You bet! Corporations spend millions of dollars each year protecting their names, trademarks, and logos from infringement by others. Just because your business may be small doesn't mean your corporate name isn't worthy of protection. Be optimistic. Your corporate name could become the next household word.

Reserving Your Corporate Name

When you file your corporation's articles of incorporation, the corporate name receives a small amount of protection. Once filed, and as long as the corporation remains in good standing, no other corporation or business can organize in your state of incorporation under your name or one deceptively similar to it. (What is deceptively similar? Unfortunately, it's very limited. Wild Bill's Coffee Express, Inc., for example, may be substantially identical to Wild Bill's Coffee Express, Corporation, but not to Wild Bill's Tea Express, Inc.)

As soon as you select a name for your corporation, contact the secretary of state's office to verify that the name is available. It's a good idea to have two or three alternate choices, since your first choice may be unavailable.

Once you have verbal confirmation that a name is available, reserve a corporate name for up to 60 days (longer in some states) by filing the appropriate form with your secretary of state's office and paying the required fee. If you begin the name reservation process yourself, it will be difficult to hand over the reins to a lawyer or service company later because the business name is reserved under your name. Only you can file the incorporation documents. If you ask a service company or lawyer to pick up after you reserve the name, the state will show it as unavailable, and you'll have to waste time and effort to unscramble the confusion.

If you think you might be doing business in more than one state, reserve your corporate name in each state where you might be doing business. If your corporate name is not available in the other state, you will have to choose another name before you do business there.

If you're hoping to franchise or otherwise create a national business, you should consider reserving your name in every state prior to incorporating in any state. This may be the only way to be sure that your name will be available in each state.

Reserving your corporate name in 50 states plus the District of Columbia can be a daunting task. If you believe this is appropriate for your corporation, consider using a service company to assist you. Some service companies are well equipped to help you with this multistate task. And using a service company for this task will save time and money.

Federal and state laws also allow for the registration of trademarks, service marks, and copyrights. These laws provide for greater protection of corporate names and marks, although any state protections provide coverage only within the particular state. For businesses hoping to franchise or have national coverage, consider using federal laws to protect your distinctive name, logo, trademarks, copyrights, or service marks. You may want to use an experienced intellectual property lawyer or service company to assist you in this task. And if a national scope is a real possibility for your business, make this contact early. If you wish to try this on your own without assistance, contact the U.S. Patent and Trademark office to obtain the necessary forms and instructions. You can find contact information in Appendix B.

Choosing a Fictitious or Assumed Business Name

Have you ever wanted an alias? Think of it — John Smith (aka Mad Dog Smith). Many corporations do business in other states using names other than their incorporated name. For example, ABC Corporation might want a more descriptive name, one that describes the different products or services it provides in the other state or one that creates a bit more buzz in the marketplace. If ABC's business is computer hardware and software, perhaps it would like to be known as Creative Solutions or Synergistic Software. If these names are available in a particular state or states, ABC Corporation could do this. First, ABC Corporation could amend its articles of incorporation and insert the new name. ABC Corporation would become Creative Solutions Corporation.

Alternatively, the corporation could register one or more of these other names as fictitious or assumed business names. All states have a process by which businesses can register fictitious or assumed business names, usually by filing a form with the secretary of state's or other government office and paying the required filing fee. As with other state forms, you can obtain fictitious or assumed business name forms from the secretary of state's office or other appropriate government office (see Appendix B).

Why wouldn't you just amend the articles of incorporation? Some businesses engage in more than one line of business within a single corporation. Using a different assumed business name for each business line allows the business to achieve product or service identity, which more accurately identifies the product or service offered.

Think about ABC Corporation. Assume that it provides computer hardware and software sales and service. What if it were also an Internet service provider? It might choose to use one or more assumed business names to identify the various aspects of its business. It might also determine whether to create a separate corporation for each of its separate business undertakings — a decision it would make after careful consultation with its professional team. For example, the software sales and service side is called Creative Solutions, while the Internet service provider could be Fast Track Corporation.

If you decide to register an assumed or fictitious business name, remember that the corporation is the applicant. This is important. If someone has a claim against Creative Solutions, they are entitled to know who the claim should be filed against. By contacting the proper government office (commonly, the secretary of state's office), a claimant would learn that Creative Solutions is an assumed business name of ABC Corporation. The claimant would also learn the corporation's registered agent's name and address for purposes of pursuing the claim. If you register the assumed business name in your individual name, you'll be the facing the claim.

Keep in mind that assumed or fictitious names provide protection only within the state or parts of a state in which they are registered. In some states, such as Oregon, you can register an assumed business name throughout the state or limit it to certain identified counties. If you have a business with national scope, consider using federal laws to obtain broader protection.

Registering Internet Domain Names

Here's a choice businesses didn't have to address just a few years ago. Increasingly, corporations and other business entities are including domain name registration as part of their incorporation process. It's important not only to know if your corporate name is available within the state or states where you will do business, but also if the Internet domain name will be available for the corporation. Many companies register more than one domain name for purposes of advertising, misspellings, or multiple product lines to help direct their clients intuitively to their Web sites.

Ideally, your corporate name and domain name will be the same. This will make it easier for your customers to find you, and it keeps it simpler for you — you only have one name to remember for compliance purposes. The longer you wait to reserve the domain name, the less likely it is to be available.

A number of private companies can help determine domain name availability and register names. Some service companies can also handle this task. An important advantage of service companies is that they have the resources available to determine name availability for all 50 states and the District of Columbia, as well as ascertain domain name availability, within a very short period of time. This advantage is especially useful for businesses needing national name coverage and hoping to get up and running within a short period of time. Once you confirm name availability, you can finish your articles of incorporation and domain name registration.

Selecting a Domain Name Provider

The easiest way to find a domain name provider is to do a simple Web search under **domain name registration.** You'll find hundreds of ICANN (Internet Corporation for Assigned Names and Numbers) accredited registrars. ICANN is the oversight body for domain name registration. Registrars have a name-search function on their sites where you can check availability. If your preferred name isn't available, many sites will offer suggestions for available alternatives.

In 2001, new Top Level Domains (TLDs) similar to the current .com will be released. They will include .info and .biz for general use and .pro for professionals. Also added will be .name for personal Web sites, .museum for museums, .aero for airline groups, and .coop for business cooperatives. These may offer additional alternatives to get your first choice in the overpopulated .com space. Most registrars will be able to assist you with these new TLD registrations.

Typically, the cost for a domain name ranges from $15–$35 per year. This includes the right to use the name for a 12-month period. Many registrars offer multiple-year registrations at discount rates.

After you get the domain name, you'll need to host it. Many Internet service providers (ISPs) provide hosting services. They may also offer free or low-cost Web pages to get you up and running. It takes about 24 hours until your name is available worldwide. If you have specific questions, contact your local ISP, which may be found online or in your local phone book.

Many providers also provide both e-mail services and e-mail forwarding options that will forward messages to your current e-mail account via your Web site. An example of this would be info@yourdomainname.com. Even if your Web site is still under construction, for the purposes of letterhead and business cards, you can begin receiving your e-mail messages almost immediately. It's important to understand that a domain name, Web site, and e-mail may be used independently or together to have a complete online presence. Most registrars can provide these services in one location.

Be sure to list your company as the owner/operator of the site. This will maintain proper separation between you and the corporation.

Want to learn everything there is to know about domain names? Look for *Domain Names For Dummies,* by Susan Wels with GreatDomains.com (IDG Books Worldwide, Inc.).

Chapter 7

Getting Down to Business with the Articles of Incorporation

. . . .

In This Chapter

▶ Defining articles of incorporation

▶ Including what's required

▶ Deciding whether to include other bits in your articles

▶ Amending your articles of incorporation

. . . .

*I*n this chapter, you'll learn much of what you'll ever need to know about articles of incorporation. In fact, some of you will be so confident after reading this chapter that you'll be ready to file your articles and form your corporation. Preparing articles of incorporation is as simple as it sounds. In fact, we provide you with an example of articles in Appendix A just so you can see for yourself.

Alas, a little information can be dangerous, and while what you learn here is important, it shouldn't be acted upon without the other information contained in this section. Keep in mind that your articles are just one piece of the puzzle — an important and necessary piece — but you should include other puzzle pieces as well, as you'll see in the next few chapters. Be patient.

The Basics Behind the Articles of Incorporation

Under all state corporation laws, a corporation forms when the appropriate state office approves and files the articles of incorporation. All states require a single written document, called the *articles of incorporation,* to be filed. In most states, you file with the secretary of state for the state in which the corporation is to be formed.

Filing articles of incorporation is a simple process. Nearly all states offer preprinted forms of articles of incorporation with blanks to complete. Today, you can obtain most of the forms online from your local secretary of state. Even if your secretary of state's office doesn't handle corporate filings, the office can direct you to the appropriate state agency for obtaining and filing articles. A complete directory of offices of the secretaries of state, together with mailing and e-mailing addresses, can be found in Appendix B. Service companies have a list of them too.

You must file articles in the right office. Again, this is usually the secretary of state's office, but not always. The name of the office and address are always on the form. Keep in mind that the information requested varies slightly from state to state, so don't send Vermont's form of articles to Ohio.

Many states now permit electronic filings, which can save time. Articles must contain the information required by the statute. This information is always on the form. We describe it later in this chapter. You must type or print in English the necessary information on the form. If you write it out by hand, be neat. The form must be signed by someone with authority to file the articles, and the form usually contains language where the signer attests to his or her authority. Usually, an incorporator must be at least 18 years of age. Finally, you must pay a filing fee to incorporate. This can range from $74 in Delaware to $300 in Texas.

Articles of incorporation are generally effective when they are filed if they comply with the state statute. This includes payment of the applicable filing fee. It's possible to direct that the corporation have an effective date other than the filing date. For example, if you know you wish to start business in corporate form on July 1, you could file your articles prior to that date and simply specify in the articles that the effective date is not to be until July 1. Check your state statutes to be sure your state allows advanced effective dates.

Avoiding an amendment to the articles

Articles of incorporation are public documents. Anyone who wants to read the articles can. For this reason, many corporations minimize the information they include in the articles and choose to reflect more sensitive items in the bylaws or minutes of the corporation. We discuss bylaws in Chapter 8 and minutes in Chapters 11 and 16.

When you seek to change the articles of incorporation, you must go through a similar process of submitting articles of amendment to the secretary of state. Although this is usually not a difficult process, it can become more complicated if a large number of shareholders must approve the amendment. For this reason, corporations will seek to minimize the information contained in the articles because it's generally easier to amend the corporate bylaws than to amend the articles. We discuss amendments to the articles in this chapter.

In most states, only one person, known as the incorporator, needs to sign off on the articles. A few states may require up to three. In addition, several states require that the incorporator be at least 18 and a real human being. (Sorry, Rover!) Other states permit corporations or other legal entities, such as limited liability companies or corporations, to file articles of incorporation. When this occurs, the age of the incorporator is no longer a factor.

Understanding What's Required in the Articles of Incorporation

You may be wondering, "So, what is required?" The easy answer is whatever the statute requires. The state's preprinted form of articles will ask you for the bare minimum. As you'll see, not much is requested. Sounds simple, doesn't it? Don't be fooled by the apparent simplicity. You have other important issues to consider that don't involve the articles of incorporation.

Basic issues

Here are the basics you should include for your articles:

- ✔ The name of the corporation, which usually must include one of the following: Incorporated, Company, Limited, Corporation, or some abbreviation of one of these terms (such as Co., Inc., Ltd., or Corp.). You may not use the words bank, trust, or education without approval from the appropriate state regulatory agency. State requirements vary. See Chapter 6 for much more on names.

- ✔ The number of shares the corporation is authorized to issue and their par value.

  Before you write down a gazillion shares, be aware that some states charge initial incorporating fees and annual franchise tax fees based on the number of shares and their par value. For example, in Delaware, your corporation will be authorized to issue up to 1,500 shares of no par value stock for minimum incorporating fees and annual franchise taxes. For more information about additional initial fees and annual franchise tax fees, contact your secretary of state or a service company.

- ✔ The name of the corporation's registered agent and the street address of the registered agent, which must be an address located in the state of incorporation.

- ✔ The name and address of each incorporator (each person who is signing his or her name to the articles of incorporation).

If this seems simple, that's because it is. Modern corporation statutes streamline the information you need to include in the articles. States want you to do your business there — they realize that they should make it easy to get you there. Once they get you there, it might be a different story (but that's not the subject of this book). If incorporating were so simple, why would anyone ever consider hiring a lawyer, accountant, or service company to do this work for them? Ah, yes. Now you know there must be more to this incorporating business!

State-specific issues for your articles

What other things might a particular state require you to include in the articles? Here are some examples:

- Whether the corporation will have cumulative voting or preemptive rights (see Chapter 14)

- The par value, if any, for shares of stock to be issued

- Whether the corporation will offer different classes of shares of stock (see Chapter 14)

- The duration of the corporation, if it won't be perpetual

- The number of and the names and addresses of the directors

- The Standard Industrial Classification of the corporation (sometimes known as the SIC code). The *SIC code* is a government attempt to classify types of businesses by code name and number. If your state requires a SIC code for your business, your state will be able to provide you with the SIC code form. The code helps government officials keep statistical data on what types of new businesses are starting up.

- Close corporation language (see Chapter 1) if the corporation elects to be governed by these provisions

Some states require more; some require less. Check the form that comes from the state office. Most states also include reasonably self-explanatory instructions to help you. If in doubt, talk with a professional to hammer out these issues.

Revised Model Business Corporation Act issues

The Revised Model Business Corporation Act (RMBCA), described in Chapter 1, generally requires that the articles of incorporation always include the following provisions if the powers and obligations listed below are to exist in any corporation:

- ✔ Provisions that would eliminate the board of directors or otherwise restrict the function of the board

- ✔ Provisions that would restrict or eliminate the power to compensate members of the board for services rendered

- ✔ Provisions to authorize cumulative voting in the election of board members

- ✔ Provisions that would require greater than a plurality vote in the election of directors

- ✔ Provisions that would provide that certain directors were elected solely from the holders of a particular class or classes of shares of stock

- ✔ Provisions limiting the ability of shareholders to remove a director except for cause

- ✔ Provisions providing for staggered terms for directors

- ✔ Provisions that deny the board to fill board vacancies

- ✔ Provisions that seek to limit directors' and officers' rights to indemnification

We discuss most of these provisions elsewhere in this book, especially Chapters 13, 15, and 16. If any of these items are of interest to you and your corporation, keep in mind that they will need to appear in the articles of incorporation. Most won't appear in the preprinted forms that you receive from the official state office. You'll need to add the language you want — perhaps an indicator that professional assistance would be helpful!

Adding Additional Pieces to the Puzzle

Before you decide whether to include other bits in your articles, keep in mind two things: First, the articles are a public record subject to review by anyone. If you feel information about the corporation or the makeup of its directors is sensitive, don't include it in the articles if you aren't required to do so. Second, anytime the information in your articles changes, you must amend your articles of incorporation. This process requires you to file a written document with the secretary of state or other state office and pay additional fees. It's also public. Before you elect to include every last detail about your business in your articles and allow any Joe Schmoe to read about your company, keep these two things in mind.

Keeping those two things in mind, here is a list of a few things you might choose to include:

- ✔ Any of the matters described in the preceding section that aren't already required to be included.

✔ Any other provision you wish to include, as long as it is consistent with law. (Don't advocate the violent overthrow of the country or hold yourself out as the one-stop shop for criminal activity.)

✔ Elaborate purposes and clauses that may include such things as mission statements, corporate values, and similar items.

✔ Required language if your state recognizes close corporations, and you elect to be subject to those provisions.

✔ Language that states that the corporation will indemnify corporate officers, directors, employees, or agents.

✔ Language that limits the liability of directors to the corporation or its shareholders for action taken or action that the director fails to take on behalf of the corporation. (We cover these important concepts of indem

✔ Language allowing fewer than all shareholders to consent and authorize corporate action by consent (discussed further in Chapter 16).

✔ Any other provision you wish so long as it's consistent with law. (We know we have already mentioned this, but it's worth repeating.)

Amending Your Articles

What if you want to change something in your articles? This happens routinely. Occasionally, the officers or board makes mistakes when the articles are filed, requiring a change to correct the error. More often, the officers or board modify the articles later on down the road to add or remove a provision. Common examples of changes requiring amendments to the articles include:

✔ Increasing the number of authorized shares of stock

✔ Adding or deleting requirements such as preemptive rights or cumulative voting (see Chapter 16 for information about director and shareholder meetings)

✔ Modifying any other term contained in the articles

✔ Changing your registered agent

Amending corporate articles requires the same type of formality you were required to use when the articles were filed in the first place. You must request a copy of the state's preprinted form for amendment to the articles of

If the amendment is made before the corporation has shareholders, a board of directors meeting must be convened to authorize the amendment (see Chapter 16). If the corporation has issued shares of stock, both the directors and shareholders must approve the proposed amendment. You will be required to comply with the requirements for meetings and amendments contained in your bylaws. (See Chapters 8 and 16 for more information on these areas.)

Since the process of amending articles is formal and requires a public filing, many corporations will include the least amount of information required in corporate articles. Instead, they will include other information in corporate bylaws or minutes — documents that require less formality to change in the future and no public filing.

Chapter 8

Getting to the Nitty-Gritty with Your Bylaws

In This Chapter

▶ Defining bylaws

▶ Deciding what to include in your bylaws

▶ Presenting additional "ideas" for your bylaws

*W*hile articles of incorporation require you to include specific information and file that information with the state, bylaws are for the benefit of your company. They are full of process and procedure — technical rules that seem miles away from the day-to-day activities of your business. For many business lawyers, years may pass before a client raises a question regarding something found in the bylaws. In fact, for many corporations, no one will ever raise a question about the bylaws. Be certain, though, that when such a question arises, the lawyer will take it seriously. It may well be that something has gone wrong, which requires immediate attention. Sometimes, the issues involve who will gain control over corporate decision-making processes.

Bylaw Basics

Corporate bylaws usually set forth rules and procedures that the corporation and its officers and directors must follow. Bylaws describe how you are going to regulate and govern your corporate business and affairs. We discuss what you should include in your bylaws in the next few sections, but here are a few examples:

✔ A discussion of when, where, and how to conduct meetings of the board of directors

✔ The circumstances upon which officers or directors may be shielded or reimbursed by the corporation

    ✔ The voting rights of shareholders

    ✔ Quorum requirements (see Chapter 16 for more on quorum requirements)

Unlike the articles, bylaws aren't public records. You aren't required to file them with the secretary of state. Generally, only officers, directors, and shareholders can review the bylaws. When things are going great, folks tend to forget that the bylaws even exist. So remember where you keep them.

Corporate statutes, as described in Chapter 1, provide corporations with wide latitude to shape rules and procedures to meet their specific needs. The statutes may act more as a default provision, applying only if the articles or bylaws don't provide an alternate process or procedure. The language, "unless otherwise provided . . ." appears in many of the corporate statutes. This language empowers you to be creative when preparing your corporation's bylaws.

Unlike articles, corporation statutes don't mandate specific requirements for corporate bylaws. Rather, the statutes may provide default provisions that apply if the bylaws fail to address a particular area. For this reason, bylaws will occasionally contain references to the corporation statutes. For example, you might see a provision that says something like, "Shareholders will be notified of meetings in accordance with state law." While this might be effective to let a shareholder know that he or she is entitled to some notification, it's ineffective to provide any details. For this reason, bylaws tend to be more detailed and include specific statutory language so that a shareholder isn't left scratching his or her head, wondering what is missing.

Many individuals who form their own corporations never realize the opportunity for flexibility. If you incorporate yourself or hire a service company to do it for you, review the documents carefully, and feel free to ask questions to make certain you understand what you have. A professional team can also be helpful to you in this area, although there's no assurance you won't be given a preprinted set of bylaws from a professional unless you ask for specific provisions.

Make a mistake with your bylaws? You can always amend your bylaws, which we discuss later in this chapter.

What Should Be Included in the Bylaws

What must you include in the bylaws? We're trying not to sound coy, but how about nothing! Corporation statutes contain default provisions specifying the obligation to conduct meetings of directors and shareholders and the notice requirements for each type of meeting. Statutes also address voting rights of shareholders and directors, quorum requirements, and the like. With statutes covering your bases, use the bylaws to focus on details mentioned in the statutes and other issues that you haven't addressed elsewhere.

Having said this, corporate bylaws should include basic pieces of information. Much of this information falls into one of four categories: shareholders, board of directors, officers, and general information.

Common provisions

Here are a few common provisions you might want to include in your bylaws:

- ✔ A description of the corporation's principal business location, together with a statement that such location can be changed from time to time by the board

- ✔ A requirement for an annual shareholder meeting to be held on a day and time designated (for example, the second Tuesday in December or as an alternative, December 10 of each year) or within a range of dates (within 60 days following the close of the corporation's fiscal year, for example)

- ✔ The process by which shareholders, officers, or directors may compel a special meeting (any meeting other than the annual meeting) of shareholders

- ✔ A description of providing notice of a shareholders' meeting, usually described within a range of days specified by the statute (for example, not less than 10 nor more than 60 days prior to the scheduled meeting date)

- ✔ A means by which convened meetings may be adjourned without new notification

- ✔ Requirements for fixing a *record date,* which is the date on which it is determined that shareholders are entitled under the bylaws or state law to notice and to vote on matters brought forth at a meeting

- ✔ The right of shareholders to inspect corporate records, describing the nature and types of records that may be inspected, and the process by which shareholders may exercise this right

- ✔ A description of any dissenters' rights or appraisal rights a shareholder may have

- ✔ The ability of shareholders or directors to conduct business without a meeting through the preparation of written corporate resolutions that are consented to by the shareholders and/or directors

- Quorum requirements (described in Chapter 16) for shareholder meetings
- A description of the powers of the board of directors
- The manner of conducting and noticing regular or special meetings of the board of directors
- Quorum requirements for board meetings
- The number, term, and qualifications for directors
- The process for removing directors or filling vacancies of the board
- The titles and duties of corporate officers
- The process by which officers are appointed (not elected) and removed
- Provisions relating to corporate indemnification of its directors, officers, employees, and agents
- The process by which directors or shareholders can amend corporate bylaws

You may sense that bylaws are somewhat formalistic. And you're correct. They are full of process and procedure. Bylaws need to be carefully drafted, and they should never be ignored. Failure to follow your bylaws could result in activities of the corporation to be disregarded by courts or creditors and potential personal liability for these activities imposed upon individual officers, directors, or shareholders.

Make sure that you understand what the bylaws say. If you see provisions that don't make sense to you or which you believe could create problems down the road, ask questions. More than likely, you can modify those provisions to satisfy your needs.

Sample sets of bylaws are available from a number of resources listed in Appendix B. Appendix A also provides a sample set of bylaws. A word of advice: Read and familiarize yourself with the sample sets of bylaws that are readily available before you get started.

Additional provisions

Holy smoke! How could you possibly want to include more in your bylaws than those things we have already listed? When will it end? Good question — maybe it won't if you don't take control. Here are some other things to consider (remembering that bylaws aren't public and may be more easily amended than the articles of incorporation):

✔ Supermajority voting requirements, which may apply to certain important matters like voting for board members, making decisions to dissolve the corporation, borrowing lots of money, and so on for which you might like to require more than a majority vote.

✔ Emergency bylaws, by which the board is authorized to act without meeting, in the event of some catastrophic event.

✔ Restrictions on the ability of shareholders to sell or transfer their corporate stock. (Many shareholders in small corporations want to know who they are going to be doing business with.)

✔ A description of the cumulative voting process if the statute or articles of incorporation require cumulative voting for the election of directors (see Chapter 16).

✔ Corporate mission or values statements

✔ Provisions that allow meeting notices to be sent electronically and persons to attend meetings via telephone or other electronic means.

✔ Any other provision not consistent with the articles of incorporation or law.

In the event of a conflict with the articles of incorporation, the articles will prevail over the bylaws. In the event of a conflict with the statute, the statute will prevail over the articles and the bylaws. Like everything else, incorporation has a pecking order.

To illustrate these concepts, check out the sample corporate bylaws in Appendix A. Keep in mind that different states have different requirements, so don't just photocopy the form and stick it in your minute book. Check it out to make certain that it does what you want it to do and that it complies with the law of your state of incorporation.

Chapter 9

Capitalizing Your Corporation

● ●

In This Chapter

▶ Finding out what it means to capitalize your corporation

▶ Understanding the differences between debt and equity

▶ Avoiding unintended termination of S corporation status

▶ Documenting your corporate records

● ●

*T*he moment you have the articles of incorporation filed with and accepted by the appropriate secretary of state, your corporation springs into existence. At this point, there may not be much to show for the corporation. Quite possibly, it lacks assets or capital and may not have its own bank account, letterhead, telephone number, or any of the many other characteristics of an operating business. Plainly, one of your first steps will be to provide the corporation with the capital and resources with which it can conduct its business.

In this chapter, we'll explore alternatives available to you to capitalize the corporation. You'll discover important differences between debt and equity that will affect your choices. We'll also consider the importance of documenting your corporate capitalization activities.

Show Me the Money

Simply speaking, *capitalization* refers to the task of providing your corporation with resources necessary to conduct business. Capital will most likely come from two sources:

✔ **Contributions by shareholders in exchange for corporate stock:** To become a shareholder, you must own stock in the corporation. The amounts shareholders pay to the corporation or the value of property contributed to the corporation in exchange for stock become part of the corporation's capital. The corporation's capital increases by the value of any property contributed to it.

> ✔ **Loans to the corporation:** Shareholders, banks, and others loan money to corporations. Loan proceeds are also used as part of the corporation's capital, enabling the corporation to conduct business and acquire additional assets required by the business. You may want to contact your local Small Business Administration (SBA) office for information about business loans.

How you capitalize your corporation is important. Shareholder contributions don't saddle the corporation with loan repayment obligations or other demands on how you operate your business, which might be imposed by its lenders. Shareholders also have rights, however, and as an officer or director, you owe your shareholders a duty to act in a careful and loyal manner using good business judgment. Chapter 15 covers the board's duties and responsibilities to shareholders. Some business owners prefer the arm's-length arrangements imposed by lenders compared to the requirement to report to and be responsive to questions and inquiries of shareholders.

The Battle of the Century: Equity versus Debt

When a shareholder buys shares of stock, either by paying cash or contributing property to the corporation, the corporation gains equity. The corporation has no obligation to repay amounts contributed by shareholders, and shareholders have no expectation of repayment. For shareholders, equity contributions are made for a number of reasons — job security, hope of future gains as the corporation grows and succeeds, or a sense of ownership. Equity also exists to the extent that the value of the corporation's assets exceed its liabilities. Just as you have equity in your house equal to the difference between the market value of the house and the mortgage amount assessed against it, a business can have equity in this excess.

We are all familiar with debt. Many of us have too much of it and spend much of our lives trying to get rid of it. Debt indicates an obligation to repay something. In a corporate sense, this commonly exists as a loan by a shareholder or others to the corporation. In either personal or business loans, there is a lender and a borrower. The lender expects the borrower to repay the borrowed amount, with interest, within a defined period of time.

Here's some good news: For most corporations, it's relatively easy to distinguish between debt and equity. Here's some bad news: This isn't always true, and the consequences can be serious. The following sections describe some of the nuances.

Equity

When a shareholder acquires stock, the shareholder is contributing to the equity of the corporation. The shareholder has no right to repayment. The monies paid or property contributed to the corporation belong to the corporation. In return, the shareholder acquires an ownership interest in the corporation and reserves the rights and privileges of a shareholder under the corporation statutes, the articles of incorporation, and the bylaws of the corporation. The rights and privileges may vary greatly from corporation to corporation and state to state.

Stock represents ownership of a corporation. It's commonly evidenced by the issuance of shares of stock although many states don't require that a certificate actually be issued. Stock can have many characteristics: common, preferred, convertible, and so on. If the articles permit it, corporations may issue different types of stock, each containing different rights and preferences.

Common stock

Most small business corporations issue a single class of *common stock,* in which one share is identical to any other share of that corporation's stock. Among the benefits of ownership is a right to vote on important corporate matters, such as the election of directors. Voting rights are usually parceled out at the rate of one vote per share. The shareholder has voting rights provided for in the corporation statutes, and he or she has a right to receive meeting notices, inspect records, and be bought out if certain events prescribed by the statute occur and diminish the value of the shareholder's stock.

There can be different classifications or series of common stock within a corporation. Whether this exists is dependent upon whether the articles of incorporation provide for separate classifications. For example, Class A Common Stock might allow shareholders to vote for certain directors while Class B Common Stock might allow Class B shareholders to vote for other directors. Alternatively, Class A could elect all directors with Class B shareholders having no voting rights at all if the articles of incorporation so provide.

It's unusual to see different classifications of common stock in newly formed small corporations. For these corporations, there simply isn't much of a need to create classes of stock. It's also unlikely that these corporations will see a need to create a different class of stock in the future.

Shareholders owning common stock have no right to compel a corporation's board of directors to declare a dividend or payment of profit to shareholders at any time.

As a corporation grows and succeeds, the value of its shares also grows, increasing the likelihood that shareholders will receive this enhanced value when the shares are sold. Most corporate shares aren't publicly traded on a stock exchange. As a result, the corporation has no readily identifiable market for the shares of its stock. Common buyers include existing shareholders seeking to increase their ownership interest in the corporation or outside third parties looking to buy the corporation. Friends and family members can also purchase corporate shares.

Preferred stock

Preferred stock is stock that contains one or more preferences. The most common preference is the right to receive annual dividends. Common shareholders have no ability to compel the corporation to pay dividends. On the other hand, preferred shareholders may have rights that lead to the payment of dividends, if adequate surplus exists, and the terms and conditions of their preferred shares require payment. This type of preferred share can be further classified as *cumulative* or *noncumulative*.

Corporate dividends generally cannot be paid lawfully if there is insufficient surplus from which the amount of dividends is to be paid. If a preferred share is noncumulative, and if there is insufficient surplus, no preferred dividend is paid to the noncumulative shareholders. If the preferred shares are cumulative, and if there is insufficient surplus to pay a dividend, the amount that would have been paid is credited to the shareholder. Once adequate surplus is available and dividends are paid, the shareholder receives his amount, even if that is years down the road. Preferred stock may also have preferences that relate to redemption (cashing in) or liquidation. Insufficient surplus exists whenever the corporation is insolvent or the payment of the dividend would cause the corporation to become insolvent. A corporation is insolvent if it's unable to pay its debts as the debts become due or, if following the payment, the corporation's total assets are less than the corporation's total liabilities.

Business succession plans often use preferred stock. Older shareholders surrender their common stock in exchange for preferred shares. Unlike common shares, which can increase in value, preferred shares often have a fixed value that doesn't rise or fall. The trade-off for preferred shareholders is the ability to receive current dividends rather than future growth.

Determining whether to issue preferred shares can be a creative and flexible process. Like common stock, the corporation can create various classes of preferred shares. Your shareholders will tell you what they want (long-term growth or current income). When setting up your corporation, you decide what you want the corporation to offer. Just remember, the articles of incorporation should describe the preferences. S corporations cannot have a second class of stock, making preferred stock unavailable for corporations seeking S corporation status.

Assume that you own cumulative, preferred shares. Although you are entitled to dividends, the corporation has been unable to pay dividends, resulting in unpaid dividends to you of $1,000. You would like to sell your shares. Who is entitled to receive the unpaid dividends? Generally, the dividends follow the stock. Make sure that your sale contract with your purchaser identifies who is entitled to the dividends when they are ultimately paid. As an alternative, have the purchase price reflect the value of the unpaid dividends.

Debt convertible to stock

Some of your investors may want the best of both worlds. Cautious in the beginning, they seek the security of a loan instrument with its current repayment and interest. They also thirst for the adventure of a successful business and the potential increase in stock value. You can often find this type of investor in a venture capital firm. To satisfy this desire, your loan agreement gives the lender a right to convert all or some part of the debt into stock of the corporation. The loan agreement sets forth the specific exchange rate. For these types of transactions, it's vital that the loan agreement detail how the market value of corporate stock will be determined from time to time.

Stock options

Most of us have some understanding of stock options. For some, it's a distant notion of a young "techie" cashing in on the dot.com craze. A *stock option* is merely an option that allows an individual to purchase shares of corporate stock for a price set forth in the option agreement. Corporations commonly use options as an incentive to retain key employees or to reward employees for good performance.

If a corporation has different classes of stock, whether common or preferred, options can be used for any of the classes. The corporate board of directors determines whether to use options and determines the terms and conditions of the option. Compliance with these terms and conditions is important. Common terms and conditions include the purchase price per share and the time frame within which the person must exercise his option. The option lapses if it isn't exercised within the required time.

Debt

For purposes of this chapter, debt is a loan. Its chief characteristic is repayment of principal and interest within a defined period of time. A loan is a particular type of corporate liability. A corporation will have other liabilities besides debt that will require repayment.

Where do you find lenders?

Despite a world where mailboxes overflow with applications from credit card companies, lenders don't always find you. Moreover, for start-ups, no traditional lender, such as a bank, will be interested in loaning you money. If you don't have an operating history and sufficient personal assets to secure a loan, traditional lenders like banks may not be available. So, who *will* loan your corporation money? For corporate start-ups, you may be your own biggest lender. Next in line, you might work with family and friends who are willing to loan money to the corporation. Some of these folks might even put money at risk and buy stock.

If you have an operating history, banks may make loans to you. Venture capital firms also exist to provide financing. For venture capitalists to be interested, your business must show great promise to increase in value within a few years. Venture capital often comes to you as a loan with features that allow the venture capital firm to convert the loan to equity in order to be able to benefit from increases in the value of the corporate stock. Lenders can demand a great deal from corporate borrowers. Lenders may impose restrictions on amounts that can be paid as salaries to corporate officers, on the ability to declare and pay dividends, and on the maintenance of certain asset-to-liability ratios during the duration of the loan.

Many corporations may also be eligible for government-guaranteed loans through the Small Business Administration (SBA). Contact your local SBA office to find out their requirements for a loan. It's easier to interest a bank in making a loan to your corporation if the SBA guarantees loan repayment.

Federal, state, and local economic development programs also have access to funds available for loans. Most states have economic development agencies that can provide you with information about eligibility. We offer contact information about some of these programs and agencies in Appendix B.

Debt characteristics

Most loan arrangements include a loan agreement and promissory note. The note sets forth the specific repayment provisions and the penalties for failure to comply with the loan terms. Traditional lenders often require security for loans. Security means pledging real or personal property in the event you can't make payment and includes a mortgage on real estate, a security agreement and financing statement for personal property, a pledge of stock, or a combination of these things. You may also assign life insurance on the life of the key shareholder as security for the loan.

The key characteristic for a debt obligation is an expectation on the part of the lender to be repaid with interest. Loans by shareholders or family members are often made without any real expectation of repayment. When this happens, is there really a loan or debt created? If no loan is created, what does exist? Is it a contribution to the capital and equity of the corporation? Is it a second or third class of stock? What rights does the borrower have? All of these questions are difficult to answer, and we suggest you seek advice.

With a loan, interest paid by the corporation is deductible to the corporation. Amounts repaid to a lender as principal aren't income to the lender. Only that portion of the loan that represents interest is taxable to the lender as income. If a corporation pays money to shareholders based on share ownership, it's considered a dividend. Dividends aren't deductible to the corporation. Amounts paid to shareholders as dividends are taxable to the shareholders.

S corporation issues involving debt and equity

S corporations provide special challenges when dealing with issues of debt and equity. For example, an S corporation can't have more than one class of stock. While certain tolerances are permitted relative to voting rights, a second class of stock will automatically terminate an S corporation election. Suddenly, the IRS treats your S corporation as a C corporation for income tax purposes. The pass-through attributes of an S corporation no longer apply.

What could cause the IRS to characterize corporate debt as a second class of stock? Here are some key factors:

- ✔ Failure to document loan transactions in corporate minutes and through loan agreements and promissory notes

- ✔ No expectation of repayment — usually demonstrated by a lack of any payments of principal in contravention of loan agreement terms or efforts on the part of the lender to collect the debt

- ✔ Loans by shareholders to the corporation in direct proportion to the shareholders' interest in stock ownership

- ✔ Debt repayment tied to profitability or success of the corporation

- ✔ Extremely favorable loan conditions made without normal lender safeguards such as documentation or security

- ✔ Loans by family members

Debt that is recharacterized as equity isn't always considered an impermissible second class of stock. If it is, however, serious consequences can follow these consequences.

S corporations also result in differing tax treatment in other areas. For example, because S corporations are pass-through entities, they don't pay tax at the corporate level. C corporations pay taxes at the corporate level and receive no deduction for dividends paid. With S corporations, dividends are taxable at the shareholder level, as are C corporations, with no tax at the S corporation level.

And while C corporations can deduct loan interest, S corporation shareholders are eligible to deduct their pro rata share of corporate interest payments at the shareholder level and not at the corporate level.

Documenting What You Do

We can't overstate the importance of documenting corporate activities involving debt and equity. This is a vital compliance area for corporations. Here is a list to get you started:

- Corporate minutes authorizing the issuance of corporate stock should include a description of the number of shares to be issued and the money paid or value of property contributed as payment for the shares.

- Corporate minutes authorizing any borrowing by the corporation should identify the lender, amounts borrowed, interest rate, loan term, and loan purpose. The corporate minutes also should direct specifically named officers and directors to sign loan documents and promissory notes on behalf of the corporation.

- Loan transactions should include a loan agreement, promissory note, and copies of any security documents securing the loan, all properly signed by authorized corporate officers or directors.

- Records should exist so that the corporation can identify its shareholders and the shares they own, outstanding loans, loan repayments, and dates of loan repayment.

See Chapters 18 and 19 for more about corporate minutes or records.

Chapter 10

Doing Business in Other States

· ·

In This Chapter

▶ Understanding the concept of doing business

▶ Qualifying your corporation to do business in other states

▶ Failing to qualify your corporation and its consequences

· ·

So you've set up shop in your home state. Business is doing great, and you're starting to venture into nearby states. Good for you — you're realizing the American Dream! And since it's America, you are free to do business wherever you want, right? Wrong! You may have to qualify to do business in those other states. This chapter presents the concept of doing business, which will help you decide whether you should qualify for incorporation in another state.

Deciding Where You Are Doing Business

Before you start the process of qualifying to do business in another state, you have to determine whether you are actually "doing business" in that other state. Here's a question that's challenged legal scholars and judges for years because you can approach it in a number of different ways. The best way is to use good common sense, and ask yourself a few questions:

✔ Do you have an office in the other state?

✔ Do you meet with customers in that state?

✔ Do you have employees physically located in that state?

✔ Does the corporation generate revenues and expenses in that state?

✔ Are the business activities continuous and systematic as opposed to isolated transactions?

If you answer, "Yes," to any of these questions, common sense suggests that you are doing business there.

However, what if you never set foot in the other state, relying instead on the mail or telephone to contact individuals or businesses there? Are you doing business in that state? Common sense suggests that you aren't doing business in the other state even though you may be generating revenue.

What about the myriad possibilities that lie between these examples? Consider an e-business: Where does a corporation that does business only on the Internet do business? Certainly, it has reporting and compliance responsibilities in the state where it is incorporated. Quite possibly, the e-business corporation would qualify to do business in any state where it maintains offices and employees. The law in this area is still developing. As you can tell, it's not always easy to know. You may want to talk with your lawyer.

The Revised Model Business Corporation Act (RMBCA) provides illustrative examples of activity, which standing alone will not require a corporation to qualify to do business in another state (see Chapter 1). Some examples include:

- ✔ Suing, being sued, or settling any claim
- ✔ Conducting meetings of the board or shareholders within a state
- ✔ Selling through independent contractors (another tricky area that might require a visit to your lawyer)
- ✔ Maintaining a bank account in another state
- ✔ Selling or obtaining orders by mail or through employees or agents, if the orders require acceptance outside of the state before becoming binding (see your lawyer)
- ✔ Borrowing money
- ✔ Securing or collecting debts
- ✔ Owning real or personal property
- ✔ Conducting an isolated transaction that is completed within 30 days and that is not one in the course of repeated business transactions
- ✔ Transacting business in interstate commerce (another highly complex area that requires professional guidance)

Although any one of these factors might not be enough to require your corporation to qualify to do business in a state, a combination of factors may require qualification.

What happens if your corporation should qualify to do business in a state but fails to do so? The corporation can't sue anyone else. Try to use the local courts to sue for breach of contract or other damages if the corporation isn't qualified. You'll find the courthouse doors are locked. Once you qualify, the doors spring open, and you can file suit, unless the applicable statute of limitations — the amount of time you have under state law to file a lawsuit — has expired. The corporation will pay fines and possible interest on amounts that should have been paid. The fines and penalties can be pretty steep if you have been doing business without qualifying for several years. Many states are lenient and will waive fines and penalties in exchange for compliance.

If you should qualify, but you fail to do so, corporate activities, including contracts made by the corporation, are valid. You might not be able to gain access to a local court until you qualify, but the actions are good. If you haven't qualified and you are sued, the corporation will have access to the court to defend itself.

Qualifying to Do Business in Other States

States want your business. They make qualification easy. In fact, the qualification process is nearly identical to the process of filing articles of incorporation. Only the names have changed, presumably to protect the innocent.

To qualify to do business in another state, corporations submit an application for a certificate of authority. Forms are available from the applicable secretary of state's office, or a service company can supply and file them for you. Required information may include:

- The name of the corporation
- The name and address of the registered agent (service companies can provide this for you if you don't have a physical presence in the state)
- The date and state of incorporation
- The duration of corporation
- The corporation's permanent address
- The names and addresses of corporate officers and/or directors
- The number of shares authorized, itemized by class and series, if any
- The date on which the corporation will begin doing business in the state

In addition to the application and the filing fee, the corporation may be required to submit a certificate of good standing, which is sometimes referred to as a certificate of existence. Some states also require a certified copy of the articles of incorporation. The secretary of state of the domestic state issues these documents. The fee for these documents ranges from $5 to $50, depending on your state of incorporation. The time frame varies from state to state and can take as little as one or two business days, if you pay a state expedite or express fee, or sometimes three weeks or more to receive the documents. As part of their standard menu of service, a service company routinely performs what is commonly referred to as "document retrieval" services for its clients. This may be a viable alternative if you don't have time to take care of the legwork yourself.

In a few states, filing fees for foreign corporations may be significantly higher than fees for domestic corporations.

Like a domestic corporation that receives a certificate of incorporation, the secretary of state issues a certificate of authority to the foreign corporation. In the event that the foreign corporation ceases to do business in that state, the corporation will file an application for certificate of withdrawal.

Living as a Foreign Corporation

Foreign corporation: Sounds exotic, doesn't it? Before you start envisioning business meetings held on a sunny, tropical beach, think again. A *foreign corporation* is simply a corporation that does business outside its state of incorporation. If your corporation is engaged in business in states other than your state of incorporation, you must qualify the corporation to do business in those other states. If you were to do business only within your state of incorporation, your corporation would be a *domestic corporation*.

If you do business in more than one state, a number of consequences follow. Duplication of administrative efforts is one consequence of doing business in the corporate form. You'll be filing annual reports, franchise, and income tax reports in each state where the corporation is qualified to do business. You'll need to be aware of licensing and permit requirements in each state, as well (see Chapter 12 for more information on licenses, permits, and registrations).

Whether you do business in one state or several, you will need to keep a calendar of important events. All states require that corporations file annual reports or other reports. In addition, your corporation must renew licenses and permits periodically. Assign a reliable employee to this task or do it yourself. You can find calendaring software or a service company to assist you. The Company Corporation, for example, provides a service called Compliance Watch, which provides an online state-specific calendaring service for your use. A special feature tracks company activity in multiple states.

Doing business in more than one state involves more paperwork, more compliance issues, and more cost (usually associated with the time required to prepare paperwork and pay filing fees). But, if the business is good, the additional time and cost will be worth it.

Business owners often don't have a choice about whether to qualify to do business in another state. The simple fact is that, if you are incorporated and do business in a state other than the state of incorporation, you must qualify to do business there. If the volume of business in that other state is sufficient, you won't hesitate to expand your business even if you are required to qualify. The additional expense and paperwork involved in qualifying in another state will be more than offset by revenue generated from the added business.

Domestication

Say you formed your Delaware corporation and qualified it to do business in Oregon. Several years later, you realize that all your business activities are in Oregon, with no connection to Delaware. You're paying fees and filing reports in both states. What are you going to do? Through a process known as *domestication*, many states make it possible for a foreign corporation to become a domestic one, giving you the opportunity to free yourself from reporting obligations and annual fees to the state with which you have no connection. If this paragraph describes your corporation, consider using the domestication process to terminate your Delaware corporate status and preserve your Oregon corporate status. You'll save time and money.

Part III

I've Incorporated My Business, Now What?

The 5th Wave   By Rich Tennant

"In the interest of a future stock issuance, I highly recommend you _NOT_ use your family name as part of your corporate identity, Mr. Defunct."

In this part . . .

You've incorporated your business, and now you're wondering what's left to do. Plenty! In this part, you obtain required identification numbers, register your corporation with state agencies, create effective shareholder agreements, conduct board and shareholder meetings, get money in and out of your corporation, and learn the importance of a business plan. This part provides you with the knowledge to finish the job of incorporating.

Chapter 11

Conducting an Organizational Meeting

The articles have been filed. You've drafted your corporate bylaws. You're ready to issue shares of stock, open bank accounts, file an application for an identification number, and formally get your corporation up and running. How do you tie all these organizational pieces together? Your best bet — conduct an annual meeting and document your organizational activities with meeting minutes. In this chapter, you'll understand why a meeting is helpful and how to document the results of the meeting.

An Organizational Meeting: Is It Worth My Time?

You betcha! This is your chance to set the tone for your whole organization. Organizational meetings provide you with an opportunity to formalize the organizational activities of the corporation. While a meeting isn't always required, it's a good idea. Use the organizational meeting to bring together everyone to consider and approve those matters described in the following section. Here's your chance to make sure that all of the players — directors, officers, and shareholders — are all on the same page as the corporation prepares for launch. Discovering disagreements or misunderstandings at this stage will be helpful in the long run, and could save time and money.

Many small corporations skip the actual meeting, choosing instead to formalize actions through consent resolutions (see Chapter 16). By using consent resolutions, you miss the chance to bring all of your big players together at this key juncture of your corporation's development.

Whether you conduct an actual meeting or use consent resolutions, you should end up with a good set of organizational minutes that document those matters described in the next section. Corporate minutes should go hand in hand with an organizational meeting or any other meeting of the corporate board or shareholders. Minutes become the record that documents and memorializes action taken at a meeting.

Let's Talk About . . . : Discussion Items for Your Organizational Meeting

Corporation statutes don't require any specific information to be discussed at an organizational meeting or included in the organizational minutes. As noted above, an organizational meeting, while not required, can be an important opportunity to make certain you consider important beginning matters.

Corporate minutes, whether resulting from an organizational meeting or later meeting, are an important part of your ongoing corporate compliance. If the corporation or its officers or directors are challenged on a particular matter, it's always nice to be able to go back to the minutes to point out that a particular action had, in fact, been authorized by the board or the shareholders. You can bet that if the corporation is ever sued, you'll be asked to produce corporate records, including minutes.

Expect that your minutes will be reviewed carefully, looking for opportunities to allege that certain activities weren't authorized or that the person performing them lacked the authority to do so. The failure to have organizational minutes could be used as evidence that the corporation is merely a sham and that personal liability should attach to the officers, directors, or shareholders.

Here are the basics you should usually discuss at an organizational meeting:

- Election of directors by the shareholders or appointment of initial directors by the incorporator
- Appointment of officers by the directors
- Acceptance and approval of corporate bylaws
- Approval of the form of corporate stock if stock certificates are to be used

✔ Authorization to sell shares to named individuals in exchange for money, property, or other consideration, all of which should be listed in detail in the minutes

✔ Authorization to establish corporate bank accounts (most banks will provide their own preprinted form of corporate resolution)

✔ Authorization to prepare and submit any required tax election forms such as an election to be treated as an S corporation

✔ A general statement authorizing designated officers or any officer to execute any and all documents and take any and all actions that may be required to effectuate any other resolution contained in the organizational minutes

✔ A general statement ratifying and approving the acts of officers, directors, and incorporators for proper actions taken on behalf of the corporation prior to the date of incorporation, through and including the date of the organizational minutes

What About . . . : Other Matters to Consider

There is no limit to the types of matters you may want to consider during your organizational meeting. The list will depend entirely on your corporation and its needs. Most courts will presume that a corporation can do anything required in the ordinary course of its business. A corporation formed for the purpose of selling widgets doesn't need to authorize or document each and every widget sale in its minutes. That would be silly.

However, some actions extend beyond what might be considered the ordinary and customary business of a corporation. The organizational meeting and the minutes should reflect these types of actions if they relate to start-up activities of the business. Otherwise, they would appear in later minutes that document actions of the board or shareholders. Here are some examples:

✔ The corporation agrees to borrow money.

✔ The corporation agrees to lend money (unless that is its principal business).

✔ The corporation makes a significant capital expenditure (buys automobiles, trucks, expensive equipment, computer system, and so on).

✔ The corporation contracts to purchase another business or to sell all or substantially all of its own assets to another business.

- ✔ The corporation buys, sells, or leases real estate (again, unless this is a principal part of its business).

- ✔ The corporation determines to enter into employment agreements with any of its officers or key employees.

- ✔ The corporation agrees to guarantee the indebtedness of another.

- ✔ The corporation determines to apply to do business in another state (see Chapter 10).

This list is by no means exhaustive. For record-keeping purposes, it probably makes sense to defer in favor of putting something into the organizational minutes rather than leaving it out.

To help you, Appendix A provides a sample form of organizational minutes. Again, as with all samples and forms, customize them. Read it carefully, and make changes that you feel are more appropriate to your corporation.

Documenting Organizational Activities

Do you remember reading that a corporation must act solely through the actions of others, most notably its directors, officers, employees, or agents? Minutes document the authority and approval for these corporate "agents" to act in a written summary. In some instances, the minutes ratify actions already taken by these agents on behalf of the corporation.

Organizational minutes are nothing more than minutes that document the essential start-up activities of the corporation. As you can guess, individuals must do a bunch of advance work to form the corporation and prepare bylaws. In addition, state and federal identification numbers have been or are in the process of being obtained, bank accounts opened, and more. The organizational minutes will generally ratify these prior acts and authorize acts that will need to occur in order to get the corporation fully up and running.

The minutes reflected for the organizational meeting are really no different from the kinds of minutes that should be prepared when the board of directors or shareholders meet or approve some activity for the corporation that isn't within its normal course of business.

No formal meeting required

As noted earlier, organizational minutes, like all minutes, don't always require a formal meeting of the board or shareholders. Many corporations owned by a small number of shareholders will simply prepare a consent resolution or resolutions for signature by all the board members or shareholders. When all necessary signatures are obtained and the contents are properly filed, the resolutions are approved just as they would have been had a formal meeting been held.

Signing off on organizational minutes

Who signs off on organizational minutes? It depends. If the corporation's initial board of directors has not been named in the articles of incorporation, the *incorporator,* the one who signed off on the articles, should prepare a document entitled, "Action by Incorporator," which designates board members and takes care of any other housekeeping matters. If the articles identify the board members, they would sign the organizational minutes. As we mention earlier, there generally aren't any shareholders at this point because one of the organizational meeting purposes is to authorize the issuance of shares to shareholders.

Chapter 12

Getting Started: Numbers, Elections, Registration

- -

In This Chapter

▶ Filing requests for corporation identification numbers

▶ Making effective S corporation elections

▶ Getting the necessary licenses and permits for your business

- -

Congratulations! You've filed your articles of incorporation, created bylaws, and prepared your organizational minutes. Now it's time to tackle the necessary actions to get your corporation up and running. This chapter starts your journey of corporate details, maintenance, and compliance. The other chapters in Parts III and IV continue this trek to the Land of Incorporation.

In this chapter, you'll be introduced to some parts of the puzzle that you'll be required to complete before you can begin doing business as a corporation. For example, any new business requires federal and state identification numbers. If you wish to become an S corporation, you'll need to file the appropriate form with the IRS within a short period of time after incorporation. Finally, almost every state, many counties, and some cities require numerous licenses and permits before you can begin operation. While the details aren't complicated, there can be a number of details you'll need to address.

 Know what numbers you'll need *before* you file the articles of incorporation. This will enable you to get the corporation up and running more quickly. What kinds of numbers? You'll need state and federal identification numbers available from the IRS and your local secretary of state. You may also have numbers assigned to you for purposes of unemployment or workers' compensation. You may need state or local permits or licenses, each of which will probably have a number assigned to them. For state or local numbers, check with the secretary of state's office. Your state may also have a one-stop shop to assist you in obtaining all required state numbers, registrations, licenses, and permits. The resources listed in Appendix B can guide you in the right direction.

Obtaining Federal and State Identification Numbers

You need numbers to start business as a corporation. How many numbers you need depends on your business. Here's a look at some of the more common types of numbers.

Charter number

Within a space of days to weeks after filing the articles of incorporation, you'll receive a Certificate, which is the state's acceptance of your articles of incorporation. The Certificate should be attached to a copy of your articles. In most states, a number, usually referred to as the corporation's charter number, will be attached to the articles or the Certificate. Not all states issue a Certificate. Some states merely attach a file stamp from the secretary of state's office, and the number will be stamped there.

To many, the purpose of the charter number remains a mystery. It's a part of the secret filing system for the secretary of state. When you file subsequent documents with the secretary of state, such as amendments to the articles of incorporation, you may be asked for the charter number. If you don't have it, the secretary's office will usually fill it in for you. Beyond that, the number probably has little significance in many states.

Identification numbers

One of the first things you'll do once you have filed the articles is apply for a federal identification number. It's a must. No bank in the country will let you open a corporate bank account until you get one. The form is available from the IRS (downloadable from its Web site at `www.irs.org`) as Form SS-4 Application for Employer Identification Number. Service companies also can often provide you with these forms and will file them for you as part of your fee.

The form is pretty self-explanatory, as IRS forms go. Here's a sampling of the information you'll be asked to provide:

- ✔ Name of the applicant (this will be the corporation's name, not yours).
- ✔ Trade name of the business (more on this in Chapter 6).
- ✔ Mailing address.
- ✔ Name and social security number of the principal officer.

✔ Type of entity (most likely, you'll check "other corporation" and indicate whether its an S or C corporation).

✔ List the state where incorporated.

✔ Describe the reason for applying (most often, you'll check the box which reads, "Started new business").

✔ Date the business started; defined to be the first date on which the corporation acquired a new business, had assets, or actually commenced business.

✔ Identify the first date on which wages were paid or are to be paid.

✔ List the highest number of employees you expect to have within the following 12 months, and break this number down to identify which will be in the categories of agricultural, nonagricultural, or household.

✔ Describe the principal activity of the corporation (an example would be advertising agency or sod farm).

✔ Identify to whom most of your products are sold or services provided (categories are public retail, business wholesale, or the ever-popular "other").

✔ Indicate whether the applicant has ever applied for a federal identification number before. (For most, the answer is "No," remembering that the applicant is the newly formed corporation and not you.)

Why in the world are all of these questions relevant? Good question. Some of your responses will plug you into other parts of the IRS, especially those concerned with whether you're making required quarterly tax payments and withholdings. Some of the information is statistical in nature, helping track new businesses.

Once assigned, the federal identification number belongs to the corporation forever. Think of it as being the corporate counterpart of your social security number.

Many states have a similar form for you to complete. Few will ask as many questions as the federal form does, so if you're ready to answer the federal form, the state form shouldn't be much of a challenge.

Filing S Corporation Elections

If S corporation status is for you, filing your S corporation election form on time is a biggie. Corporations seeking S corporation status must file Form 2553 Election by a Small Business Corporation within a narrow window of time. For new corporations hoping to achieve S corporation status from the outset, the election must be filed on or before the fifteenth day of the third month of the tax year. For most start-ups, this will be 75 days following the earliest date the corporation first had shareholders or assets, or began doing business. Of course, it isn't always easy to tell when these events occur, so professionals most often recommend that, to be safe, you file your election within 75 days following the date of incorporation.

What is an S corporation election? As discussed in Chapter 2, a corporation can choose to be taxed as a distinct legal entity or to allow the tax to be levied and assessed at the shareholder level. This is an S corporation. You make your choice by completing IRS Form 2553 and submitting it to the IRS. The form is available online from the IRS at www.irs.org.

Be prepared to answer these questions for your S corporation election:

- The name and address of the corporation
- The tax year for which the election is to be effective
- The identity and contact number for a corporate officer who can respond to IRS questions about the filing
- The date on which the corporation first had shareholders or assets, or began doing business, whichever date occurred first
- The name, address, and social security number of each shareholder
- The signature and date of signature of the shareholders, all of whom must consent to the filing of the election

S corporations choosing a tax year other than a tax year ending on December 31 must complete Part II of the election form to describe why a different tax year-end is appropriate. Most S corporations have December 31 as the year-end date.

Your accountant or lawyer can advise you regarding S corporation election. Service companies can also often provide applications for SubChapter S filings.

Registering Your Corporation in the State of Incorporation

The registration process doesn't end with identification numbers. Depending on the corporation's business, expect to contact a number of state agencies to register and obtain numbers, licenses, or permits before doing business.

It's not possible to list all of the possible agencies you may need to contact. Truly business-friendly states have one-stop shops where you can access a single contact or form to complete required state registrations. Other states make you go agency to agency to accomplish this task. Expect to visit state employment departments, workers' compensation divisions, revenue departments, and the like. Depending on the business, permits and licenses may be necessary (whether or not your business is incorporated) from federal and state agencies dealing with environmental quality, land use, and so on.

In addition, some states (like Oregon) license anything that shows signs of life. Some permits and fees merely require the payment of a fee. Others require proof of education, experience, and possibly the passage of a state or federal examination. Doctors, lawyers, contractors, barbers, restaurant operators, hot dog stand vendors, and virtually every other occupation or business imaginable require licensing. Some licenses apply to individual operators and not the corporation, some apply only to the corporation, and others apply to both. You'll need to check with your state to see what types of licenses or permits you may need.

Again, your secretary of state's office should be a good starting point for accessing information about licenses and permits. Most states have Web sites that provide directories for all the different state agencies.

Knowing what licenses and permits you'll need to conduct your business will save you time in the long run. It won't help you much to have the corporation formed and ready to go if it doesn't have required licenses and permits. To speed up the process, research, in advance, which permits and licenses you'll need.

Shareholders: Do's and Don'ts

Shareholders are the true owners of the corporation. They are your equity investors, contributing money, property, or other things of value in exchange for a stock ownership interest in the corporation. Sometimes, a shareholder receives stock in exchange for the performance of services.

Shareholders of small corporations often wear other hats as well: Officer, director, or employee are the most common. If you're wearing more than one hat, know which hat you have on at any moment in time. As you'll see, different hats mean different rights and responsibilities.

Did you know that not all states have shareholders? It's true. Some states have stockholders instead. The only difference is the name. In this book, we use the term *shareholder*. If you incorporate in a stockholder state, you might want to modify your corporate documents to refer to stockholders instead.

So what do you need to know about your shareholders? How do shareholder roles and responsibilities differ from those of officers and directors? How do close corporation statutes affect the roles and responsibilities of shareholders? This chapter covers all these issues and also looks at shareholder lawsuits, both derivative and direct actions.

The Making of a Shareholder

Some shareholders are born, and some are made. Virtually any legal entity can be a shareholder — including individuals, other corporations, limited liability companies, partnerships, trusts, and so on — unless your corporation elects S corporation status. With limited exceptions, S corporation shareholders must be individuals.

For smaller, start-up businesses, your shareholders will likely be key individuals involved with getting the business up and running. Most will be active in the day-to-day operation. Those not active are likely to be family members and close friends. Many small corporations have Mom and Pop as shareholders.

People become shareholders for a number of reasons. Here are a few examples:

- ✔ It's your business, you decided to incorporate, and state corporation laws require that you have to have shareholders. You're it.

- ✔ The prospect that a dollar invested today might be worth many dollars in the future spurs investors to become shareholders.

- ✔ People want to acquire shares in something that makes them feel special. For example, shareholders might seek to acquire stock in businesses that support their view of the environment or a local sports franchise.

- ✔ Someone wants to see you succeed. Your mother, father, or friends may offer to help you by buying shares in your fledging corporation.

Corporations with significant operating history or great promise for success may be able to attract outside investors, such as venture capitalists or private investors with no other relationship to the corporation. A number of corporations have registered their shares of stock publicly with a national stock exchange. If this sounds like the right path for your company, expect to spend time and money attracting venture capitalists or registering your corporation with a national stock exchange.

Do you see your corporation going public? Recruit an experienced professional team early on to help guide you. You may be able to take steps upfront to facilitate this process down the road.

Shareholders own stock. That doesn't necessarily mean that they hold stock certificates. Most states no longer require a paper stock certificate to prove ownership. However, the majority of corporations do provide shareholders with paper stock certificates for proof of ownership. The issuance shares also provide a tangible indication of ownership, important to some investors.

State and federal securities laws regulate the offer and sale of securities, including corporate stock. While a number of exemptions exist, visit with your lawyer to discover which exemptions will benefit you. Failure to comply with securities law can result in civil and criminal fines and penalties.

We Know Our Rights!

Shareholders are special. Look at state law, the articles of incorporation, and the corporate bylaws for their rights. Generally, state corporation statutes provide a number of shareholder rights unless, of course, the articles of incorporation or bylaws say otherwise. Here's a list of some shareholder rights:

- ✔ The right to vote for corporate directors
- ✔ The right to inspect certain corporate records (discussed in Chapter 19)
- ✔ The right to vote on proposed bylaw or articles amendments that seek to alter shareholder voting or quorum requirements (discussed in Chapter 16)
- ✔ The right to cumulative voting in the election of directors (see Chapter 16)
- ✔ The right to vote on significant actions such as a proposed sale, merger, reorganization, or dissolution
- ✔ Preemptive rights (see the next section)
- ✔ Dissenters or appraisal rights (which we cover later in this section)

Preemptive rights

Preemptive rights allow shareholders to maintain their percentage stock ownership. In effect, where preemptive rights exist, a corporation must first offer existing shareholders the right to purchase new shares before it offers the shares to third parties.

Consider Michael, Nina, and Eric, each owning 100 shares of stock in ABC Corporation. Assume that ABC Corporation wants to issue another 600 shares of stock. If preemptive rights exist, Michael, Nina, and Eric would each have the option to buy 200 shares of the 600 proposed to be offered by ABC Corporation. The purchase price would be equal to the price at which ABC Corporation intended to sell the shares to third parties. If the shareholders don't buy, the corporation is free to issue the shares to third parties.

Here's an important catch about preemptive rights. In some states, preemptive rights exist automatically unless specifically excluded in the articles of incorporation. In other states, preemptive rights don't exist at all unless they are expressly provided for in the articles of incorporation. How do you know for sure? You must check the state's corporation law and the articles of incorporation. Alternatively, your articles could simply state that preemptive rights are included or that they are excluded.

Even if your corporation provides for preemptive rights, these rights only attach to newly issued shares by the corporation. They don't attach to sales by shareholders (see Chapter 14 for a discussion of shareholder agreements). In some cases, preemptive rights might not apply to sales within the first six months following the date of incorporation.

Preemptive rights are a favorite of small corporations like ABC Corporation. Shareholders appreciate a tool intended to lessen the possibility that their ownership interest can be diluted.

Dissenters or appraisal rights

Consider this situation: You own 100 shares of ABC Corporation, representing about 20 percent of the issued and outstanding stock of the corporation. Your minority interest subjects you to the whim of those holding the other 80 percent. What if the majority group decides to sell or merge the corporation, something you think makes no sense at all? Welcome to the world of dissenters or appraisal rights.

State legislatures adopted *dissenters* or *appraisal rights* to protect the interests of minority shareholders. These statutes provide a mechanism by which a minority shareholder can compel a corporation, in effect, to buy her or his shares in the event of a sale, merger, or related activity.

If you're a majority shareholder, don't look for ways to oppress or harm your minority counterparts. Similarly, know that your minority shareholders may compel the corporation to buy shares in the event the corporation plans a sale or merger.

For minority shareholders, you may have the opportunity to have your shares purchased if the corporation undertakes a significant act like a sale or merger. You'll also have this opportunity if you feel that the value of your shares is compromised.

Other shareholder rights

Your corporate articles or bylaws may include or exclude any other shareholder rights the corporation chooses. As Chapter 1 notes, corporate articles and bylaws can create different classes of stock, each possibly providing for different rights and preferences. For example, corporate articles could authorize preferred stock, creating certain preferences in favor of the preferred shareholders.

Different classes of stock can have different voting rights. For example, class A might have the right to elect a board member, and class B might not have any voting rights at all. If different classes of stock are to exist or if you choose to create preferences in favor of some shares over others, you must include this information in the articles of incorporation.

You have creative opportunities available here if you choose to use them. For most small corporations, especially S corporations, expect to find a single class of common stock with no additional preferences or rights.

Duty Calls

Do shareholders have responsibilities or duties? Here's a lawyer's favorite answer, "It depends." Generally speaking, a shareholder has no responsibilities or duties as a shareholder. A notable exception exists for a majority shareholder who actively works to oppress, defraud, or otherwise harm the interests of minority shareholders. A majority shareholder can do these things through voting control; he may be able to cause the corporation to do whatever he chooses. To the extent that the motive for these actions is to harm the minority shareholder, the majority shareholder could be sued. It's not easy to prove bad motive or intent, and most of the court decisions holding a majority shareholder liable have involved serious misconduct on the part of the majority shareholder.

Keep in mind which hat you are wearing. As a shareholder, you have little or no responsibility or duty to the corporation or your fellow shareholders. However, if you also serve as an officer or a director, you have responsibilities and duties to the corporation and to the shareholders. In many small corporations, the same individual wears all three hats: shareholder, officer, and director. What if you're all three? You're not out of the woods yet; you must be careful.

One of the principal benefits of incorporation is limited liability for shareholders. From time to time, courts pierce the corporate veil, disregarding the corporation's legal existence, to impose personal liability on shareholders. Here are a few examples of when this is likely to happen:

- The same individuals serve as shareholders, officers, and directors (which by itself is never enough to pierce the veil).
- Personal and business funds are commingled.
- Corporate actions aren't documented.
- Shareholders hold themselves out publicly as the owners of the business, creating the impression that the business is a sole proprietorship or partnership.
- Employees, creditors, and others dealing with the business think the shareholder is the owner.

> ✔ The corporation lacks adequate capital or insurance necessary to meet reasonably foreseeable claims.
>
> ✔ Shareholders make personal use of business assets.
>
> ✔ Somebody or something is seriously harmed, either is personally injured or suffers significant economic loss.

No one of these factors is determinative. For personal liability to attach, likely several must be present, and the harm must be significant. Terms like *outrageous* and *shock the conscience* describe the types of behavior that trigger personal liability for shareholders.

So Sue Me

Shareholders can sue their corporations. Shareholder lawsuits fall into one of two categories: direct or derivative actions.

Direct actions include claims that the corporation has harmed an individual shareholder. Anything that relates particularly to that specific shareholder would fall in the category of a direct action. For example, if a shareholder requests to inspect corporate records and the corporation refuses, the shareholder could sue the corporation to compel inspection.

Derivative actions are lawsuits filed by a shareholder or shareholders on behalf of the corporation. Remember, a corporation is a creature of statute and has no ability to act on its own. It's entirely dependent on the actions of officers, directors, employees, or other agents to act on its behalf.

What if the officers and directors embark on a course of action that they know is improper for the corporation? Consider a large manufacturer producing a potentially defective product. The officers and board members know about the defects and the potential for harm, yet they choose to do nothing about it. Since the board and officers control the actions of the corporation, shareholders might file a derivative lawsuit to compel the officers and directors to stop manufacturing the product.

To avoid potential abuse by disgruntled shareholders, derivative actions have built-in safeguards. Among them, the shareholder must be a shareholder as of the time of the alleged harm. The shareholder generally must make a demand on the corporation to take the desired action. The demand is intended to give the corporate board the first opportunity to consider the claim and take the desired action. If the corporation fails to act after the demand is made, or if the shareholder can show that a demand would be futile, the derivative lawsuit can be filed. Once filed, only the decision of the court can settle derivative lawsuits.

Duties and responsibilities under close corporation statutes

Do close corporation statutes impose additional rights and responsibilities on corporate shareholders? Before we can answer that question, two conditions must exist. First of all, your state must have a statute that allows close corporations. Second, your corporation's articles of incorporation have affirmatively elected to be treated in accordance with the close corporation statute. If neither of these conditions is met, you don't have to worry.

However, if both of these conditions are met, close corporations may eliminate a board of directors altogether or reduce or eliminate board powers and duties. When this occurs, shareholders, especially majority shareholders, step into roles traditionally filled by board members and assume board duties and responsibilities. Board duties are much more extensive than shareholder duties, including duties relating to loyalty and the exercise of reasonable care. Corporation statutes set forth standards of conduct for officers and directors, all of which we detail in Chapter 15.

Chapter 14

Preparing Shareholder Agreements

· ·

In This Chapter

▶ Introducing different types of shareholder agreements

▶ Deciding when to create shareholder agreements

▶ Understanding how close corporation statutes impact shareholder agreements

· ·

From a practical standpoint, a well-crafted shareholder agreement is a must for new corporations with more than one shareholder. For many small businesses, the corporate shareholders are also the officers and the individuals who are active in the day-to-day operations of the business. The loss of any one of these key players can dramatically affect the ongoing viability of the business.

Shareholder agreements involve control of the corporation. Existing shareholders seek to guard who their fellow shareholders will be. Genuine concern exists over who has the right to participate in business decisions, especially in small corporations where shareholders are also active in the business. Not only do outside shareholders disrupt the balance in selecting directors, they can also upset the chemistry of individuals working together to make the business succeed.

Shareholder agreements provide a direction for the corporation and its shareholders to follow in the event of a shareholder's death or disability, retirement, termination from employment, bankruptcy, or attempt to sell shares to outsiders. For many shareholders, the primary benefit of a shareholders' agreement is that it can provide a market for shares of a small corporation in the event of a shareholder's death or disability, providing needed funds for family members.

Consider this example: Eric, Nina, and Michael form ABC Corporation. ABC's business is to provide computer hardware and software solutions. Eric and Michael are master programmers, essential to the corporation's business.

Nina provides marketing expertise and sales skills necessary to attract business to the corporation. What if any one of the three die or become disabled? What if Michael decides to move on and wants to transfer his shares to his son, Bob, a high-school dropout whose idea of a full day of work is surfing at the beach? What can Eric and Nina do to protect themselves and the corporation? A shareholders' agreement can provide answers and protection.

Are you the only shareholder in your corporation? A shareholder agreement will offer nothing of value to you. Keep the concept in mind, however. You may seek additional shareholders in the future, at which time an agreement will be important.

Shareholder Agreements: Deciding Which Is Right for Your Corporation

A *shareholder agreement,* in its simplest terms, is any agreement between shareholders. It doesn't need to include all shareholders, although shareholders who are not a part of the agreement may not be bound by it. Shareholders can agree to practically anything relating to the corporation if the agreement doesn't contradict the articles of incorporation, bylaws, or state law. A corporation needn't be a party to the agreement, but if it isn't, the corporation can't be bound by the terms of the agreement.

Can some but not all shareholders enter into a shareholder agreement? The answer is "yes" although it isn't common. If the number of shareholders is too numerous, it might be impractical to get all to agree. Minority shareholders (those who own less than 50 percent of the outstanding corporate stock) might enter into an agreement to preserve voting control. In any of these instances, the corporation will most likely not be a party to the shareholder agreement.

Shareholder agreements are essential. They promote smooth working relationships among shareholders, especially those who are active in the day-to-day activities of the business. They also provide a market for corporate shares where none may otherwise exist.

Shareholder agreements enable shareholders with different interests the opportunity to craft an agreement that addresses those interests. Imagine three shareholders: Eric, Michael, and Nina. One is looking for long-term employment while another is seeking a source of retirement income. A good agreement can help address these different interests.

We describe the two general types of shareholder agreements in the following sections:

- ✔ **Pooling and voting trust agreements:** The principal thrust of these agreements is to control voting for a corporate board of directors.
- ✔ **Buy sell or stock purchase agreements:** These attempt to deal with a broader variety of circumstances.

Most important, shareholder agreements are an area where your professional team can provide invaluable service. You can find a buy sell or stock purchase agreement out there in books, through service companies, or elsewhere. These sample agreements may not be appropriate for all corporations and their shareholders, so consider turning to your professional team for more complex options.

Pooling or voting trust agreements

A *pooling agreement* is any shareholder agreement where shareholders decide to pool their votes together on matters presented to the shareholders for decision. Most often, the pooling agreement will relate to the election of corporate directors.

A *voting trust agreement* is similar to a pooling agreement. The principal difference is that the shareholders transfer their shares to a trustee who votes the shares in accordance with the agreement. Again, the principal focus of such an agreement is the election of directors.

Through these agreements, shareholders are able to maintain a certain level of control over who serves on the corporate board. Unlike buy sell agreements or stock purchase agreements, which we describe in the next section, pooling or voting trust agreements are unlikely to regulate who your other shareholders will be or provide for buyouts in the event of a shareholder's death.

Most state corporation laws provide specific requirements for pooling or voting trust agreements. The most common restrictions are that the agreements be in writing and that the duration can't exceed a certain time limit, often ten years. The agreement can generally be renewed for additional ten-year periods.

Buy sell or stock purchase agreements

Perhaps the more common form of shareholder agreement is the *buy sell* or *stock purchase agreement*. This type of agreement identifies the terms and conditions under which a shareholder may sell shares and the corporation or other shareholders are required to buy shares. Only the imagination of the shareholders limits the scope of an agreement. Here are some of the more common types of provisions considered.

Restrictions on lifetime transfers

For small businesses, the shareholders, officers, directors, and employees are often the same group of individuals. You want to control who your fellow shareholders are. Michael, Eric, and Nina are important to one another and to the success of the corporation's business. In the previous example, Eric and Nina don't want Michael's son Bob to have an ownership interest in the business. Bob won't contribute anything to the day-to-day operation and success of the business. For Michael, Nina, and Eric, restrictions on lifetime transfers will be an important part of their agreement.

Most states won't allow shareholders or corporations to use agreements to absolutely prohibit sales or transfers of corporation stock. As a result, restrictions on sales or transfers must be reasonable in nature. A common restriction relating to lifetime transfers creates a right of *first refusal*. Any shareholder seeking to sell his or her shares must first offer the corporation and/or the remaining shareholders the opportunity to purchase the shares on the same terms and conditions offered to a third party. If the shareholders or corporation exercises its option to purchase shares, the third party doesn't become a shareholder. If the corporation or shareholders decide against purchasing those shares up for sale, a third party can purchase the shares or the shareholder can transfer the shares to the third party.

When creating the shareholder agreement, the agreement must include specific provisions that describe the type of notice a seller seeking to sell must provide to the corporation and remaining shareholders. It must also include time limitations within which the option to purchase must be exercised.

The agreement should also address whether a shareholder can make transfers to a trust created by the shareholder or to a spouse or other family members. Shareholders must determine whether they want to be shareholders with another shareholder's spouse or children. The general rule, in this case, is if the spouse or children aren't actively engaged in the business, these types of transfers should be restricted. Common restrictions include limitations on who can acquire shares and the conditions that must occur before shares can be transferred.

Put up or shut up clause

Think of the Put up or shut up clause as an old Western-style shootout on Main Street. Shareholders don't always agree. Some disagreements relate to fundamental business issues such as proposed expansion, sale, or acquisition. For shareholders who believe that a system of checks and balances would be useful, consider a Put up or shut up clause.

Here's how it works: Michael, Eric, and Nina each own one-third of the outstanding shares of stock of ABC Corporation. Nina and Michael have reached a place where neither believes that they can continue to work with the other. Using the Put up or shut up clause in their shareholders' agreement, Michael offers to buy Nina's shares of stock for $100 per share. Nina has a choice. She must now put up or shut up — sell her shares to Michael or buy Michael's shares (which Michael must sell) for the same $100 per share that he offered her.

With a Put up or shut up clause, a shareholder had better believe he presents a fair offer or he may end up selling his own shares rather than buying shares from the other shareholders. In principle, one shareholder may end up being separated from the corporation but has hopefully received fair value for his or her shares in exchange.

Shareholder bankruptcy

In most instances, when an individual or corporation files for bankruptcy, the bankruptcy court appoints a trustee. The trustee's role is to gather assets of the bankrupt individual, identify creditors of the bankrupt individual, and pay creditors. Without a shareholders' agreement to the contrary, a trustee could endeavor to sell the bankrupt individual's shares in the corporation. Once again, the possibility presents itself that the corporation would have a new shareholder to contend with, one who might not share the same values, goals, or long-term business plan of the other shareholders.

A shareholders' agreement could provide that upon a shareholder's bankruptcy, the corporation or the remaining shareholders would have the option to purchase that individual's shares in accordance with a purchase price formula set forth in the shareholders' agreement. If the formula is reasonable, the bankruptcy trustee would most likely be bound by this provision.

Death of a shareholder

What happens if one of your shareholders dies? Without an agreement, shares of stock would be distributed in accordance with the will of the deceased shareholder. If no will exists, individuals identified by state law, most often the surviving spouse and children, receive the distributed shares. If the shareholder doesn't have a spouse or children, look to siblings or nieces and nephews of the deceased shareholder.

You have to ask yourself, "Do we want to operate our corporation with these folks?" In some instances, you might be quite comfortable with a surviving spouse or child, especially if they have already been active in the business. If you are the deceased shareholder, would you rather have your surviving spouse and children receive shares of stock that have no ready market value instead of dollars for your shares so that the survivors have funds on which to live? It's a difficult question. As you can see, the interests of the surviving shareholders and corporation aren't necessarily the same as the interests of the surviving relatives.

In many agreements, the corporation or remaining shareholders must buy the shares from the estate of a deceased shareholder based on a formula contained in the agreement. The purchase requirement is often supported by an obligation on the part of the corporation to carry life insurance on the lives of its shareholders.

Shareholder disability

Shareholder disability is a tough area. At what point does a shareholder become disabled? How do you tell? What if you think your fellow shareholder is disabled, but she disagrees? How do you resolve the disagreement?

Death might not be good, but at least it's certain. Disability, on the other hand, isn't good, and it's far less certain. Shareholder agreements that provide for disability provisions usually attempt to define disability, often paralleling the definitions found in a disability insurance policy that the corporation maintains on each shareholder. Definitions might include:

- A licensed physician's medical opinion that the shareholder can no longer perform the essential functions of his or her position with or without reasonable accommodation

- The inability of the shareholder to perform his or her job for a defined period of time such as 90 consecutive days or 180 days within any 12-month period, whether or not consecutive

- The disabled shareholder and the corporation agree that the shareholder is disabled and unable to perform essential job tasks

- A determination under the terms of a disability insurance policy insuring the shareholder

- The decision of an agreed upon arbitrator if the parties can't agree whether a shareholder is disabled

As upon death, the corporation or remaining shareholders would either have the option or be required to purchase the disabled shareholder's shares in accordance with a formula provided in the agreement.

Termination of employment

Although many shareholders of small corporations are also employed by the corporation, the roles and responsibilities of shareholders are different from those of an employee. Without a shareholders' agreement to the contrary, a shareholder doesn't have to be an employee. In publicly held corporations, for example, most of the shareholders have no employment relationship with the corporation. However, with small corporations, the corporation often actively employs shareholders.

So, what do you do when a shareholder/employee quits or is fired? What if the shareholder/employee simply stops coming to work? To the extent that active, day-to-day involvement by the shareholder in the business operations is important, you'll want a shareholders' agreement to address this topic.

A common provision creates an option in favor of the corporation and remaining shareholders to purchase the shares of the retiring or fired shareholder/employee upon retirement or termination. Termination includes voluntary termination, when the employee quits, or involuntary termination, when the employee is fired.

A formula included in the agreement or on any other value that the parties can agree upon determines the purchase price.

Determination of share's worth

An essential component of a stock purchase or buy sell agreement is a means by which shareholders and the corporation can tell how much the shares are worth. Keep in mind that most nonpublicly traded corporations don't have a ready market for shares. People don't line up to buy a minority interest of a small business that may be dependent on its shareholder/employees for its success.

Your accountant is a good person to help you determine the value of your corporate stock. A number of methods to value your corporation exist, and many accountants can fine-tune any formula to fit a particular business. Possibilities include the book value of the corporation or a formula based on the earnings history of the corporation.

It's often preferred that shareholders agree annually as to the value of the corporation's stock, usually as part of the annual shareholders' meeting. No one has a better feel for what the corporation is worth than the actively employed shareholders — let them have the first stab at it. As a backup, the agreement could provide that, if the shareholders haven't agreed to a valuation within the preceding two years, they use a default formula to determine value.

Payment distribution

If you're a shareholder whose shares are being purchased, you want to get your money fast. If you're a corporation or a remaining shareholder, you may want to stagger the payments over time to ease pressure on corporate cash flow. It's not in the interest of anyone to create a financial burden on the corporation, which could cause the business to fail.

Buy sell and stock purchase agreements often allow for payments to be made on an installment basis. Here are a few possibilities:

- If insurance monies are available, these dollars get paid in full as soon as they are received.

- Pay a certain amount (10 percent, for example) up front, with the balance paid in equal monthly installments over a set period of time (60 months, for example).

- Provide for payment in full at such time as the outstanding balance falls below a predetermined amount, such as $5,000.

A promissory note that sets the payment obligation and interest rate is used to document the deferred obligations. Occasionally, remaining shareholders are obligated to pledge their shares of stock as security for the payment obligation.

A payment formula and deferred payment option don't apply to restrictions relating to lifetime transfers. A lifetime transfer is any transfer that occurs during the lifetime of the person transferring shares. It could be a sale or gift of shares to another. With a lifetime transfer, the third party seeking to purchase the shares sets the price and payment terms, and the corporation or remaining shareholders seeking to purchase shares must match the third party's offer.

Restrictive language on stock certificates

Whenever a stock purchase or buy sell agreement is used, two things must occur to enhance the enforceability of the agreement. First, the corporation should be one of the parties. This is especially true where the agreement imposes an obligation to purchase on the corporation. Second, the stock certificates must contain language that clearly indicates that the transfer of the shares is subject to the terms and conditions of a stock purchase or buy sell agreement. Without this language, the agreement may not be binding on third persons who acquire the shares. The corporation or remaining shareholders might have a breach of contract claim against the transferring shareholder but no recourse against the third party acquiring the shares. Don't forget to add this restrictive language to corporate stock certificates.

It's All in the Timing: Adopting a Shareholders' Agreement

When people first incorporate their businesses, they focus on getting the corporation up and running. There's an immediate need to get the corporation functional so it can begin generating income. They want to minimize upfront fees and costs, seeking to defer other expenses until the business can pay for it. As a consequence, many choose to wait a while before developing a shareholders' agreement.

 Many times, this is a mistake. At the time the corporation is formed, the prospective employee/shareholders must come together to agree on a number of matters already considered. Strike while the iron is hot. When prospective shareholders are coming together to agree on other issues, it's easier to reach agreement on issues you'll include in the shareholder agreement.

By considering the issues we discuss earlier about who can be a shareholder and all of the what ifs (lifetime transfers, bankruptcy, death, disability, termination), a prospective shareholder can consider issues that might be vitally important to him or her as well as his or her family. This discussion might also point out different interests for each of the shareholders that might not otherwise be uncovered. For example, think of Michael, Eric, and Nina of ABC Corporation. Without a discussion about a stock purchase agreement, Michael might not learn that Eric is interested in long-term employment with less emphasis on building the value of the business. At the same time, Nina wants retirement income, believing that she could retire in a few years and use her stock as a long-term investment. With this information, Eric, Nina, and Michael might determine that their long-term goals are so different that they may be better off seeking different business associates or working to redefine their relationship.

Worse yet, if you don't address these matters upfront and early in the process, a shareholder may die, become disabled, or quit. What happens then? It's better to have a path that is certain and within the contemplation of the shareholders than to fly by the seat of one's pants.

Close Corporations: A Different Set of Rules

A number of states permit corporations to elect to be treated under close corporation statutes, if the corporation includes the election in the articles of incorporation. When this election is made, stock certificates must also conspicuously reflect that the close corporation election has been made and that the rights of shareholders in close corporations may differ materially from the rights of shareholders in other corporations.

Among the key differences between shareholder rights of close corporations and regular corporations are restrictions on stock transfers, which affect shareholders of close corporations. These restrictions are similar, but not identical, to ones described earlier and contained in buy sell or stock purchase agreements. Close corporation statutes may automatically restrict lifetime transfers by creating a right of first refusal in favor of the corporation and requirements for the corporation's purchase in the event of a shareholder's death.

Close corporation statutes also empower corporate shareholders to make agreements under which shareholders assume roles traditionally performed by corporate directors and officers, possibly eliminating the corporate board altogether.

State laws vary both as to the content and method by which close corporations can elect to be governed under the various statutory provisions. Don't assume that because your corporation has elected close corporation status that the shareholders will be subject to all of the close corporation provisions. Talk to your lawyer to find out if close corporation status is for you and what it includes.

Close corporation statutes may lessen the need for a shareholders' agreement in certain areas. However, you need to be certain what you are getting or not getting under the statute before you choose to rely on it over a separate written agreement among the shareholders.

Chapter 15

Understanding the Role of Directors and Officers

Corporations are creatures of statute with no power to act on their own. They must rely on individuals to do their work. For example, you may own a Ford, but don't assume Ford, the corporation, made it. Individuals and other entities working on behalf of Ford, the corporation, designed, manufactured, and marketed your vehicle.

At the top of the corporate pile, you'll find the board of directors acting on behalf of corporations. Next in line are corporate officers appointed by the board, followed by managers, rank and file employees, professional agents such as lawyers and accountants, and independent contractors including suppliers and others.

In a small corporation, the same individuals may serve as directors, officers, rank and file employees, *and* shareholders. When you serve in many different roles, keep in mind which hat you're wearing at any point in time. Different hats mean different responsibilities and different legal duties.

If your corporation has a single officer, director, and shareholder, you must still maintain corporate formalities, some of which include documenting separate activities of the corporate board or shareholders. In some respects, wearing all the hats of the corporation adds to your challenge. How do you know which hat you have on or which role you're playing at any time?

Putting Together a Board of Directors

Your corporate board is important. All corporate power is exercised under the authority of, and the business and affairs of the corporation are managed under, the direction of the board. The buck stops with the board. While the board may delegate tasks to officers, outside professionals, and others, the board is ultimately responsible.

Corporate boards set policy and direction. Boards paint with a broad brush. Corporate officers appointed by the board handle the day-to-day operations, filling in the details of the board's broad-brush strokes.

Corporate board members and officers are often the same individuals in small corporations. As you'll see, the legal duties and responsibilities of officers and directors are quite similar.

Directors: Insiders and outsiders

Larger corporations are more apt to have a larger number of outside directors than inside directors. *Outside directors* include individuals from outside the corporation, persons with no significant daily link to the corporation with the exception, perhaps, of being a minority shareholder. *Inside directors* include individuals who also serve as officers or majority shareholders of the corporation.

Outside directors provide an objective perspective of the corporation. They may also provide guidance in a special area of expertise such as legal, financial, or marketing. Inside directors are well versed in the ongoing operations of the business.

Smaller corporations can also benefit from the use of outside directors. Objective viewpoints and special expertise can aid a small business as it moves forward.

Finding directors

Where do you find your directors? In a small corporation, your directors probably will be your officers and shareholders. You might consider bringing in one or more outside directors to provide objectivity and subject matter expertise. First, determine areas of outside expertise that would be helpful to the business. Second, look for individuals who are team players, willing to work together with other board members in the corporation's best interests. Outside directors include bankers, lawyers, accountants, marketers, insurance agents, financial planners, and presidents of other businesses.

When you recruit an outside director, make it clear what you're seeking. For example, don't recruit a lawyer because you want free legal advice. Instead, look for a lawyer who can provide business advice and guidance or analytical, problem-solving skills. If it's legal advice you want, hire a lawyer. The same is true for other professional outside directors as well.

Limiting board size

With directors, the more is not the merrier. Board size varies greatly. Most states now permit single-member boards. Other states require a minimum of three. Board size for many smaller corporations falls within these parameters.

How big is too big? Going beyond 10 to 12 may be pushing it. Boards can only act if a quorum (a minimum number or percentage of directors specified in corporate bylaws) is present at a meeting or if all directors consent to action in writing. The more directors you have, the harder it may be to get enough board members to constitute a quorum or the longer it may take to circulate a written memorandum of action for signature.

Larger boards can provide greater perspective and expertise, which is important in making good business decisions. On the other hand, more voices may spell greater dissension and difficulty in reaching consensus.

While size of the board may vary, use an odd number for board decision. With an odd number, you reduce the risk of deadlock on important board decisions.

Appointing Officers

Unlike corporate board members who are elected by shareholders, the board appoints corporate officers. They serve at the board's will and pleasure. Corporate boards can terminate an officer at any time, without cause, despite the existence of an employment agreement between the officer and the corporation. While the board can fire the officer/employee, the officer retains the ability to sue the corporation for breach of the employment contract.

Corporate officers most often include a president, secretary, and treasurer, although other officers such as a vice president, assistant secretary, or treasurer can be appointed. Corporate bylaws describe the duties of each officer, usually in general terms. Some of the common duties assigned to corporate officers include:

- ✔ **President:** The corporate president generally presides at all meetings of the board and shareholders unless the bylaws provide for another person to do this. The president signs stock certificates, corporate contracts, and other legal documents. In addition, the president tackles tasks assigned to her or him by the board. For significant tasks, corporate resolution normally directs the president to act on behalf of the corporation.

- **Vice president:** If one exists at all, the vice president generally fills in whenever the president is unavailable. The vice president also handles any other tasks delegated to him or her by the board or the president. In many larger corporations, vice presidents may be in charge of a certain department or division within the company.

- **Treasurer:** Responsibility for maintaining corporate financial records and rendering financial reports for the board, officers, and shareholders usually belongs to the treasurer. For many corporations, especially larger ones, the role involves oversight rather than daily contact with corporate financial matters. With smaller corporations, the treasurer may be the day-to-day financial officer as well.

- **Secretary:** Maintenance of corporate records, updating shareholder records, and preparing and distributing meeting notices are among the duties of corporate secretaries. Like the treasurer, many of these tasks require more oversight than daily interaction, but oversight is important to verify that these actions are properly completed.

Hiring, Firing, and Replacing Board Members and Officers

Corporate shareholders elect directors. Directors appoint officers. Unless the articles or bylaws require otherwise, shareholders can vote to remove directors, with or without cause. Directors can remove officers, and directors and officers can resign at any time. Shareholders can't be touched, generally.

From time to time, corporate officers sign employment contracts with the corporation. The board retains the right to fire the officer, although the officer may sue for breach of contract. If an officer under contract resigns, the corporation may assert a breach of contract claim against the officer.

Some corporations use a process known as cumulative voting (see Chapter 16) to elect directors. *Cumulative voting* is a tool that increases the voting strength of minority shareholders in the case of electing and removing directors. If cumulative voting applies to your corporation, shareholders cannot remove a director unless the number of votes in favor of removal equals or exceeds the number required to elect the director in the first place.

Corporate bylaws may also provide standards of conduct by which members of the board may seek to remove a wayward board member.

When a vacancy arises, the board typically has the power to designate an individual to fill the remaining term of the vacated directorship, unless the articles or bylaws require an election. The board fills officer vacancies as well.

Knowing Who Has Authority

Because a corporation can't act on its own, knowing at any moment in time who has the authority to act on behalf of the corporation is important. Think of Nina, Michael, and Eric, equal shareholders of ABC Corporation. They are also officers and directors of ABC Corporation. Who has the authority to act on behalf of ABC Corporation? Who can borrow money? Who can withdraw money from the bank? Who can order the company jet? Imagine if Nina purchases a new computer system for the business at the same time Michael is buying the corporation a deluxe copier, and Eric is signing a contract for the construction of new corporate headquarters. Who's gonna pay for all of this? Let's find out.

Identifying the types of authority

Authority is the permission or right to act. For purposes of this chapter, authority is the permission to act on behalf of the corporation since a corporation has no ability to act on its own. Who has the authority depends on the situation. As you'll see, there are different types of authority. Since persons with authority can legally bind the corporation, knowing who can act on behalf of the corporation is important. Here are the types of authority that exist.

Express authority

Express authority derives from an expressed direction or command. For example, a board meeting resolution directs the president to establish a $100,000 line of credit with Community Bank, with interest not to exceed 11 percent per annum. Or, the corporate president instructs an employee to ship product to a customer. In these examples, the president has express authority to establish a line of credit, and the employee has the express authority to ship the product.

Implied authority

Implied authority is less clear than express authority because there is no specifically expressed direction. Rather, the authority comes from the nature of the task or from the circumstances of the task. Consider this example: Concrete, Inc. has supplied concrete to We Build Them Strong, Corp. for five years, always on the verbal or written request of the company president. We

Build Them Strong, Corp. pays for the concrete each time it's provided. No one can deny that the president has the implied authority to order concrete from Concrete, Inc. without a corporate resolution. The years of doing business with Concrete, Inc. suggests that the president has the implied authority to keep paying that company.

Consider our example in the "Express authority" section above: The employee is expressly authorized to ship product to a customer. Presumably, that express direction of authority carries with it the implied authority to select a shipper and incur shipping fees. Implied authority often arises to help fill in the gaps that may exist when authority isn't clearly or fully delegated.

Apparent authority

Apparent authority is no authority at all. Yet, it costs corporations millions of dollars a year. Over the last few years, the executive directors of several large nonprofit corporations have bilked lots of money from the corporations to pay for lavish hotels and meals, home remodels and improvements, and other areas.

How could this happen? Several things usually come into play. First, the board was asleep at the wheel, failing to ask important questions or analyze corporate financial information. We discuss this breach of corporate duty later. Second, the board effectively cloaked the executive director with apparent authority to act on its behalf. Individuals and others relying on this apparent authority used it to their advantage. If the reliance is reasonable, the corporation pays.

Corporate presidents are often cloaked in apparent authority. Most businesses or individuals dealing with the corporation assume that the president has full authority to act. Fine lines separate implied authority from apparent authority as well.

If your corporate president or other key officer or employee resigns or leaves the corporation, notify your major customers or suppliers. By letting others know, you're removing any apparent authority of the former officer or employee to act on behalf of the corporation.

Adopting policies to protect the corporation

The board should adopt policies regulating who can act on behalf of the corporation and under what circumstances. For example, suppliers should receive a written policy from the corporation indicating the names of individuals authorized to purchase on behalf of the corporation. The policy might indicate that two or more individuals must sign the authorization if it exceeds a certain dollar amount. By distributing a written policy, the supplier can only rely on the policy itself and not on the individual requests from one or more officers or employees.

Corporate officers and board members must review financial reports and records carefully, and ask questions whenever something unusual appears or when certain line-item dollar amounts seem to be inconsistent with budget projections.

Understanding the Legal Duties and Responsibilities

Failure to comply with legal duties and responsibilities can subject board members and officers to personal liability. By and large, the duties and responsibilities are the same for officers and directors.

General duties and responsibilities

Here are some examples of the kinds of general duties and responsibilities out there. Officers and directors must:

- Act in good faith and in a manner reasonably believed to be in the best interests of the corporation. This is sometimes known as the *Business Judgment Rule,* which simply means that if you serve on a board you must exercise good common sense and actively participate in board meetings and discussions.

- Discharge corporate duties with care that a person in a like position would reasonably believe to be appropriate under similar circumstances.

- Avoid conflicts of interest with the corporation and when conflicts arise, disclose them fully and accurately.

- Demonstrate loyalty to the corporation.

- Deal fairly with minority shareholders.

These duties and responsibilities sound tough, but they don't guarantee that the corporate officers and directors will make the corporation successful. Corporate directors and officers merely agree to act in good faith, exercise care, treat other directors and shareholders fairly, and demonstrate loyalty to the corporation.

Things that spell trouble for officers and directors

It's easy to provide a list of duties and responsibilities. While most are relatively self-explanatory, it's probably more useful to describe specific activities that have put officers and board members at risk of personal liability. Some of the activities we describe are outrageous, while some are more subtle. All involve the breach of one or more of the duties we describe in the previous section.

Here is a list of things that spell trouble for officers and directors:

- Misappropriation of a corporate asset for personal use or the use by another business
- Unreasonable compensation for board members or officers
- Loans from the corporation on terms more favorable than those commercially available
- Loans to the corporation on terms and conditions more favorable to the lender than those commercially available
- Failure to disclose actual or potential conflicts of interest (for example, an interest of a director in a corporate supplier)
- Actions of the board that dilute or reduce the value of a minority shareholder's shares in the absence of any justifiable business purpose
- Commingling of personal and business assets
- Serving as a rubber stamp without using independent judgment in reviewing corporate reports or failing to ask questions to gain additional information

Board members have a duty to be reasonably informed about corporate activities. It isn't enough to show up at meetings. Board members must act affirmatively, reviewing reports and asking questions. They may rely on reports and information provided by others if the information is reasonably believed to be reliable and competent.

Board members should never be reluctant to ask questions about matters presented at board meetings. Common sense suggests that if you are confused or uncertain about matters being discussed, others may be too. Board members are often hesitant to ask questions about financial matters or financial statements for fear of appearing ignorant. There are no dumb questions, only dumb people who fail to ask questions. Your failure to ask could result in personal liability. Speak now or forever hold your peace!

Defining conflicts of interest

Board members and officers must disclose actual and potential conflicts of interest. Do you own stock in a competitor? Do you have any interest in corporate suppliers? How about your spouse, son, or daughter — do they have conflicting interests?

To define a conflicting interest, the Model Business Corporation Act (MBCA) looks at transactions of such financial significance that the interest would reasonably be expected to exert an influence on the director's judgment. The interest might be those of the director or the director's spouse, parent, child, grandchild, trust, or other related person or entity. In other words, could you gain some personal, financial, or other benefit by virtue of your decision? If so, a conflict may exist.

When a conflicting interest is present, directors must disclose the following:

- The existence and nature of the conflicting interest
- All known facts that a reasonably prudent person would reasonably believe to be material to a judgment about whether to proceed

If you believe you may have a potential conflict of interest, regardless of how remote, keep yourself out of trouble by letting the corporation know — you've nothing to lose by disclosure, but you increase the possibility for personal liability if you don't disclose. Make the smart choice and disclose.

Board members with conflicting interests generally abstain from voting on matters involving the conflict. They may continue to have a voice, however, expressing opinions about the subject. Your corporate bylaws should indicate whether board members with conflicting interests are eligible to participate in the discussions regardless of whether they have a right to vote.

Disclosing corporate opportunity

Over the years, a legal doctrine known as the *corporate opportunity rule* has developed. Corporate statutes don't refer to the doctrine. Rather, statutes speak more of corporate loyalty, which includes concepts of fair dealing and corporate opportunity. Under the corporate opportunity doctrine, corporate officers, directors, and employees who learn of a prospective business opportunity by virtue of their role as officer, director, or employee may not pursue the opportunity without first offering the opportunity to the corporation.

Here's an example of how it works: You're a corporate director for ABC Corporation. The corporation is in the business of providing hardware and software sales and service at retail and wholesale prices. Over the years, the ABC Corporation board has discussed the possibility of expanding its business into new areas. ABC Corporation has considered several possibilities, ranging from real estate development to expanded product lines. In fact, ABC Corporation has retained additional cash reserves to help with its expansion.

One day, an old friend approaches you with a business opportunity. While the proposed new venture is outside of the hardware and software field, it is within a number of other possibilities studied by ABC Corporation. What do you do?

Here's what we know: ABC Corporation is seeking expansion opportunities and has retained funds to help with these efforts. The proposal presented to you is similar to others that ABC Corporation has studied. The smart thing to do is to present this opportunity to ABC Corporation and afford it the first opportunity to participate in the proposal or to reject it. If rejected, you can proceed with it individually, if you like.

Making Mistakes: When Directors or Officers Goof Up

Directors and officers make mistakes. It happens. Occasionally, the mistakes are purposeful. For example, a board knowingly approves the manufacture of a product with a design flaw, believing that the revenues generated by sales of the product will exceed the cost of liabilities associated with the product.

More often, mistakes are not purposeful, resulting, instead, from bad information or unintended consequences. Mistakes can also occur when the board fails to act under circumstances when it should. For example, boards sometimes aren't wearing their thinking caps, failing to exercise reasonable care. Board members fail to ask questions at board meetings or review financial reports that might otherwise uncover corporate or officer wrongdoing.

Deciding when an officer or a director is liable

Once again, the RMBCA provides guidance as to when an officer or a director may be liable. What follows may seem repetitious. Nonetheless, it's worthwhile if it can keep you out of hot water with your fellow board members, officers, or shareholders. It may also help keep you on good terms with important suppliers, business lenders, and the IRS.

An officer or director may be held liable for actions taken, or in some cases for failing to act. Liability may attach if action lacks good faith or whenever a director doesn't reasonably believe a proposed action is in the best interests of the corporation. Similarly, whenever the director participates in a decision-making process without being adequately informed (especially when the director fails to ask questions), liability may follow.

Liability may also exist whenever a director's actions lack objectivity and independent decision making due to the director's familial, financial, or business relationships. An officer's or a director's sustained failure to provide reasonable oversight of the business and affairs of the corporation, or to devote timely attention to corporate matters by asking relevant questions or other inquiry, may also subject the officer or director to liability.

Failure to present the corporation with business opportunities related to the corporation's line of business (existing or proposed), knowing that the corporation has the financial capacity necessary to undertake the opportunity, can prove costly to the director who fails to disclose the opportunity.

Finally, if an officer receives a financial benefit to which she or he is not otherwise entitled, the officer or director can be liable to the corporation for breach of duty.

When in doubt, disclose! Ask questions! If you're not satisfied with the answer, ask more questions or request an outside professional's opinion.

Indemnifying officers and directors

If corporate officers and directors can be sued for so many things, why would anyone want to be an officer or director? You're not alone in asking. Many years ago, state legislatures recognized that corporations would have a difficult time attracting talented individuals to serve as officers and directors unless something was done to limit their liability. Legislatures also realized that corporate insurance for the actions of officers and directors would skyrocket in cost without some limitation on liability. Voilà — corporate indemnification was born. Today, it exists everywhere.

Indemnification is a repayment or reimbursement of expenses incurred by corporate officers or directors defending claims brought against them for actions undertaken while serving as a corporate officer or director. In some instances, the corporation can pay these expenses as they occur rather than reimburse them later.

Unfortunately, each state varies as to when and if it applies. The RMBCA says permissive indemnification exists whenever the director or officer:

- ✔ Acts in good faith
- ✔ Reasonably believes that his or her conduct was in the best interests of the corporation or, at least, not opposed to the best interests
- ✔ Had no reason to believe conduct violated a law, if criminal charges are involved

An officer or director receiving an impermissible personal benefit from the corporation or from another individual or entity to influence corporate action is ineligible to be indemnified by the corporation.

The corporate statutes and the bylaws hold indemnification provisions. Some state statutes also allow the articles to contain language that directors aren't liable to the corporation or its shareholders. This exculpatory language is intended to keep lawsuits from being filed against directors in the first place rather than reimburse or indemnify costs or expenses. This language can eliminate board liability for most actions, but not actions taken in bad faith or actions resulting in an impermissible personal benefit to the director.

Insuring Your Directors and Officers Against Mistakes

Few corporations would consider conducting business without a general liability insurance policy. It makes sense; accidents happen, and when they do, it's good to have insurance to cover the costs of defense and pay any liability.

But suppose your corporate board makes a mistake. For example, your board adopts a personnel policy that has the unintended effect of discriminating impermissibly against a protected class of individuals. Quite likely, the general liability policy won't cover the liability associated with this claim. More important, the corporation gets stuck with hiring lawyers to defend against the claim.

Directors' and officers' insurance is a product you should consider for your corporate board. In a sense, directors' and officers' insurance provides protection for claims that result from errors in judgment. Your general liability

---

Eliminating the board in a close corporation

A key component of close corporation statutes is the ability of a close corporation to eliminate the board of directors entirely (see Chapter 1 for a refresher of close corporation law). If the board isn't eliminated, its powers and authority can be restricted in virtually any fashion that the shareholders may desire.

When shareholders elect to eliminate the board, they effectively rise to the level of the board. The former board members' duties and responsibilities now fall upon the shoulders of shareholders, especially shareholders active in the decision-making aspects of the corporation. One consequence: Shareholders in close corporations assume greater responsibility and potential liability for their actions than corporate shareholders of general corporations.

In a close corporation, a shareholder's actions will be judged using the same standards of conduct imposed on corporate officers and directors. Understand those duties and responsibilities and follow them.

Remember the value of a good professional team. One of the team members should be a good insurance agent. Like so many other things, insurance is a complicated industry. It takes a trained professional to help you decide the types of insurance coverage appropriate for your business.

Chapter 16

Director and Shareholder Meetings

*I*t's a busy world where finding the time to get everything done is a constant struggle. Contemplating another set of meetings for the corporate board and shareholders may be the furthest thing from your mind. But because corporations are entirely dependent upon corporate directors, officers, and agents to act for it, and many of these actions need to be authorized by the board of directors or shareholders, you'll need to host meetings or meeting substitutes.

Keep in mind that meetings don't always need to be formal. In a typical small corporation, the same individuals probably serve as corporate officers and directors, and they may also be corporate shareholders. Most likely, all are active in the day-to-day conduct of the business. They see each other every day, and each has a sense of what's going on with the business. Meetings for this group can be quite informal.

If you are the sole officer, director, and shareholder, you'll conduct most of your meetings using consent resolutions without formal or informal meetings. The consent resolutions will merely document the action approved. Why would you need to hold a meeting or use consent resolutions if you're the only officer, director, and shareholder? That's a good question. Remember, corporations are creatures of statute and entirely dependent upon others to act for them. Meeting minutes and consent resolutions provide the formal authorization for you to act on behalf of your corporation. Does this seem like form over substance? It probably is, but when you deal with corporations, form or formality is important.

Other corporations have less daily communication. Shareholders may not have any involvement with the business. Disgruntled shareholders may disapprove of corporate actions and seek to remove one or more board members. Here, meetings are likely to be quite formal, following all of the procedural rules and dotting each *i* and crossing every *t*.

Corporate bylaws provide the principal source of information about how to conduct meetings. Expect your bylaws to describe how meetings should be called together, what type of notices must be provided, and the timing for notices. The bylaws also discuss concepts like record dates and meeting adjournment.

The corporate bylaws will also tell you if corporate meetings can be conducted electronically or without a meeting by consent of directors or shareholders. If the bylaws are silent on these areas, check with the corporation statute to see if the statute can fill in the missing pieces.

This chapter will give you a greater understanding of meeting specifics. Failure to abide by meeting requirements described in your corporate bylaws or state law can undo corporate actions, create shareholder and director unrest, and waste time and money.

Hosting a Shareholder Meeting

Corporate bylaws and statutes provide for meetings of shareholders. Shareholder participation in meetings is often limited to electing directors and approving actions of the corporate board and officers during the previous year.

Be careful, however. Your corporation's articles of incorporation, bylaws, or state law may give shareholders greater rights and a more active say in certain corporate activities. For example, the Revised Model Business Corporation Act (RMBCA), adopted in whole or in part by many states, requires shareholder participation in these areas:

- Increasing or decreasing meeting quorum requirements
- Authorizing special voting groups
- Modifying cumulative voting requirements
- Restricting corporate distributions or share dividends
- Altering or creating preemptive rights

As you can see, most of these provisions safeguard shareholder rights by requiring their input on actions that could negatively affect shareholder voting rights or rights to receive dividends or distributions. Presumably, any corporate action could require shareholder approval if the articles of incorporation or bylaws so direct. This would be cumbersome and rare, however.

Corporations must conduct an *annual meeting* of shareholders. Its purpose is to elect individuals to serve on the corporate board. Annual meetings also update shareholders on matters of interest relating to the corporation, such as financial reports, industry trends, and upcoming events.

Some corporations prefer to conduct meetings within a certain amount of time following the close of the corporation's fiscal year. This gives the officers time to disclose year-end financial information, which helps shareholders understand whether the corporation was successful for that year.

For small corporations with a limited number of shareholders, an annual meeting within four to six weeks prior to the fiscal year-end is advisable. Consider inviting members of your professional team. Here, the corporation can report on its year-to-date activities. Potential problem areas can be red-flagged in advance of year-end, and tax-saving strategies can be generated with time to implement them. Corporations with large numbers of shareholders generally tend to hold annual meetings following the close of the fiscal year so that year-end financial information can be discussed. Throughout the fiscal year, the board of a large corporation would consider tax-savings ideas and potential red flag issues.

A *special meeting* is any meeting other than an annual meeting. You don't need to hold a special meeting unless the articles or bylaws specify. You would want to call a special meeting if an extraordinary event, such as the sale of the corporation's assets, merger, or liquidation, requires shareholder approval. Similarly, board members or shareholders may seek to oust a wayward director. Whenever a special meeting is to be held, the meeting notice must specify the meeting's purpose.

Getting the word out

So far, we've talked about annual and special shareholders' meetings. You know what they are, but how do you find out when a meeting is going to be held or what's going to be discussed? The next few sections should shed a little light. After all, you'd hate to miss your own meeting.

How's Hawaii this time of year?

First, look at the corporate bylaws to see if they indicate a specific location. If not, the meeting can be held almost anywhere the board or shareholders like. Meeting notices must clearly indicate the date, time, and location of the meeting. If your corporation's shareholders are local, you may not want to set a meeting for 3,000 miles away without a clear understanding that they are comfortable with a distant meeting. But, you'd be surprised how many Midwesterners welcome an annual shareholders' meeting in Hawaii, especially in winter.

Here's your invitation!

Shareholders should receive notice of annual and regular shareholder meetings. Your bylaws or state law will prescribe the content and timing of required notices. Failure to comply with notice requirements can invalidate or delay corporate action. For example, if shareholders aren't properly notified of a meeting, any action approved at that meeting could be challenged by shareholders who didn't receive proper notice. In addition, if shareholders don't receive notice, no one will show up, and no action could be approved due to the absence of a quorum. Pay attention to detail here.

Meeting notices often must be in writing and specify the time, day, and place of the meeting. For an annual meeting, the notice will most likely indicate that the meeting is the annual meeting for the purpose of electing directors and considering any other business that might come before the meeting. Contrast this with a special meeting notice that must specifically describe the purpose of the meeting. If matters come before a special meeting that weren't described in the notice, don't take formal action on those matters.

Your bylaws or state law usually will tell you when and how notices must be sent. Common provisions require that notices be delivered, not less than 10 nor more than 60 days, prior to the date of the meeting. Delivery can usually be accomplished in several different ways: regular mail, personal delivery (harder to prove without a receipt), certified mail, and possibly electronic mail.

If a shareholder shows up at the meeting, he generally is deemed to have waived any objections he may have to the holding of the meeting, unless the sole purpose for being at the meeting is to object to the corporation's failure to provide appropriate notice.

To save time, if any purpose of a shareholders' meeting is to consider an extraordinary corporate event such as sale, merger, or dissolution, think about including a copy of the proposed sale agreement or plan of merger or dissolution along with the notice.

Meeting electronically or by consent

The ability to conduct shareholder meetings using electronic means isn't entirely clear. The trend is to permit meetings using e-mail and other electronic sources. To be sure, your corporate bylaws could state whether shareholders can participate in meetings by telephone conference calls, e-mail, or other electronic means. For example, Delaware, the leading corporate jurisdiction, recently revised its corporation law to permit stockholder meetings with remote communications. State laws don't always allow shareholder meetings using electronic means. If not, you'll still have to meet the old-fashioned way.

Similarly, shareholders may consent to action without a meeting. In a sense, consent resolutions aren't meetings at all. To authorize action without a meeting, in general a written memorandum of action setting forth the actions to be agreed upon must be circulated to, and signed by, every shareholder. In some states, the consent resolution need only be signed by at least a majority of all shareholders. The actions must be separately listed. For example, a memorandum of action consenting to corporate actions could read:

✔ Resolved, the following persons are elected as directors of the corporation: Nina Martin, Michael Ross, and Eric Spencer.

✔ Resolved, the acts of the corporate officers and directors, prior to the date of this memorandum and subsequent to the date of the last consent memorandum, are approved and ratified.

For small corporations with few shareholders, this is the most common means to document corporate action. Remember: All shareholders may have to sign the consent for the memorandum to be effective to authorize or ratify corporate actions.

As a practical matter, don't get in the habit of formalizing all shareholder actions by consent. Conduct an actual meeting from time to time, especially if you have shareholders who aren't active in daily business operations. These shareholders will feel a greater sense of ownership and loyalty to the corporation, characteristics that can save the corporation time and money in the long run. Cultivate good relationships with corporate shareholders. It makes good sense.

Attending meetings from afar

Shareholder and director meetings are similar in the areas of electronic meetings or actions by consent. Whether electronic means are available for the conduct of a meeting depends on state law and corporate bylaws. Plainly, the clear trend is to accommodate meetings by any viable means.

In addition, directors can act by consent. Just as with shareholders, a memorandum of action setting forth the actions approved by the board must be circulated, signed, and dated by each board member to be effective.

When board members, officers, and shareholders are the same people, board actions by consent can be an efficient means of action by the board. Like shareholder meetings, it's a good idea to meet periodically and include the professional team to make sure all board members are up to date with corporate activities.

I sent out notices and nobody came; now what?

What do you do if you don't have a quorum? If an inadequate number of shares is represented at the meeting, no action can be taken. A couple of possibilities present themselves:

> ✔ You can continue the meeting, setting a new date, time, or place so long as you announce the new date, time, or place prior to adjourning the meeting. Any continuation of the meeting must occur within a limited time, usually within 60 days of the original date.
>
> ✔ You can set a new record date for the meeting. If you do, shareholders must be sent meeting notices again.

Voting in meetings

Now you know about shareholders' meetings: what they are, what types of meetings exist, and how you receive notice about the meetings. Are you entitled to vote at the meeting? The next sections provide useful information about voting and voting rights.

Setting a record date

For corporate purposes, a *record date* is a date set by the board of directors for determining whether the shareholders should vote at the meeting, receive dividends, or participate in any corporation action. Individuals and entities shown as shareholders on the corporate books and records on that date receive meeting notices. Those who become shareholders after that date aren't entitled to notices. Only shareholders as of the record date receive the dividend, even though others may subsequently become shareholders.

If the board fails to set a record date, look to your corporate statute to help you determine the record date. Possibilities include:

> ✔ The day before the first notice is delivered to shareholders
>
> ✔ The date the board authorizes a dividend or distribution

Following quorum and voting requirements

Once again, corporate bylaws should address quorum and voting requirements. If the bylaws are silent, a majority of shares constitutes a quorum, which is the percentage or proportion of voting shares required to be represented to constitute a valid shareholders' meeting. No action can be taken in the absence of a meeting quorum. If a quorum is present, a majority of the quorum can authorize action unless the articles, bylaws, or state law require a greater majority or supermajority.

Quorums are based on the number of corporate shares issued and outstanding. If Eric owns 100 shares of ABC Corporation stock, and Nina and Michael together own 200 shares of ABC Corporation stock, none of them alone would own enough shares to constitute a quorum. However, any two of them would be sufficient to create a quorum. Assume that a special meeting is held, and only Eric and Michael show up. A quorum exists. If the shareholders have a matter to approve, Eric doesn't have enough shares of his own to approve the matter. Michael does, however, since he owns two thirds of the shares represented at the meeting. Tough luck, Eric.

If your corporation has created multiple classes of stock (see Chapter 9), you may have to meet quorum requirements for each class. Similarly, meeting notices may or may not have to be directed to each class depending on the matters to be considered and whether a particular class has an interest in such matters. You'll need to check the corporate articles or bylaws to see if restrictions are imposed on shareholders.

The largest majority of corporations provide for a single class of common stock. For these corporations, shareholders are entitled to one vote per share of stock unless the articles of incorporation or state law provide differently.

Cumulative voting

Cumulative voting is a tool intended to help minority shareholders (those holding less than 50 percent of the issued and outstanding shares of a corporation) elect a representative to the corporate board.

Here's how it works: Nina, Michael, and Eric each own 100 shares of the issued and outstanding stock of ABC Corporation. Corporate bylaws provide for three directors, and state law allows cumulative voting. With cumulative voting, Nina, Michael, and Eric can cast up to 300 votes apiece for the election of directors. Why 300? In cumulative voting situations, you're allowed a total number of votes equal to the product obtained by multiplying the number of shares you own (100) times the number of directors to be elected (3). They can sprinkle these 300 votes any way they choose. However, if they want to preserve their seats on the board, each will likely cast their 300 votes for themselves. What if ABC Corporation only allowed two directors? The results could get interesting. Here, each shareholder could cast up to 200 votes for the election of directors. If each shareholder cast all 200 votes for himself or herself, no director would be elected. This would be a good place for a well-drafted shareholders' or pooling agreement discussed in Chapter 14.

If cumulative voting exists for your corporation, it also applies to actions to remove a director from the corporate board. A director can't be removed unless the number of shares seeking to oust the director are at least equal to the number of shares required to elect the director in the first instance.

Cumulative voting is an area where many incorporate-yourselfers slip up. In some states, cumulative voting exists unless the articles of incorporation say that it does not. In others, it's just the opposite. How are you supposed to know? You may want to contact your legal professional for advice on this because it may vary from state to state.

Supermajority

Any majority requirement greater than a simple majority is a *supermajority*. A simple majority is anything more than 50 percent. Remember, if a quorum is present, a simple majority of shares represented by that quorum is generally sufficient to authorize corporate action.

Supermajority requirements are generally set forth in the articles of incorporation or corporate bylaws. They exist most often as a protection for minority shareholders.

Let's look again at Nina, Michael, and Eric. Each owns 100 shares of ABC Corporation stock. When the corporation was formed, our three shareholders expressed concern about the possibility that any two of the three could authorize corporate action and disregard the opinion of the third. To address this concern, Nina, Michael, and Eric determine to include supermajority requirements in the articles and bylaws.

Fortunately, our three shareholders recognized that supermajority voting requirements would be cumbersome for most corporate actions. Instead, they chose to subject certain major or extraordinary actions to a supermajority requirement, including:

- The sale of the business
- A merger, consolidation, or dissolution
- Borrowing in excess of $10,000
- Contracts with a term exceeding two years
- Purchase of any single asset exceeding $5,000 or any group of assets which in the aggregate exceed $15,000
- A hiring or firing
- Declaring corporate dividends or making distributions
- Increasing salaries of shareholder/employees

This list is illustrative, and it's not exhaustive. Think of situations unique to your corporation that might justify a supermajority requirement.

What supermajority will you choose? Unanimous? Eighty percent? Two thirds? The choice is up to you. You'll want to test the possibilities, before you choose, to make certain that the supermajority requirements provide the protections you desire.

What if you own more than 50 percent of the issued and outstanding stock already? You may not want supermajority requirements. Whether supermajority requirements will exist is largely a matter of negotiation between shareholders. If they exist, the range of subject matters to which they will apply and the supermajority percentage are also open to negotiation.

Consider including supermajority requirements in your bylaws or articles from the beginning if you wish to enhance the voting strength of minority shareholders or preserve a balance of power among different shareholders.

Letting a proxy vote for you

Shareholders don't actually have to go to a meeting to vote. They can get someone to vote for them with a *proxy,* a written authorization given by one person to another party, directing the party to vote on behalf of him. Do you own shares in a publicly traded corporation or mutual fund? Does your mailbox fill periodically with meeting notices and solicitations for your proxy? When this occurs, it may be a sign that disagreements among board members or other shareholders have occurred and individuals are actively contesting for seats on the corporate board.

Proxies must be in writing. Don't expect to call the corporate secretary an hour before the meeting and tell her that you'd like your Aunt Matilda to vote your shares. Written proxies must be delivered to the corporation before the scheduled meeting or presented at the time of the meeting.

A proxy generally expires after 11 months unless the written proxy includes an earlier expiration date. If you grant a proxy, you can revoke it at any time unless the proxy is irrevocable and "coupled with an interest"; a nice legal phrase. A proxy is coupled with an interest if the proxy is issued, for example, as part of a sale of the stock to another person, or pursuant to a voting trust or pooling agreement.

Proxies count for purposes of determining whether a quorum exists. If a shareholder who has executed a proxy dies and the corporation is unaware of the death, the proxy is counted for quorum and voting purposes.

Proxies don't use magical language. A writing signed by the shareholder or his or her attorney (usually under a power of attorney) is probably enough. The writing should identify the person who has the authority to vote the shareholder's shares of stock.

Who can act as a proxy? Very few restrictions exist as to who can be a proxy. Where restrictions do exist, they commonly require that a proxy be at least 18 years of age. Some states require that proxies must be individuals rather than corporations.

Holding a Meeting for the Board of Directors

Board meeting requirements are similar to shareholder meeting requirements. The good news is that there aren't nearly as many requirements for board meetings.

One of the regular meetings may be the *annual meeting* of directors. The annual meeting is often held in conjunction with the annual shareholders' meeting. For small corporations with some or all of the same individuals serving as directors, officers, and shareholders, this may be the only regular meeting during the year.

As noted earlier, the annual meeting is a good time to invite your professional team. Use the time to update the team on corporate activities, and give them the chance to offer suggestions and ideas that could help you save time and money.

Special board meetings are any meeting not regularly scheduled. The president or one or more directors may call a special meeting. If the bylaws so provide, a certain percentage of shareholders may also be able to call a special meeting. Special meetings are held to address important matters that may need to be addressed and may not be able to wait until the next regularly scheduled meeting. Common examples would be a financial crisis, death of a key employee, or the possible sale or merger of the business.

Holding meetings: Time and place

Corporate boards of directors often meet at regular intervals. For example, the board might meet on the second Tuesday of each month at 5:00 p.m. at the corporate office. A corporate resolution or the bylaws usually prescribe the interval. Once prescribed, you don't need to send out another notice, although, as a practical matter, most corporations will send out a reminder to board members.

Board meetings can be held wherever the board chooses. Convenience dictates that the meeting location be at whatever location is most accessible to the board members to facilitate attendance and ensure that a meeting quorum will be present.

Regularly scheduled meetings don't require notice, although it's usually provided. Special meetings, however, do require notice. Look to the corporate articles, bylaws, or state law to tell you how much notice may be required. Unlike shareholder meetings, board-meeting notices are less formal and require less time, perhaps as short as two days. Board meetings are not encumbered by concepts like record date since shareholders aren't required to receive notices of board meetings.

A board member's presence at the meeting generally waives any defects in the notice requirements unless the board member appears specifically to object to the improper notice. Similarly, participation in the meeting will waive future objections to the meeting unless the director states his objections at the outset of the meeting.

To be continued . . . at another meeting

Like shareholder meetings, the board members present can continue the meeting if they specify the new time, date, and place before the meeting is adjourned. As an alternative, nonurgent matters can wait until the next regularly scheduled board meeting.

Making your vote count

Corporate articles of incorporation or bylaws tell you how many individuals serve on the board. Sometimes, the articles or bylaws present a fixed number, such as three. More commonly, the board provides for a range of possible numbers. For example, a board might require a minimum of three members and a maximum of five.

With a fixed board number, a quorum exists whenever a majority of that number is present unless the articles or bylaws require a higher number. If the articles or bylaws provide for a variable range, the quorum is based upon the number fixed within that range. If the variable range runs from three to five, and four have been elected by the shareholders, the quorum is two unless the articles or bylaws specify a higher or lower number.

Each board member usually has one vote on matters presented to the board. And unless the articles of incorporation or bylaws provide otherwise, a majority of the votes of the quorum. Articles and bylaws can require a supermajority for board votes as well as shareholder votes. For examples of the types of activities that might require a supermajority, see the discussion, in this chapter, of supermajority voting for shareholder meetings.

Unlike shareholders, board members can't vote by proxy. However, they may be able to participate in a board meeting by telephone conference call and be counted for quorum and voting purposes if the bylaws or state law permit it.

What Every Meeting Should Include

Whether you're conducting a shareholders' or board meeting, certain things are constant. We discuss a couple of ideas in this section.

Create an agenda

A written agenda is a must. With it, you'll be better organized and capable of conducting a more effective and time-efficient gathering. Shareholders and directors appreciate meetings that get to the point.

Here's a list to get you started:

- Call the meeting to order.
- Review and approve prior meeting minutes.
- Go over the president's report.
- Let the treasurer present her report.
- Discuss other officer, board, or committee reports.
- Announce action items for consideration and approval (list each one separately).
- Present other news or announcements.
- Remind everyone of the next meeting date, time, and location.
- Adjourn the meeting.

The chair of the meeting conducts the meeting. If you're the chair, check off your agenda to make certain you cover all items.

Impact of close corporation statutes on board and shareholder meetings

If you've elected to subject your corporation to your state's close corporation statutes, how much do you need to know about board and shareholder meetings? A good lawyerly answer is, "It depends."

Close corporations may elect to eliminate the board of directors entirely. Make this election, and you can ignore the discussion on board meetings. Rather than eliminate the board entirely, you might take away some of the board's role and authority, but not all of it. If you eliminate some of the board's role but not all of it, the discussion of board roles and meetings still applies. Why eliminate a board? If you wear three hats as officer, director and shareholder, why not simplify matters by removing one hat?

Even if you eliminate the board of directors, close corporations must have an annual shareholders'

meeting. You'll need to revisit the discussion on shareholder meetings to be certain that you comply with shareholder meeting requirements.

Many close corporation statutes contain language which states, in general, that failure to observe the usual corporate formalities is not a ground for imposing personal liability on the corporate shareholders. Conducting board and shareholder meetings and documenting these meetings are corporate formalities. Most lawyers recommend that even if you've selected close corporation status for your corporation, don't disregard corporate formalities like board (if there is one) and shareholder meetings. Despite the statutory language, you're running the risk that personal liability will attach to you if you fail to follow these formalities.

Get a copy of Robert's Rules of Order

Corporate bylaws speak generally to rules and procedures to be used at corporate meetings. Bylaws paint with a broad brush. The best authority on the ins and outs of meetings is a book entitled, *Robert's Rules of Order,* by The Princeton Language Institute (Dell Publishing). Don't go to a board or shareholder meeting without it.

Have you ever been to a meeting where folks shout numerous ideas back and forth? Motions are made, and attempts to amend or table motions follow. Pretty soon, you've lost track of what item is currently before your board or shareholders. The chair of the meeting or more detailed bylaws (or detailed rules for meetings put in place pursuant to the bylaws) can help you stay on track in your meetings if you don't have a copy of *Robert's Rules of Order.*

For small corporations, a thorough knowledge of parliamentary procedure is unnecessary. Many items you'll consider aren't controversial. Those that are will often lead to consensus without procedural motion. For those rare moments when procedure takes precedence, have your *Robert's Rules* ready.

Documenting Board and Shareholder Meetings

You've done a great job conducting board and shareholder meetings. All meetings were properly noticed, quorums were present, and you fielded all the procedural questions. Now what do you do? Take minutes!

Corporate minutes are a written reflection of actions taken and approved at a board or shareholder meeting. This documentary evidence can be used to prove that the meeting occurred and that the actions described were authorized.

Corporate minutes are vital. If your corporation is sued, expect a demand to review corporate meeting minutes. Shareholders have a statutory right to review corporate meeting minutes.

Meeting minutes should be prepared as soon as possible following the meeting's conclusion. At a minimum, meeting minutes should include:

- The date of the meeting or action by consent
- A list of board members or shareholders present
- A statement that a quorum was present
- A recitation of action taken at the meeting

✔ Approval of prior meeting minutes

✔ Other action taken, including such things as: election of directors, appointment of officers, issuance of shares, purchase or sale of significant corporate assets, borrowing or loaning money, and so on

✔ Signatures by the president and secretary if an actual meeting was conducted, or the signatures of all directors or shareholders if the actions are being approved by consent

Preparing corporate meeting minutes isn't complicated. Old time legalese may include big dollar words such as, whereas, heretofore, and an all-time favorite, towit, in meeting minutes. These words don't add anything to the minutes. Use short declarative sentences to state the action approved.

For example, the board authorizes its president to buy a Chevrolet Silverado truck for a purchase price of $25,000, an amount that will be financed through Community Bank for five years. Your corporate minutes might read something like this:

> Resolved, this corporation shall purchase a 2000 Chevrolet Silverado truck for a purchase price of $25,000.

> Further resolved, this corporation will borrow funds necessary to purchase the truck from Community Bank for a term of five years with interest payable at the rate of 10 percent per year.

> Further resolved, the corporation authorizes its president to take whatever steps may be required and sign any documents required to effect the preceding resolutions.

Still sound too legalese? Try it yourself; you'll do fine.

Don't backdate your corporate meeting minutes. If no meeting was held, the consent to action should be dated when it was actually signed by a shareholder or director. The consent is effective on the date the last shareholder or director signs it. Use current dates even if the action authorized in the consent has already occurred. Backdating a single corporate document can undermine the credibility of all of your corporate records.

Chapter 17

Getting Money (And Other Items of Value) In and Out of the Corporation

. . . .

In This Chapter

▶ Getting money into the corporation

▶ Getting money out of the corporation

. . . .

ou're probably anxious to get into this chapter. Who wouldn't be focused on getting money out? Before you get started, however, you have to remember that corporations are creatures of statute. Corporate existence is dependent upon compliance with corporate requirements, spelled out in the corporation statutes, articles of incorporation, or bylaws. The U.S. Department of Treasury, acting through its Internal Revenue Service (IRS) and the Internal Revenue Code (IRC), also provides rules and regulations governing the tax treatment of money and other property going into and coming out of the corporation.

You have a number of accepted ways to put money or other items of value into the corporation or to take it out. Different tax consequences may follow depending on the choice you make. Because of the varying tax treatments, you'll want to consult your tax advisor for guidance.

Getting Money or Other Items of Value into the Corporation

This section is relatively straightforward. We consider contributions to the capital of the corporation, sales of stock, loans to the corporation, and some hybrids.

Contribute to the corporation's capital

Simply stated, you can contribute money or any other property of value to the corporation. All kinds of things qualify as property of value: personal or real estate, accounts receivable, and contract rights.

You determine the value for cash with the amount of the cash. For property contributions, determining value can become a little more complicated. Value can be determined by agreement of the corporation and the person making the contribution. This method works fine unless the person contributing the property is also a director, officer, or shareholder of the corporation. The IRS might not concur with your agreed-upon value.

You can appraise property, formally or informally. Formal appraisals may use the skills of a licensed appraiser. Informal appraisals rely on guestimates of value by someone who deals regularly in the purchase and sale of similar property. For example, licensed real estate appraisers can provide formal appraisals of value. Licensed real estate agents or brokers may not provide a formal appraisal but can offer an informal opinion as to value based on experience in a certain area and comparable sales of property.

When someone contributes cash or property to the capital of the corporation, the contribution is usually in exchange for corporate stock, as we discuss later. This doesn't have to be the case, however. Corporate shareholders may contribute additional monies or property without receiving additional stock. Additional contributions to capital increase a shareholder's basis in his or her stock (discussed in the next section). When capital contributions are returned to a shareholder, her or his basis in corporate stock is reduced.

It would be rare for an individual or other entity to contribute money or property to the corporation without a prior relationship to the corporation as shareholder, officer, or director. These types of contributions are frequently made to tax-exempt, nonprofit corporations in exchange for tax deductions. That's another story.

The corporation considers contributions to its capital to be equity contributions, which are generally unrestricted and may be used by the corporation for any legal purpose. The corporation is under no obligation to return capital contributions at any time, so shareholders have no rights to ask the corporation to return contributions to capital.

What if you contribute property to your corporation that is subject to a debt? For example, John contributes computer hardware and software worth $5,000. The property is subject to a loan of $2,000. What's the impact of the debt? If John agrees to repay the debt directly, his contribution is valued at $5,000. If the corporation assumes the debt, John's contribution is only $3,000.

Be careful when contributing property subject to a debt. If the corporation agrees to pay your indebtedness, you may have to pay income tax on the loan amount assumed by the corporation.

Sell corporate stock

The most widely recognized means of getting money into a corporation is through sales of corporate stock. Remember Nina, Michael, and Eric: our shareholders, officers, and directors of ABC Corporation? At the time of incorporation, Eric contributed $10,000 in cash in exchange for 100 shares of ABC Corporation stock. At the same time, Michael contributed $5,000 in cash and computer hardware and software valued at $5,000 in exchange for 100 shares of ABC stock. Nina didn't contribute any money or property for her 100 shares. Instead, she did most of the preliminary, pre-incorporation work, and she received her stock in exchange for her services.

As a result of these transactions, ABC Corporation has $20,000 worth of capital. In addition, Eric and Michael have a basis in their stock equal to $10,000 each. Nina may have zero basis in her stock, because she contributed services. More importantly, Nina might have to report income in her personal tax return equal to the fair market value of the stock received.

Basis is an accounting and tax concept that represents the amount of cash or property contributed to the corporation, generally in exchange for stock. It's important because when you sell your stock, your gain or loss on that sale is measured against your basis. If Eric sells his stock for $12,000, he has a $2,000 gain. Similarly, if he sold his stock for $8,000, he would have a $2,000 loss.

S corporation shareholders are treated somewhat differently. In Chapter 2, we describe S corporations as pass-through entities. Items of income, gain, loss, deduction, or credit are passed through and taxed at the shareholder level rather than the corporate level. If Eric's basis is $10,000, and $2,000 of loss items are passed through to him, his basis is reduced to $8,000. If he sells his shares for $12,000, he'll now have a $4,000 gain.

Using Eric as an example, again, assume that ABC Corporation has had a good year. Eric will receive pass-through income of $2,000. However, ABC Corporation determines it must retain the income rather than pass it through. Eric will have to pay tax on this $2,000 even though he never receives it. On the other hand, Eric's basis increases from $10,000 to $12,000.

As for Nina, her basis may be $0 since she received stock in exchange for services. If so, she has no basis against which to take advantage of pass-through losses (they can carry forward to future years). If Nina sells her stock for $10,000, she has a $10,000 gain upon which she must pay tax. She may have been better off borrowing money to pay for stock rather than receiving it for services.

Concepts like tax basis are complicated. Tax rules and regulations contain numerous traps for the unwary. Examples presented here are oversimplified to aid in your understanding. Consult with your tax advisor before acquiring or selling corporate stock to avoid unnecessary tax problems.

Loan money to the corporation

A popular tool for getting money into the corporation is a loan. For smaller corporations or start-ups, you can look to shareholders, officers, directors, parents, and friends for loans.

Why a loan instead of purchasing stock? The purchase of stock represents an equity investment. The corporation has no obligation to repay it, and if the corporation fails, the shareholder will receive little or nothing. The investment is said to be at risk. The good news about equity is that if the corporation succeeds, the investment can increase dramatically.

When a loan is made, borrower and lender must each intend that the loan be repaid. Loan repayments consist of principal payments and interest payments. Principal payments represent a return of capital. The lender doesn't pay tax for principal payments received. Interest represents the cost of borrowing to the corporation. Generally, interest payments are deductible by the corporation and included in the income of the lender.

Loans aren't considered to be at risk. They require ongoing repayment. The reality, however, is that unless a loan is secured, the lender runs the risk that the loan may not be repaid if the corporation fails.

Since many lenders are also shareholders, officers, or directors, it's important that the corporation and the lender comply with certain formalities, including:

- ✔ Using a written promissory note (a written document containing a promise to repay amounts borrowed) for the loan
- ✔ Providing for the repayment of the loan with interest in the note
- ✔ Preparing a corporate resolution authorizing the borrowing and directing the president or other officers to sign the promissory note and other related loan documents
- ✔ Complying with the terms and conditions of the promissory note and loan agreements

Failure to follow these formalities might result in the IRS disregarding the loan, treating it instead as a contribution to the corporation's capital or a second class of stock. For S corporation shareholders, recharacterization of a loan as a second class of stock could result in the loss of S corporation status, leading to disastrous consequences.

If the corporation's lender is also a shareholder, make sure loan transactions are at arm's length, containing terms and conditions comparable to those offered by banks or other commercial lending operations. Make certain that the corporation can make loan repayments in a timely fashion.

For S corporations, don't require shareholders to make loans in proportion to their stock contributions. For example, Eric and Michael each contributed $10,000 in cash and property in exchange for 100 shares of ABC Corporation stock. If the corporation requires that they loan $10,000 each, the corporation increases the risk that the IRS may assert that the loan is a second class of stock rather than a loan.

Consider a hybrid

Like so many things corporate, many possibilities are available. Just as corporate articles and bylaws may be modified to supercede contrary language of corporate statutes, corporations can create hybrids. Is it debt or is it equity? Only the IRS may know for sure.

Hybrids aren't often used, especially for small, start-up corporations, but here are a few examples:

- ✔ **Loan that is convertible into stock:** Typically, such an instrument complies with all loan formalities. The promissory note or loan agreement contains additional language giving the lender, in most cases, the option to convert all or some part of the loan into shares of stock. The promissory note or loan agreement sets the formula for conversion.

- ✔ **Stock option:** A stock option is a right to purchase corporate stock in the future. The option specifies the number of shares that person may acquire, the purchase price to be paid or a formula by which the purchase price can be determined, and a time frame within which the option must be exercised. The option will also describe the manner in which it is exercised.

   Options are popular incentives for employees and are commonly part of a stock option plan. They may also be granted to lenders and other non-employee shareholders.

- ✔ **Securities:** The term *securities* can include many different types of things, including corporate stock, options, and certain loan transactions. Federal and state laws regulate the offer and sale of securities.

   Talk with your lawyer before offering the sale of securities to see if exemptions may be available to you. Civil and criminal penalties exist if you're required to comply with federal and state laws, and you fail to do so.

Make money

This could probably be unspoken. Assuming your business buys or sells products or performs services, the corporation will generate income when it is paid for these products or services. The money that comes in belongs to the corporation, not its shareholders, officers, and directors.

Some shareholders, officers, and directors fail to grasp the concept that money coming in belongs to the corporation. You perform services on behalf of the corporation, but the corporation gets the money. Get it? If you don't understand this concept, expect the corporation or other creditors of the corporation to sue you — for misappropriating corporate funds or commingling personal and business assets.

Getting Money or Other Items of Value Out of the Corporation

Getting money in is relatively simple. Getting money out is more complicated. Yet, people get money out of corporations every day.

Pay yourself a salary

You work hard, so you should be entitled to be paid reasonable compensation for services you provide to the corporation. Once every two to four weeks, someone comes along, puts a paycheck on your desk, and life is good. Of course, you're always amazed at how many other groups are getting a piece of your paycheck, most notably the federal and state governments.

Before you begin paying your employees, visit with your accountant or other payroll specialists. Federal and state laws specify how often your employees must be paid and determine what you may deduct from your employees' paychecks. Learn the ropes before you get started.

S corporation shareholders who also serve as officers and employees present some complications. Because S corporations are pass-through entities, the corporate level has no tax to pay. The shareholder level addresses all items of income, expense, deduction, or credit. As a result, an S corporation treats its shareholder much like a general partner for income tax purposes.

This is significant because distributions from S corporations are considered to be salary or dividends. For salary, recipients must pay self-employment taxes. For dividends, no self-employment tax is due.

How do you know which is which? If there is an employment agreement, look to see what it provides for compensation, subject to self-employment tax. If no employment agreement exists, look to see if a board resolution provides a compensation amount. If there is neither an agreement nor a resolution, the IRS will determine what a reasonable amount of compensation is for the services provided. The IRS also has the right to step in and reallocate these amounts.

Amounts distributed (or in the case of an S corporation, deemed distributed) over and above compensation amounts are *dividends*. While dividends will be subject to income tax, they won't require payment of self-employment tax.

Can I treat all S corporation distributions as dividends? You'd like to, wouldn't you? It'd be nice to avoid self-employment taxes. If you're an S corporation shareholder with no active involvement in the corporate business, your distributions are almost certainly going to be considered dividends. However, if you're active in the daily corporate business, a certain amount of the distribution must be regarded as salary, subject to self-employment tax.

How do you draw the line between dividends and compensation? What you would be paid if you performed the same work for someone else is a good indicator of the amount you would treat as compensation. Anything less than that may subject you to audit and the possibility of penalties and interest on unpaid taxes.

When dealing with S corporations, items of income, gain, loss, deduction, and credit pass through to the shareholders in proportion with their shareholdings. Regardless of whether the corporation actually distributes income to you, you're deemed to receive it. Imagine that, paying taxes on money you never received! The good news is that your stock basis will increase — even though you might rather have the money to pay the tax.

Declare a dividend

A *dividend* is a distribution by the corporation to its shareholders. They are paid out of accumulated or current corporate earnings and profits. Common forms of dividend include cash, stock, and occasionally other property.

Dividends relate to stock. Most small corporations, and all S corporations, use a single class of stock called *common stock*. More complex models may use preferred stock. In addition, the articles of incorporation can provide for an almost unlimited variety of classifications of stock, each with different rights and preferences. (See Chapter 9 for more about preferred stock and other forms of classifications.)

Board action is required to declare a dividend. If the board determines to declare a dividend, the board should adopt a resolution authorizing the dividend and identifying the date on which the dividend will be paid, the form of the dividend (cash, stock, or other property), and the shareholders eligible to receive dividends.

Generally, shareholders have no right to compel the board of directors to declare a dividend. If the corporation has issued preferred stock, however, the corporation may be contractually obligated to make dividend payments in accordance with whatever preferences are provided. You should also review corporate bylaws and state laws to determine any additional procedural or substantive requirements.

Chapter 16 introduces the concept of record date. For meetings, only shareholders as of the record date are entitled to meeting notices. For dividend purposes, shareholders as of the record date are the ones who will receive dividends. A common dividend record date is the day prior to the date the board approves the dividend distribution.

Corporations can't declare dividends if the dividend payment would render the corporation *insolvent*. This is true for common stock and preferred stock. You can use two tests to measure insolvency for dividend purposes:

- ✔ Will the dividend render the corporation unable to pay its debts as they fall due?

- ✔ Are corporate assets sufficient to meet corporate liabilities plus the amount of any preferred dividends required to satisfy the rights of preferred shareholders?

A corporate board that declares and pays a dividend in violation of corporate articles or state laws may be personally liable to reimburse the corporation. More important, board members may be unable to be indemnified by the corporation for these costs unless board members can demonstrate that they relied reasonably on financial records that were prepared using acceptable accounting practices and principles.

Repay a loan

If you loan money to a corporation, you have the right to be repaid. In fact, you better be repaid — if an expectation of repayment never existed, the loan is likely to be recharacterized as a second class of stock.

Loan repayments consist of principal and interest. *Principal* represents a return of capital, and it's not taxable to the lender. *Interest* is the cost of the loan, and the lender must report its receipt as income. From the corporation perspective, the interest, not the principal, is deductible.

Redeem shares

A *corporate redemption* occurs when a corporation chooses to purchase its own shares from its shareholders. The corporation and one or more of its shareholders must agree to it. When a shareholder sells some, but not all, of her or his shares to the corporation, a partial redemption results. A redemption is a corporate distribution subject to the limitations on insolvency similar to those described in the "Declare a dividend" section.

A shareholder might want to convert some of his or her shareholdings to cash. The corporation and remaining shareholders are concerned about the possibility of the shares being sold to a third party. If the corporation has the money to fund the redemption without compromising other business obligations, and the corporation seeks to avoid the addition of new shareholders, a redemption may make sense. The selling shareholder gets money from the corporation, the corporation buys back its own shares, and no new shareholders are added to the mix. If all the selling shareholders shares are purchased, the remaining shareholders would see a proportionate increase in their percentage ownership of the corporation as a result.

When a redemption occurs, the shareholder will recognize gain or loss, depending on whether the redemption price is greater or less than the shareholder's basis in the stock (see the "Sell corporate stock" section earlier). Just as a shareholder can pay for stock with cash or anything of value, a corporation can redeem stock for cash or other property of value.

While redemptions tend to be voluntary, they may be involuntary, as well. Chapter 13 discusses shareholder appraisal rights, sometimes known as dissenters' rights. Minority shareholders may compel a corporation, in effect, to purchase the shareholders' shares in the event of a corporate merger or sale. Here, the shareholders may be able to compel a redemption of shares.

Liquidate assets

Liquidation occurs when a corporation chooses, or is forced, to go out of business. Liquidation and dissolution are related concepts. Both the corporate board and shareholders must approve plans to liquidate and dissolve the corporation, although a court may order it in certain circumstances (see Chapter 21).

Generally, when a corporation liquidates and dissolves, the corporate board oversees the following activities:

- Gathering all corporate assets
- Liquidating assets (selling for cash) that won't be distributed in their current state

- ✔ Identifying creditors of the corporation, including persons who might have claims against the corporation

- ✔ Paying secured creditors and creditors with priority such as state and federal taxing authorities

- ✔ Paying or making provision for the payment of other creditors or potential creditors, possibly including the payment of unpaid dividends to the holders of preferred shares

- ✔ Distributing any remaining assets to corporate shareholders on a pro rata basis

- ✔ Filing an official dissolution with the state

As you can see, shareholders come last whenever liquidation and dissolution occur. Nonetheless, it is a means of getting money out of the corporation.

Corporate redemptions and liquidations involve complex tax issues. Be sure to work closely with your tax advisor to avoid getting into a fix.

You need to plan for success

This chapter makes it seem so easy — the ebb and flow of money in and out of your corporation occurring effortlessly, like the rise and set of the sun. For most businesses, it's a struggle. Banks will only loan so much money, and you can't find enough friends or relatives to loan you the difference or buy your corporation's stock.

Getting money out of the corporation isn't a walk in the park either. First, money must be available. You have to know if there is enough money to purchase inventory, equipment, or supplies. And you need to know whether you can afford to pay your employees and business creditors.

Some people are surprised to learn that new businesses rarely make money during the early months of operation. In fact, many new businesses fail. How do you enhance your chances for success? In a word, *plan*.

Every business, new or old, should have a detailed business plan. With no plan, you're planning to fail. Even a bare bones plan is better than no plan at all.

Consider including a detailed description of the business, its operating history, if any, and a list of products or services provided in your business plan. Describe the background and experience of officers and directors. Provide financial information including a balance sheet, a profit and loss statement, and cash flow information. Include financial projections for the business, and clearly state any assumptions upon which those projections are based.

Identify business opportunities and competitive threats. Be realistic, and consider best-case and worst-case scenarios.

You need a plan if you're going to succeed. Fortunately, you'll find no shortage of resources available to help you prepare your business plan (see Appendix B for a few examples). You can also check out self-help books with computer-ready templates, government publications and programs such as SCORE, and community-based programs and services designed to help you create your plan.

SCORE for your business

The SCORE (Service Corps of Retired Executives) Association provides free small business counseling and low-cost entrepreneurial education to both existing and start-up businesses. Through its network of 389 office locations across the country, plus numerous branch locations, SCORE likely has a presence near you. Formed in 1964, SCORE is both a nonprofit association and a resource partner of the U.S. Small Business Administration. Since its inception, SCORE has helped nearly 4.5 million entrepreneurs across the United States. SCORE's free business counseling services are available to all U.S. citizens and resident aliens.

To find a SCORE counseling location, call toll free at 800-634-0245, e-mail SCORE at contact. score@sba.gov, or visit their Web site at www.score.org. On the Web site, you can use the Locator function under the Find SCORE tab. Simply enter your zip code or city and state to search for a location near you, then pull up a map and contact information for that SCORE office.

SCORE offers free e-mail counseling through its Web site, as well. Visit Get E-mail Counseling on their Web site and ask a business question, or search by key words. Find a SCORE business counselor who has the skills and experience you are looking for. Then, just e-mail your question to that SCORE e-mail counselor of your choice. You will get a response to your inquiry within 48 hours. The Web site also provides small-business articles, tips, trends, resources, and tools to help your business grow and succeed.

Part IV
Compliance Issues —
The Paper Trail
Continues

In this part . . .

Your paper trail continues. This part offers hints on how to put your corporation's best foot forward. You see how to prepare and retain good corporate records, off- and online, which may possibly save you from headaches on the road ahead. We also show you how to keep appropriate financial records. If things don't work out, we discuss how to dissolve the corporation. And don't think you have to do all this alone; we offer suggestions for finding help on compliance matters.

Chapter 18

Documenting Corporate Actions

· ·

In This Chapter

▶ Preparing minutes of corporate meetings

▶ Executing corporate documents

▶ Holding the corporation out to the public

· ·

*L*ike people, corporations have the legal authority to engage in a wide range of activities and are subject to possible sanctions and penalties if they run afoul of state and federal laws. Unlike people, corporations have no ability to act on their own, remaining entirely dependent on the actions of others — most often, officers, directors, employees, and agents.

You're an individual. You also happen to be the president of a corporation. How would anyone know when you are acting on your own behalf or on behalf of the corporation? Is that important? The distinction may be critical in determining whether to impose liability on you individually, subjecting your personal assets to loss, or whether liability should be imposed instead on the corporation, subjecting the corporation's assets to loss. If one of the reasons for your decision to incorporate is limited liability, you want to be sure to dot your corporate *I*'s and cross your corporate *T*'s.

Sounds easy, doesn't it? You'd be surprised how many folks fail to document corporate activity, exposing themselves to personal liability. In this chapter, we cover meeting minutes, corporate documents, phone numbers, business cards, and other crucial pieces. Read on, and you'll understand how to properly document corporate actions.

Protecting Yourself with Documentation

When you incorporate your business, you create a separate legal entity. Your corporation is not you. Be sensitive to how you project your corporation to the world. If you don't hold the corporation out as a separate legal entity, you make it easier for creditors and other claimants to assert personal liability against you rather than corporate liability against the corporation.

By simply documenting corporate activity, you save yourself from possible personal liability later down the road. Create meeting minutes, sign corporate documents correctly, and present your company as an incorporated company in its letterhead, business cards, and Web sites. Business cards, letterhead, telephone listings, and Web sites may seem like small, almost insignificant things, but they aren't. More importantly, you have complete control over these items.

Interestingly, your failure to do any one of the items mentioned in this chapter may not subject you to personal liability. That's the good news. The bad news is that your failure to do lots of these little things adds up. The cumulative weight of failure to do these little things can cause your corporation to be disregarded and personal liability to be imposed on individuals.

Moreover, when someone is hurt or damaged, creative minds look for ways to turn a corporation on its head and impose liability on individual officers, directors, and shareholders. Don't make the victim's task easier by failing to observe the small details, or you'll find yourself the victim.

Creating Corporate Meeting Minutes

Because corporations lack the ability to act for themselves, others must act for them. In small corporations, the actors tend to be corporate officers or directors.

Officers and directors have several sources of power to act. Here are a few examples:

- ✔ The power to act might be implied by virtue of the corporate office held. One might imply that a corporate president is authorized to obligate the corporation to a wide range of actions.

- ✔ The power might be implied through a long course of dealing. If you work with a single supplier, the supplier could reasonably assume that the person who has authorized prior shipments has the right to order additional shipments.

- ✔ Authority can also be expressed in corporate meeting minutes. While corporate minutes don't need to make specific reference to those things that arise in the normal, day-to-day business operation, extraordinary items or matters that fall outside the category of daily activity should be expressly authorized in corporate minutes. For example, corporate meeting minutes should authorize the purchase or lease of large or expensive equipment or real estate, loans, agreements to purchase another business or sell substantially all of the corporation's assets, or merge the corporation with another.

REMEMBER

Corporate shareholders elect directors and ratify acts of the corporate board and officers. Unless the bylaws provide otherwise, shareholders rarely authorize specific corporate action to take place. The corporate board will assume this role. When we speak about meeting minutes in this context, we refer almost exclusively to minutes of the corporate board.

Meeting minutes should clearly identify the action to be taken and the names or titles of the individuals authorized to carry out the action. Most often acts are approved and people authorized to carry the acts out through corporate resolution. Corporate resolutions should be presented as simple declarative sentences. Don't be a lawyer — leave your "whereas," "heretofore," and "to wit" at home.

Assume that your corporation needs office space. You have presented a proposed lease to the board for its consideration. After the board has reviewed the lease and asked questions about it, board members vote to approve the lease. Here's an example of a corporate resolution the board might consider:

> "Resolved, the corporation shall enter into a three-year lease agreement for 2,000 square feet of office space located at 123 Main St. in Grants Pass, Oregon, in accordance with the terms and conditions of a lease agreement which has been presented to the board and is to be filed with the records of this meeting.

> Further Resolved, the corporate president is authorized and directed to execute the lease on behalf of the corporation."

The resolution could also incorporate the lease agreement by referring to it in the resolution. As written, one would expect to find a copy of the lease agreement in the corporate minute book with the meeting minutes.

Meeting minutes don't always require a meeting (see Chapter 16). The board of directors and shareholders can meet by consent of all board members or shareholders. In lieu of meeting minutes, a Memorandum of Action would be prepared. The resolution would read the same. However, with an actual meeting, the corporate president and secretary usually sign the minutes. With a consent resolution or Memorandum of Action, no actual meeting takes place. Rather, the board members or shareholders agree to the action described in the resolution, and each signs and dates the Memorandum or consent resolution. The Memorandum isn't effective until the last director has signed it. The corporate president generally prepares the Memorandum or consent resolution for signature by the directors or shareholders.

Signing Corporate Documents

During your day, you are Jane Doe, private citizen. You wear lots of hats: individual, spouse, parent, and community volunteer. You are also Jane Doe, president of ABC Corporation. How you sign your name says a great deal about which hat you are wearing and indicates whether you are committing yourself individually or obligating the corporation to do something.

When you sign a corporate document, make sure you sign in a representative capacity. Consider the office lease example in the preceding section. Here are two good ways to demonstrate your representative capacity:

- ✔ ABC Corporation

  By Jane Doe, President
- ✔ Jane Doe, President of ABC Corporation

By making certain that you mention the corporate name and by adding your representative capacity (president, in this example), it's clear that the corporation is entering into the transaction. Failing to do either of these things clouds the issue, possibly exposing you to personal liability for the lease.

What if you are presented with a corporate document that lists your name but not the corporation's? Don't sign it unless you intend to be personally liable. Ask for the document to be revised to include the corporate name and not your name. If there isn't time for a revision, strike through your name, write in the corporate name, and have all parties initial this change. On the signature line, use the second example shown above.

Taking Care of Business: Letterhead, Phone Listings, and the Rest

Whoever said, "The devil is in the details," must have worked with corporations. How you hold yourself out to the public is important for liability issues. When you sign a document as "President of ABC Corporation," this signature tells the world that you're acting in a representative capacity.

What about how you hold yourself out when a signature is not required? Think about the many ways you present yourself and your business to the public. Here are a few common examples:

- ✔ Business cards
- ✔ Telephone listings
- ✔ Signs
- ✔ Letterhead
- ✔ Web sites

Do you list the corporate name on these items? Do you include the complete corporate name? Which name should you list on your business card or letterhead — the complete corporate name or the assumed business name? Chapter 6 introduces the concept of doing business using an assumed or fictitious name.

If you've complied with the state requirements to register the assumed business name, you're probably safe just using it. However, most attorneys will suggest a more conservative approach, listing both the actual and assumed names. Assume that ABC Corporation is doing business under the name, Mullet Cuts, a name that ABC has properly registered with the secretary of state. Here's what the letterhead or business card might look like:

- Mullet Cuts, a division of ABC Corporation
- ABC Corporation doing business as Mullet Cuts

You should also have a separate telephone listing for your corporation. Never confuse the people with whom you do business. Don't create an opportunity for someone with a claim against your corporation to assert, "I didn't know it was incorporated. I always dealt with Jane Doe. I thought she was the business."

Many corporations maintain Web sites, serving current and prospective customers. (Chapter 6 covers the issue of reserving a domain name.) Make sure your Web site lists the complete corporate name, as well as any registered assumed or fictitious names it does business under. And show the names of individuals in their representative capacities, such as "Jane Doe, President."

Chapter 19

Corporate Record Keeping

. . . .

In This Chapter

▶ Identifying records you'll need to keep

▶ Knowing where to keep corporate records

▶ Deciding what to do when a shareholder wants to see the corporate records

▶ Understanding the value of a corporate kit

. . . .

*E*very corporate lawyer or accountant who's been around for a while has had this experience: A client walks into the office with a box (or boxes) of files and papers. A quick glance indicates the absence of any filing system or organization. The client says one of two things. First, "I received this notice from the IRS, and I need to produce some records." Or second, "One of my customers just filed a lawsuit, and she wants to inspect my corporate records."

Let's face it. Some of us are better record keepers than others. Some require order and structure in their lives, and others are content living out on the edge.

Why is this important to you? State and federal laws require that corporations maintain certain records. In addition to these records, there are a number of other records that good business practice suggests a corporation (or any business, for that matter) should retain.

If you're not a good record keeper, you're just asking for trouble for yourself and your corporation. Failing to keep appropriate corporate records can do many things, all of them bad. You could forfeit your corporate charter; empower a court or the IRS to disregard the corporate status and impose personal liability against individual officers, directors, and shareholders; or find yourself unable to prove claims that the corporation may have against others or defend claims brought against the corporation.

Corporate Records: What to Include

Corporations are required by law to keep certain records. In this section, we'll consider records that the Model Business Corporation Act (MBCA) says you must keep.

The MBCA deals with corporate records that must be maintained. Many state and federal laws require a wide range of other records to be maintained and retained by businesses, whether or not they are incorporated. This includes workers' compensation claims or injury reports, safety committee minutes, immigration forms, tax returns, and more.

The MBCA requires that each corporation maintain:

- Articles of incorporation
- Bylaws
- Board resolutions creating classes of stock
- Minutes of shareholder meetings and consent resolutions
- All written communications to corporate shareholders within a designated time — usually the last three years — including copies of any financial statements furnished (year-end balance sheet, income statement, and statement of changes in shareholders equity)
- An alphabetical list of shareholders by class or series of shares
- A list of current board and officer names and addresses
- The most recent corporate annual report

The MBCA list is a starting point. In addition, corporate statutes may grant shareholders the right to inspect corporate accounting records. Keep them readily available for shareholder review. Check out the "Shareholders Sneak a Peek" section for more about shareholder inspection rights.

Beyond the MBCA list, the IRS and other persons with claims against the corporation may be able to compel disclosure of a much broader range of documentation, including:

- Detailed financial information
- Tax returns
- Sales records
- Repair records
- Letters and other correspondence
- Personnel records
- Company contracts and agreements

With limited exception, virtually all corporate documents and business records can be obtained if the documents or records bear some reasonable relationship to the claim presented. Now can you see why record keeping is important?

Spend time making certain that your records are complete and up to date. Don't put it off. It's hard to re-create records after the fact, and the record keeping just piles up, creating a vicious cycle. Don't backdate records. A single backdated corporate record can undermine all corporate records.

Good corporate record keeping has much to do with corporate credibility. If it's important to you that your corporate identity not be disregarded, keep good records. Poor record keeping, backdated documents, and missing documents all undermine the credibility of the corporation, perhaps making it easier for the IRS, disgruntled employees, claimants, and others to sue the corporation. It could be difficult for the corporation to prove its claims or defend against the claims of others. Moreover, poor record keeping is one more basis upon which the separate corporate status may be disregarded and personal liability imposed on shareholders, officers, and directors.

Keep Corporate Records on Site and in Sight

It may be important to distinguish records by type. Corporate records required under the MBCA should be maintained in your corporate kit at the corporation's principal business location. In addition, financial, accounting, and tax information should be retained there. Records should be kept in a safe and secure location, immune from theft, wandering eyes, and destruction. Other business records may be stored in a variety of places. For example, if you do business in more than one location, certain records related to the operation of that location are likely to be maintained there. However, if you do business in one location, all corporate records might be located there. Consider protecting your vital corporate records in a fireproof safe or safe-deposit boxes.

As noted, corporate records should be kept in a safe and secure location. Confidential information, such as the kind of information found in personnel files, medical records, and other proprietary corporate information, should be secured with limited access. All corporate records should be kept in an organized manner so that they can be easily retrieved if needed. You never know for sure which record might prove decisive in a dispute.

Shareholders Sneak a Peek

Shareholders have the right under state law to inspect records. As a general rule, the shareholders always have the right to inspect those records found in the MBCA list. Fear not, however, a shareholder can't march into your office and expect to review records immediately unless you agree to it.

Shareholders must submit a written request to inspect corporate records, usually at least five days prior to the date of inspection. The written request should state the purpose for the inspection and identify the records to be inspected.

Don't expect precision if the shareholder has prepared the request. The more precise the request, the more likely a lawyer is involved, and a claim may be imminent.

If a shareholder wants to inspect MBCA items, a stated purpose isn't required. A shareholder seeking to inspect additional records may have to state the purpose of the inspection. The corporation isn't required to produce documents if it deems the request improper or unreasonable. Shareholders investigating potential mismanagement or seeking a mailing list to facilitate communication with other shareholders could be proper. On the other hand, requests made simply to harass the board or officers would be inappropriate. Similarly, a shareholder could be denied access to company trade secrets or other proprietary information.

A shareholder's right to inspect extends to lawyers and others authorized by the shareholder to inspect on his or her behalf. If the shareholder wants copies of records inspected, the corporation can impose a reasonable charge related to the cost of copying. Inspections generally occur during normal business hours on regularly scheduled workdays.

Organization Made Easy with a Corporate Kit

For those of you who have difficulty maintaining corporate records in an organized fashion, a corporate kit will help. In one notebook, you'll find a place to keep your articles of incorporation, bylaws, all meeting minutes (both director and shareholder), stock certificates, and stock transfer records. You can also include lists of shareholders, officers, and directors.

Corporate kits also look impressive. That might not be important to everyone, but a corporate kit containing all this information can reap positive benefits. Remember the client who showed up with a box of loosely filed, disorganized records? What impression will the IRS agent have when the agent sees the box? Picture that same agent being handed a well-maintained corporate kit.

Impressions are also important when you're being sued or trying to sell your business. You want to present your corporation in its most favorable light. Organized records help immensely. A corporate kit is a great step in the right direction. It will generally come packaged with incorporation services provided by incorporation service companies.

Compliance Watch online services

Don't be dissuaded from incorporating your business because of anticipated record-keeping headaches. The Company Corporation recently released an exclusive service to help business owners keep their corporate records in compliance. It's called, aptly, Compliance Watch, and it's designed to be used in conjunction with your corporate kit. It's an ingenious online service that alerts the subscriber what compliance duties need to be taken care of and when. It is multistate specific so, for example, if you are incorporated in Florida and qualified to do business in California, Compliance Watch automatically alerts you of the dates when annual reports and franchise taxes are due in both states.

Keeping track of your minutes online helps keeps your records in order. You can even plug in your annual meeting date and Compliance Watch will e-mail your board, shareholders, and officers when the meeting will be held. Learn more about Compliance Watch online at www.compliancewatch.com.

Chapter 20

Getting Your Financial Information in Order

* *

In This Chapter

▶ Filing required financial reports

▶ Establishing and maintaining a good banking relationship

* *

*N*umbers, numbers, numbers! When you formed your corporation, you created a distinct legal entity. Already, the corporation has its own charter number and federal identification number (see Chapter 12). What about the numbers that indicate how well or how poorly the corporation is doing? Folks will be interested in those numbers. Your shareholders, for example, will want to learn if the business is making money. Your banker will care, especially if you have borrowed money from the bank. State and federal tax authorities will also want to be sure that the corporation is paying whatever income taxes and franchise taxes may be required.

For a variety of reasons, you should be able to generate accurate corporate financial reports within a short period of time to suit a number of possible audiences. Modern financial reporting software should help you handle this, allowing you to create balance sheets, cash flow statements, and profit and loss statements with a few keystrokes.

Filing an Annual Report

Each state requires domestic and foreign corporations to file *annual or biennial reports*. For many corporations, these reports change little from year to year. Annual and biennial reports provide states with updated information on such things as corporate address, business activity, and changes in the makeup of officers or directors. Your annual report may include:

✔ The corporation's name and state of incorporation

✔ The registered agent's name and address

- ✔ The principal corporate address
- ✔ The corporate president and secretary names and business addresses
- ✔ Corporate board members' names and addresses
- ✔ A description of your corporation's principal business activity
- ✔ Federal or state identification numbers

Some states ask for more, others less. Keep in mind that annual and biennial reports are public records, and the information included within the report can be reviewed by anyone requesting to do so. Because it is public, don't include more information than requested in the report.

Anyone who might have a claim against the corporation will seek to obtain the annual report so that he or she knows who to file a lawsuit against.

Most states mail the annual report form to the corporation's registered agent. If you don't receive a form before the filing date, check out the Web site for your state's secretary of state.

Make sure you clearly mark the annual report filing date on your calendar each year. If you fail to file the report or pay the appropriate fee, your corporate charter could be revoked even if the failure to file results from the fact that you never received the report form from the secretary of state. If this happens, see Chapter 21.

Where are "financial" numbers included in the annual report? Generally, the annual report doesn't require financial information. For purposes of this annual filing with the secretary of state, limited or no financial information is required.

Filing a Corporate Franchise Tax Form

A *franchise tax* is a fee paid for the privilege of doing business in the state. (Didn't you know that it's a privilege to pay taxes?) The good news is that not all states charge a franchise tax. Corporations doing business in more than one state may be subject to a franchise tax in some states and not others.

Different states use different formulas to assess this tax. A common model bases the fee on the number of authorized shares of corporation stock. If you're incorporated or doing business in such a state, you may want to limit the number of authorized shares in order to keep the franchise tax as low as possible.

Like the annual report, if you fail to file the franchise tax form or pay the required tax, the corporate charter may be revoked. This is never good. The due date for filing annual reports and paying franchise taxes varies greatly state by state. For example, Delaware annual reports and franchise taxes are due March 1 each year. Some states calculate due dates based on the anniversary date of the corporation. Check the requirements in your state.

Filing Income Tax Returns

Here's a treat you're sure to enjoy: A corporation is a distinct legal entity, and as such, it may be required to pay income taxes just like you. For general (or C) corporations, you have to file state and federal income tax returns. Since S corporations are pass-through entities for tax purposes, they are generally exempt from federal income tax. Federal income tax items pass through to S corporation shareholders who report these items on their personal income tax returns (see Chapter 2 for more information about S corporations). Most states follow the federal tax rules, applying state income tax to the S corporation shareholders.

Tax matters can be complicated. The preparation and filing of state and federal income tax returns may require professional assistance. Consult your tax advisor for help. Even if you prepare your own state and federal income tax returns, professional guidance may be useful. It's especially useful to consult a tax advisor when:

 ✔ You're humbled at the site of numbers, big or small.

 ✔ You buy another business or sell part of your business during the tax year.

 ✔ Your S corporation status was inadvertently terminated during the year (see Chapter 2).

 ✔ You dispose of a significant corporate asset, such as a piece of real estate or expensive equipment, during the year.

 ✔ You make personal and business use of a company car, and you're uncertain how to allocate the value of each use on your tax return.

At the federal level, C corporations are taxed at graduated rates based on taxable income, ranging from 15 percent to 35 percent. S corporation shareholders pay income tax based on their individual tax rate.

State tax rates vary widely. You'll need to check with your state's department of revenue to determine which tax rate, if any, applies to your corporation.

Deciding Who's Responsible

Corporations file annual reports, franchise tax returns, income tax returns, and other reports during the year. If you're the sole officer, director, and shareholder, you'll do the work or you'll be in charge of hiring a professional to help you. Either way, you're responsible.

If your corporation has a number of employees, the corporate president or treasurer is generally considered responsible for the timely and accurate preparation and filing of these reports. This is true even if professionals are recruited to do some or all of the work.

When corporations fail to file annual reports or franchise tax returns, the corporation can be administratively dissolved (see Chapter 21). Directors become statutory trustees required by law to wind up the business of the corporation.

When a corporation fails to pay state or local income tax, federal and state laws impose personal liability on responsible persons. The Internal Revenue Service generally looks to the corporate president, treasurer, or both as the responsible persons for income tax purposes.

 Make certain that your corporate calendar lists all required reports and returns and the due date for each one. Designate a reliable individual to keep track of these reports and returns and filing dates. Consider a tracking service with a service company to provide a calendar and electronic reminders to ensure your compliance with your reporting obligations.

Maintaining a Good Relationship with Your Bank

Every business needs a good banking relationship. From working capital loans to funds necessary to purchase needed equipment or property, banks are invaluable. Banks can also provide credit references and history, which are helpful in opening up doors to other sources of needed capital. If your corporation is to expand and grow, maintain a good banking relationship.

Banks also provide a host of services useful to corporations. From the basics of establishing depositary accounts to the facilitation of money transfers and related services, banks can keep your business running smoothly.

A good banker with a strong business background may spot trends and issues in your statements that may prove helpful in improving your corporation's bottom line. As a result, your banker can be an integral part of your professional team, helping you analyze what's going on in your business and identify prospective funding sources.

When you borrow from a bank, the corporation will be required to provide financial information, usually a current balance sheet and income and expense statement. You may also be required to provide prior-year financial reports or tax returns. Banks will often require that you provide corporate financial information on a periodic basis (usually annually) during the term of the loan. Failure to provide this information, if it is required, may result in a default in the loan.

As a condition to making a loan, your bank may require that the corporation maintain a certain level of income or expense, restrict increases in management salaries, limit the amount of debt the corporation can incur, and otherwise impose requirements on the operation of the corporation's business. You need to be comfortable that the business can succeed with these limitations. Over time, your good working relationship with your bank may allow these restrictions to be modified or eliminated after the bank is comfortable in its relationship with you and your corporation.

For small corporations, your bank is likely to require personal guarantees of key officers and shareholders prior to making sizeable loans. You may also be asked to pledge corporate shares or other items of value as additional security for the loan. This request is pretty common, so don't be alarmed. If you can't accept the restrictions, look for another lender.

When you borrow from a bank, expect to post security for the loan. You might be required to mortgage your house, pledge your life insurance policy, or offer other valuable personal assets as security for the loan. If you can't repay the loan, the bank may foreclose on those pledged assets, leaving you with little more than the shirt on your back. Hopefully, you'll still have your pants!

Good banking relationships aren't born, they're made. The banking industry has changed dramatically over the last few years. Big banks buy small banks. New, small banks are formed. You have national banks, regional banks, and community banks. Where do you start shopping for a bank? Ask around — talk to your friends and fellow business owners. Where do they bank? What do they like about their bank? What special needs has the bank been able to address for them?

Finding a good bank is often more about finding a good individual banker within the bank rather than the bank itself. Find out:

✔ Has the banker worked with corporate clients in businesses like yours?

✔ What is the banker's experience?

✔ Can the banker direct you to resources for low-income or guaranteed loans?

✔ Can the banker provide you with assistance in preparing business plans?

✔ What does the banker know about other community resources useful to corporate owners?

✔ Does the banker seem to genuinely care about you or your business?

Documenting Banking Transactions

Day-to-day transactions such as making deposits or writing checks don't require a written record other than the normal business records generated through ledger entries and the checks or deposit slips themselves. However, your board meeting minutes should reflect more significant transactions, such as:

✔ Establishing a checking or savings account (the bank will usually provide you with its standard form of corporate resolution)

✔ Borrowing money from the bank

✔ Authorizing a pledge or mortgage of corporate property as security for any loan

Make sure that any corporate resolution recorded in the board meeting minutes describes the activity with enough specificity to identify the transaction. The resolution should also identify the officers or employees authorized to carry out the transaction on behalf of the corporation.

Chapter 21

Closing Up Shop

*O*ne of the unique characteristics of corporations is the ability to have perpetual existence. Unlike individuals, corporations can, and sometimes do, live forever. Ford Motor Company and General Motors Corporation continue to thrive and survive despite the fact that the founding shareholders have long since departed. For most corporations, however, there is an end of the road, whether it be a merger, consolidation, dissolution, or bankruptcy that brings the company to a close.

When a corporation no longer engages in business, state statutes provide a mechanism by which the corporation is dissolved and its assets liquidated. As you will see, dissolution can be voluntary or involuntary. When a corporation is dissolved, its officers and directors are charged with the responsibility to gather corporate assets, pay off claims and creditors, and distribute any remaining corporate assets to shareholders.

State laws also prescribe procedures for merging and consolidation, but because this subject area is so complex, we suggest you talk with your professional team.

Terminating the Company with Dissolution

Some corporations are so closely tied to their key employees that the termination, death, disability, or retirement of the employee make it impossible for the corporation to stay in business. In these cases, and many others, dissolution may occur. *Dissolution* is the statutory procedure that terminates the existence of a domestic corporation, and it comes in two flavors: voluntary and involuntary.

Voluntary dissolution

Voluntary dissolution occurs with the approval of corporate directors and shareholders, each of which typically must vote to approve the dissolution. Only majority approval is required unless your articles or bylaws require a greater majority.

In rare circumstances, a corporation will dissolve shortly after it files its articles. Most often, this occurs when people change their mind or decide to do something else that doesn't require a corporation. If the corporation hasn't selected directors, state law allows the incorporators to file articles of dissolution. Since the company has no directors or shareholders, it doesn't need to hold a formal meeting.

The more common situation is that the corporation has directors and shareholders. Often, someone presents a plan of liquidation or dissolution to the board and shareholders for approval. The plan outlines the process by which assets will be gathered and claims paid or funds set aside to satisfy possible claims that may not have been filed yet. The plan generally contains a timeline that states when the assets will be sold, claims paid, and any remaining assets distributed to shareholders. The plan is generally presented to the board and shareholders for approval.

For many small corporations, dissolution and liquidation is a simple process. Bills have always been paid in a timely fashion, and no claims against the corporation are lurking. For these corporations, it's a simple exercise of paying recent bills and creditors, liquidating assets, and distributing remaining assets to the shareholders.

In a voluntary dissolution, corporations file *articles of dissolution* with the secretary of state. The articles may set forth the name of the corporation, the date the dissolution was authorized, and the number of shares voted in favor of and against the plan to dissolve.

Once the secretary of state files the articles of dissolution, the corporation's continuing existence focuses on winding up and liquidating its business and affairs. The corporation isn't able to continue its corporate business except to the extent necessary to enable the corporation to wind up and liquidate. The concept of "winding up" refers to the discharging of a corporation's liabilities and the distribution of its remaining assets to its shareholders. The corporate officers generally perform tasks related to winding up, subject to oversight by the corporate board of directors.

Involuntary dissolution

Involuntary dissolution doesn't require board or shareholder approval. A corporation can be dissolved involuntarily by order of the secretary of state or any court with jurisdiction located within the state of incorporation. When a court orders dissolution to occur, the process is referred to as *judicial dissolution.* If the secretary of state dissolves the corporation, the corporation is said to be *administratively dissolved.* Presumably, the involuntary dissolution of a corporation in the state of incorporation serves to terminate the authority of the corporation in any other state where it is qualified to do business.

Let's say you have a corporation in Delaware, but you do business in New Jersey and Maryland, two states where you have qualified to do business. If your corporation is voluntarily dissolved in Delaware, but you want to continue doing business, you will need to take steps to "resurrect" your corporation in those states and requalify your corporation to do business in the other states where it is doing business. When you qualify to do business in another state (see Chapter 10), the law probably requires a valid incorporation in some other state. If your corporation is dissolved in that state, then by definition, you can no longer be qualified as a corporation to do business in those other states.

The secretary of state might dissolve a corporation because:

- ✔ It failed to file an annual report.
- ✔ It failed to maintain a registered agent or registered address within the state.
- ✔ It failed to file required franchise tax reports.
- ✔ It failed to pay any statutory fees.
- ✔ The corporation's period of duration expired.

In most states, you will receive prior written notice from the secretary of state's or other government office and an opportunity to cure any deficiency before the corporation is administratively dissolved. If an involuntary dissolution occurs, the corporation can no longer engage in business until it reinstates, except to the extent necessary to enable the corporation to wind up its affairs, gather assets, pay claims and creditors, and distribute remaining assets to shareholders.

Make sure your corporate calendar is up to date with important filing dates and deadlines. Don't face involuntary dissolution of your corporation because you failed to file required reports.

Courts can also dissolve corporations, although it is rare. The state may seek a court order to dissolve if a corporation obtained its articles of incorporation by fraud or repeatedly exceeded or abused the authority conferred upon it under state law. For example: Corporate articles might provide that the corporation exists for the purpose of engaging in legal activities permitted by state law. In fact, the corporation's principal purpose is to facilitate illegal activity. Hopefully, you will never see one of these in your corporate lifetime.

Shareholders can seek judicial dissolution as well. Here are some examples of conduct that might trigger shareholder action:

- Board members deadlock on management decisions, creating a likelihood of serious harm or injury to the corporation or its business if the deadlock is not broken.

- Board members engage in conduct shown to be illegal, oppressive, or fraudulent.

- Corporate assets are being misappropriated or wasted.

- Shareholders deadlock and are unable to elect directors.

Involuntary dissolution isn't common. It usually results because a corporation fails or is unable to act. A corporation fails to act whenever a corporate board refuses to take requested action, and a corporation is unable to act whenever its board deadlocks.

Following the Rules: Formally Dissolve and Liquidate

Suppose you tell your lawyer, "My corporation has lost money. Why should I incur more expense just to prepare and file articles of dissolution? What if I just stop doing business without formally dissolving and liquidating the corporation?"

If a corporation ceases activity and doesn't formally dissolve, the secretary of state will involuntarily dissolve it for failing to file one or more required reports. For businesses without creditors or potential liability claims against it, this may be just fine. Anyone contacting the secretary of state's office to inquire about the corporation would be told that it is inactive or that its corporate charter had been forfeited. However, there are a number of reasons why you would want to formally dissolve your corporation:

- Technically, corporation law requires it, and failure to comply with the law could result in fines or penalties. It may also be more expensive from a practical standpoint, as creditors will not know against whom they should file claims.

- You don't want to be sued in your individual capacity (more on this later).

- You want to develop a process by which creditors can be paid and funds can be reserved for potential future claimants.

- You want to unplug the corporation from the state's system, relieving yourself of future notices and the potential for future fees, penalties, or interest.

> ✔ It's cleaner, something appreciated by the Internal Revenue Service and state departments of revenue.
>
> ✔ In the event you go back into business, you won't have to pay past due franchise taxes and interest payments required by some states.

When a corporation is in the process of dissolving, whether voluntarily or involuntarily, its corporate directors may become *statutory trustees,* responsible for making certain the corporation gathers assets and pays creditors and claims.

In an involuntary dissolution, it's possible that directors and officers aren't aware that the corporation has been dissolved. If the corporation fails to file timely reports, it will be dissolved administratively by the secretary of state. The corporation's office should receive by mail a notice warning about the possibility of the dissolution. If the directors never learn of the notice or the possibility of dissolution, they suddenly may become statutory trustees.

Directors may be personally liable to creditors and claimants against the corporation to the extent that corporate assets came into their hands. If you're a director who receives a corporate distribution during dissolution, you may be liable to others for the value of that distribution. You could be sued as "statutory trustee," and the corporation might not have the means at that time to indemnify you or to cover your legal costs. In such a case, you could have to pay back any distribution you received, either to the corporation or the creditor.

If your corporation's time is up, comply with the state's formal dissolution process. While you may incur some additional expense, you could save yourself time and the big bucks in the long run. Need help in this area? Contact your legal professional or a full-service incorporation service company for assistance in filing the required dissolution documents in your state. If you want to do it yourself, contact the secretary of state or other state incorporation office in your state and request the forms, which are generally uncomplicated, for dissolution. The hard part is carrying out the dissolution — liquidating assets and paying creditors in an orderly fashion.

Paying income tax after your corporation's death

The only sure things in life are death and taxes. The same holds true for corporations when they die. Not only are the tax issues significant, they are complex.

If your corporation seeks dissolution and liquidation, consult your tax advisor immediately to understand and plan for the tax liabilities that may be triggered.

Losing Out to Bankruptcy

Bankruptcy is complicated. What follows is a brief, oversimplified description of the process.

Like dissolution, there are two basic types of bankruptcy: voluntary and involuntary. A corporation will put itself into *voluntary bankruptcy,* while creditors will put a corporation into *involuntary bankruptcy.*

A corporation may consider bankruptcy whenever its liabilities exceed its assets or whenever it's unable to pay its bills when they fall due. In some bankruptcies, the corporation seeks to liquidate and dissolve. This process is similar to corporate dissolution described earlier.

The corporation may also seek bankruptcy protection so that it can reorganize its business operations. A few years ago, it seemed as if every major airline carrier in the United States was using the bankruptcy laws to reorganize. Reorganization provides a window of opportunity where the corporation and its creditors work to create a plan that will enable the business to continue and allow creditors to pay all or some part of amounts owed.

Whether voluntary or involuntary, liquidation or reorganization, bankruptcy provides a formal, court-sanctioned process to limit, at least temporarily, creditors from filing claims against a corporation. For anyone who has ever been hounded by creditors, bankruptcy can provide order and shelter from what may seem to be a very disorderly and demanding world. Bankruptcy can afford corporate officers and directors an opportunity to catch their collective breath while they consider options for the future of the business. Bankruptcy is an orderly process for claims to be heard and approved; assets identified, gathered, and distributed; and a corporation liquidated or reorganized.

If you're considering bankruptcy, contact your attorney. Because it's a complicated process, your professional can advise you whether bankruptcy is in your corporation's best interests, and if so, what type of bankruptcy you should consider. Don't do this on your own.

Chapter 22

Who Can Help Me with Corporate Compliance Matters?

· ·

In This Chapter

▶ Doing it yourself

▶ Getting help for compliance matters

▶ Deciding what you can do and what others should do

· ·

Your corporation is like a beautifully running roadster. To make it run like a well-oiled machine, it helps to take care of certain matters every three thousand miles. Corporate compliance is like maintaining your car. If you make a routine and follow it, your corporation will run smoothly and you can expect years of good service. If you put it off, the paperwork piles up and your corporate engine may stall. Being diligent and attending to matters as they arise makes your compliance tasks easier.

This chapter offers three roads you can take to corporate compliance: do it yourself, use a service company, or hire a professional. Read on to understand more.

Doing It Yourself

So you consider yourself a regular home mechanic. You can save your corporation a little dough by doing it yourself, and you can benefit by getting to know your business better. Here's a checklist of things you'll need to do:

✔ Keep good corporate minutes. Document important corporate activities and transactions with meeting minutes showing that the action was authorized and identifying the officers authorized to act. Include loans, dividends, sales, or mergers of the corporation or its assets, major capital expense items, election of directors, and appointment of officers in your minutes.

✔ File required reports and returns on time. Don't forget to complete and return the corporation's annual report, franchise tax return, income tax returns, and other annual filings. Develop a calendar system to help you remember.

✔ Hold the corporation out to the public as a corporation. Don't let your customers or suppliers be confused about the nature of your business. Make certain they understand they are doing business with a corporation and not you individually. If your corporation uses an assumed business name, make sure it's registered.

✔ Pay corporate bills and repay loans on time.

✔ Understand what the corporate bylaws and articles require. Don't conduct a meeting without first reviewing your corporate bylaws. Similarly, don't take action at a board or shareholder meeting if your articles or bylaws restrict the action proposed.

If you're going to be your corporation's compliance officer, establish a routine to help you keep up with compliance work. Done regularly, you shouldn't be overburdened. If you procrastinate, you and your corporation could get in trouble.

Calling an Incorporation Service Company

Service companies provide a wide range of corporation-related services leading up to the filing of articles of incorporation (see Chapter 7). Most are good at getting you up and running, but not all service companies are as efficient at providing follow-up service, especially with respect to compliance matters. Before you work with a service company, find out what it can do for your corporation *after* you're on the right track.

Here are some questions you might want to ask before you retain a service company:

✔ Do you provide registered agent services?

✔ Can you provide a calendar system to help me track important corporate dates, such as meeting, annual report, or franchise tax dates?

✔ Do you provide regular updates regarding changes in corporate laws?

✔ Do you offer required state forms, such as annual report or franchise tax forms?

✔ Can you provide samples of important corporate documents, such as a stock purchase agreement or meeting minutes?

✔ Are you set up to provide these services in all of the states where my corporation is engaged in business?

✔ What other support services do you provide?

Not all service companies are alike. To get the best value, find a service company equipped to meet your incorporation *and* compliance needs.

Hiring a Professional

Believe it or not, eventually you'll need a professional team. Ours is an increasingly specialized world filled with regulations that can trip up the most seasoned professional. Recruit a lawyer, an insurance agent, and an accountant to begin with.

Cultivate your team to work with you on your terms. Ask your lawyer and accountant to teach you things you can do for yourself. This may include keeping track of meeting minutes, basic bookkeeping, the completion of annual reports, and tasks that are often repeated.

Many small corporation owners focus entirely on running the corporate business. For these folks, professional team members are more involved in preparing all corporate-related documents. While costs will be higher, owners may have greater confidence that work is done correctly, enabling the owner to run the business without worries.

Use your professional team to draft complicated agreements, evaluate your business for liability concerns, update you on changes in the law that will affect your business, complete and file tax returns, and similar items.

Keep your professional team in the loop. An annual meeting with your team can highlight potential trouble areas and identify potential tax-saving opportunities. It will also keep your team current with you and your business.

A well-selected team generates value for you beyond your initial incorporation. As your business grows and succeeds, you'll need additional services spawned by your success. Estate planning, business acquisitions, business succession (who will take over your business when you retire), life insurance, disability insurance, and financial planning are all important issues for the business owner.

Find an insurance agent who represents a number of different companies to make sure that your insurance covers all aspects of your business. Get the most insurance for the smallest premium.

Choosing Between the Three

Before you pick one route, consider taking all three. Understand what you can do yourself — you'll save money and gain a greater understanding of the nuts and bolts of your business. Then work with a service company to provide periodic updates on law changes, forms for required reports, and a calendar system with which you can track important corporate dates. Finally, build a good professional team that will work with you on more complex corporate matters and those related issues that arise as your business grows.

Part V
The Part of Tens

The 5th Wave   By Rich Tennant

"I just never thought to incorporate my business. Then we were hit with a massive lawsuit. Fortunately, I never lost my shirt. They also let me keep these pants, shoes, and hat."

In this part . . .

Your corporation is up and running like a finely tuned machine. Now's the time for practical, easy to understand and remember tips to keep you out of trouble and moving smoothly. Know how to locate and retain a good professional team to help you when you need it, understand what not to do with your corporation, and remember ten common-sense principles that can help you in business and beyond.

Chapter 23

Ten Ways to Locate and Retain a Good Professional Team

*F*ace it. You can't do everything for your corporation. Whether it's lack of time or knowledge, you're going to need additional help and expertise from time to time. Your primary focus is on your business. How much time and energy you choose to spend on matters that fall outside of the day-to-day aspects of your business is up to you.

This chapter offers ten ways to help you find and keep a good professional team who will be able to give you that additional expertise.

Pick Your Professionals

What sort of professionals might you want to have on your team? Consider an attorney, an accountant, an insurance agent, and a financial planner. With these professionals on board, you will be able to have legal, tax, insurance, and business-planning issues addressed. Because you may have overlaps in your business and personal lives, professionals can also provide estate planning, business succession planning, and related matters for you.

Expect success, and plan to succeed. Many start-up business owners focus on the short term without a view to what lies ahead. This is a mistake. Engage your professionals early on to discover what your alternatives, options, and possibilities are. Understand what you might need to be able to accomplish your long-term personal and business objectives. Use the experience of your team to help you make informed choices and a good plan for the future.

Shop Around

You won't find a one-stop shop for professional assistance, although some professionals may try to tell you otherwise. Similarly, not all professionals are equipped to work with your corporation. In the legal world, some lawyers spend most of their careers handling personal injury claims, divorces, administrative issues, criminal law matters, and other nonbusiness-related specialties. You need a lawyer who spends most of his or her day on business-related matters. Ever heard the expression, "A jack of all trades, but a master of none"? You might not need a master, but you do want professionals who work with corporations and business owners on a regular and continuing basis. A general practice attorney or accountant might not be the best choice for your corporation.

The same is true for your other professionals. How much experience does your insurance agent or financial planner have with businesses like yours?

Talk to a number of different professionals. Find out what their experience is and get referrals. Ask accountants to refer attorneys and vice versa. Ask for insurance agents and financial planners who are actively engaged in representing corporate clients and their owners. Don't pick the professional whose face is splattered across the local bus or who has the biggest ad in the telephone directory. You may find that the larger the ad, the lesser the lawyer.

Visit with other business owners in your community. Ask for their recommendations and inquire how often they use their professional team. It's possible that these owners aren't making effective use of their team, and that could reduce the value of their recommendations.

Legal directories, such as Martindale-Hubbell, exist to provide information about attorneys. This directory actually grades attorneys on a scale of *A* to *C* based on evaluations submitted by other attorneys in the area. This scale can help identify the lawyers in your area who are highly regarded for their skills. Do you want to find a lawyer in your area? Check out Martindale-Hubbell's Web site at www.lawyers.com.

Ask Lots of Questions

Lawyers, accountants, and other professionals intimidate many people. It's not unheard of to find intelligent and competent business owners afraid to question lawyers and accountants. Many professionals want you to ask questions. When you find a good fit with your professional team, expect a long-term, productive relationship.

You can't make an informed decision about whether a professional is right for you unless you ask questions. Questions can provide you with insight into a professional's background and experience as well as provide you with a tangible sense of how well you and the professional will be able to work together.

What kinds of questions should you ask? The possibilities are limitless. Here are some examples:

- What type of work do you do?
- How long have you done this type of work?
- How many corporate clients do you represent?
- What type of services do you perform for your corporate clients?
- How much of your practice is devoted to these clients?
- What type of related services do you offer to your corporate clients (estate planning, business planning, succession planning)?

The next sections discuss additional examples of questions. Remember, there is no such thing as a dumb question; there are dumb people who neglect to ask questions, however.

Discuss Fees in Advance

Most lawyers and accountants must discuss professional fees with you in advance. It's good practice even if it isn't required. You need to know how much you are going to spend for professional advice. Know it upfront. Don't be surprised when you get the bill.

Professionals can charge fees in a number of ways. Lawyers and accountants may charge fees by the hour, by the project, or on a contingency basis. (Contingency fees are rare for corporate work and are most likely to be used in personal injury claims. A contingency fee allows a lawyer, for example, to recover a predetermined percentage of any judgment or settlement. Most of the full-page telephone directory advertisements promote contingency-fee lawyers.)

Hourly rates are much more common for corporate and business work. Hourly rates begin around $125 per hour and go up (some would say, "Way up!") from there. Basic corporate work, such as preparing and filing articles of incorporation and preparing bylaws and corporate meeting minutes, can usually be performed quite competently at the lower end of the hourly wage scale. More complicated matters (such as securities law issues, real estate or business acquisitions, or complex business reorganizations) may require greater expertise, usually at a higher hourly rate. If you're paying an hourly rate, ask for an estimate of the amount of time that your work will require.

Many corporate start-ups benefit from project billing. Here the professional undertakes to provide a range of services (articles, bylaws, and organizational meeting minutes) for a flat fee. More and more lawyers are providing project billing, so you know what your costs will be in advance. The professional accepts the risk that he or she will be able to deliver the project in a cost-effective manner. If you use project billing, make sure you have a clear understanding of what is included within the scope of the project and what is not.

Insurance agents normally receive a commission based on the premium that you will pay for the insurance project. With insurance, look for an agent with access to a number of insurance companies so that you can shop around for the best premium. Similarly, financial planners are generally compensated on a percentage of the assets that they manage. Know what that percentage is before you retain the professional.

Ask Who Will Do My Work

When you come to a lawyer's or accountant's office, ask who will be doing your work. If the office has several, or even hundreds of lawyers, how will this impact the fee structure? Don't assume that the professional you interview will do all or any of your work. Ask. New associates may handle much of your work. By itself, this is not a bad thing. However, make certain that the fees charged reflect this fact. Lawyers and accountants also retain a host of nonprofessional assistants who perform a variety of services. Find out how they bill for these services. You can also ask which of these services you can be trained to perform yourself.

Does your professional leave town for certain weeks or months during the year? What coverage is available for you if you need professional advice during this absence? Again, these are questions for you to ask when selecting your team.

Find Out What You Can Learn to Do on Your Own

Most professionals are happy to teach you to perform a variety of services, which you can then do in-house. This will help you reduce your professional costs and expenses. Common examples include such things as doing payroll, reporting financial information, and completing standardized contracts. Corporate compliance matters such as corporate meetings, minutes, and annual reports can also be taught so that you will be confident completing these tasks without professional assistance.

If there is a particular task in your business that you repeat often, ask your professional to teach you or your staff to perform the task. Commercial transactions often require documentation that can be easily performed by you, not the professional, with a little instruction.

Discuss What Other Services Are Available as Your Business Grows

Be optimistic. Your business will grow. You will have needs other than corporate formation and compliance. Business expansion, the addition of new shareholders, the sale of the business, business succession, retirement, disability — these are illustrative of the types of issues and challenges you may face. How will your professional team be able to help you with these areas?

Planning is important to the success of any business. Be certain that your professional team has been there before with other clients. It's never too late to think about the future and develop a strategy to help you meet it.

Find Out When Your Team Is Available

Not all professionals work full time. Many have other activities they pursue. Will your lawyer or accountant be available to you when you need her or him?

I have the great fortune to coach cross-country and track at the local high school. It provides wonderful balance and perspective to my life. Unfortunately, it means that I am not available to my clients after 2:30 p.m. during seven months of the year. My clients know this in advance, before they decide to work with me. While it creates occasional problems, my clients and I are usually able to work with my schedule.

Are there certain times of the day or week when you will need to meet with members of your professional team? Are they able to meet you then? If not, find a different professional who can meet your time needs. Don't assume that professionals are available to you on a 24/7 basis. Some professionals will allow you to contact them during the evening and on weekends, although they may charge a higher hourly rate.

Does your professional leave town for certain weeks or months during the year? What coverage is available for you if you need professional advice during this absence? Again, these are questions for you to ask when selecting your team.

Don't Nitpick Your Professional

Most likely, you aren't your professional's only client. Any professional budgets his or her weeks and days to accommodate the needs of many clients. Don't expect to reach your professional every time you call. Don't call your professional about everything that comes up, when it comes up. Work with your professional to learn how to use him or her most effectively.

Target the correct professional with ready answers in their specific areas of expertise. For financial questions, refer to your financial planner or accountant. For legal issues, talk to your lawyer. For insurance questions, contact your insurance agent. It's a good idea to meet with all of your professional team members together from time to time. Gain an understanding of which professional you should contact with tax questions or financial matters. Don't generate fees with the wrong professional — make sure you direct your question to the appropriate team member.

Make cost-effective use of your professionals by batching your questions as well. Your lawyer, for example, charges by the hour. For many lawyers the smallest billing unit is 15 minutes. If you call and talk for 3 minutes, you are charged as if you talked for 15 minutes. If you call your lawyer for five straight days to discuss matters that take three minutes for each call, you will be billed for 1.25 hours of time. If you compiled a list and called to discuss all of the items during the same discussion, you would have been billed for .25 hours. The difference could be as much as $100 or more.

Keep Your Professionals Up to Date

Although professionals don't want you to nitpick, they do like to be kept up to date with you and your corporation. Where do you draw the line? How do you do this? Consider investing one or two hours each year meeting with the professional team. Most often, this is done in conjunction with the corporation's annual meeting.

An annual meeting with your professional team will maximize the value of the professionals for your corporation. By describing corporate activities, your professionals can spot red flags of trouble ahead and provide recommendations to solve problems before they occur. Suppose, for example, you disclose your intention to bring in additional shareholders. Your professionals would recognize a need to make certain that you address securities law concerns. They can help you address and consider your alternatives and options. They can also identify matters that might require corporate documentation to ensure corporate compliance.

Professionals can also advise you as to personal matters that you may face related to your corporation. For example, your estate plan may need to be reviewed in light of your corporation's growth and success. A business succession plan may need to be developed to ensure that there is a market for your business when it is time for you to retire. Divorce might force a change in the makeup of corporate shareholders.

Also expect professionals to inform you about law changes that will affect your corporation now or in the future so that you can make any necessary modifications.

If you wait until a crisis to engage your professional team, you may spend more on professional fees. Without regular contact with your professionals, it will take longer for your team to learn important background information about your corporation. For your professionals, time is money. You can reduce the educational curve by meeting with them periodically to let them know what the corporation is doing. For you, time may mean the difference between a successful and unsuccessful resolution of your problems.

Many professionals will meet with you on an annual basis for a reduced fee because they want to know what the corporation is doing. They want to serve your business well. This can only happen if they know about you and your corporation. Of course, the meeting may also generate additional fees, producing work for the professionals.

Finally, such a meeting will help you remember to do the compliance work necessary for your corporate well being. It's a win-win situation for all.

Chapter 24

Ten Things You Never Want to Do with Your Corporation

Corporations are creatures of statute, owing their existence to state corporation laws and regulations. To maintain your corporation in good standing, adherence to certain corporate formalities and legal requirements is a must. Failure to do so can result in the loss of corporate status. Worse, noncompliance can open the door for disgruntled shareholders, creditors, government agencies, and others who seek to impose personal liability on the players in the corporation, eliminating one of the key benefits of incorporation.

What follows are ten common-sense tips designed to protect your corporate status and minimize the likelihood that corporate officers, directors, and shareholders will be exposed to personal liability for corporate activities.

Don't Hold Yourself Out as the Owner of the Corporation

This may sound confusing. If you are the only shareholder or the majority shareholder, you would certainly seem to be the owner. You might have a number of roles with the corporation; you could be an officer, a director, a shareholder, or all three at the same time. But remember which hat you are wearing at any given point in time.

If you sign a contract for the corporation, indicate that you are signing as president. Sign as "John Doe, president" and not simply "John Doe." Print your business cards to list the corporate name, and wherever your name appears, add your designation next to it.

Telephone directory listings should list the business name, not your individual name. If you have to include your name or picture, remember to designate your corporate title.

If the public has any reason to believe that you are doing business in an individual capacity, it may be hard to deflect personal liability in claims filed by creditors. By remembering to use the corporate name and referring to yourself with your corporate capacity, you can insulate yourself from personal liability.

Don't Commingle Personal Assets with Business Assets

Don't mix your business assets and personal assets. A corporation is a distinct legal entity. It should have its own business bank account distinct from any personal bank accounts you may have. It's much harder to demonstrate that expenditures were made for the benefit of the business when personal and business accounts are the same.

Similarly, don't fill your office with artwork, tools, or equipment that belong to you personally. These items might be considered to be business assets subject to the claims of creditors. If personal items are used by the business, corporate minutes should reflect which items are personal. If the items are used in the business operations, consider selling or leasing these items to the business.

Don't Make Personal Use of Business Property

You don't commingle personal assets with business assets, and you don't make personal use of business property. But do you use a corporation-owned car to tote your kids back and forth from school? You may want to document this for the corporate records. You may also wish to check with your tax advisor to determine if you need to report income for the personal use of the car.

Business property has certain tax attributes not available to personal property. For example, you may be able to deduct the cost of certain business property or depreciate its value over a period of time. You can't do this with personal property. Whenever you make personal use of business property, you cloud the issue, and you may lose your ability to take advantage of these tax deductions.

Business property is generally insured against loss through your business insurance policy. Your personal property may or may not be insured against loss by your homeowner's or personal automobile insurance policy. If you make business and personal use of a particular asset, which insurance company do you anticipate will step forward to provide coverage?

Don't get creative. Does your business really need a boat? Plane? Hawaiian condo? Don't try to deduct or depreciate as business assets property that is used almost exclusively for personal purposes. You're asking for trouble.

Don't Forget to Document Important Corporate Transactions

COMPLIANCE ALERT

Because a corporation is its own legal entity, important activities should be documented, usually in corporate minutes, contracts, or both. Things that a corporation would be expected to do in its day-to-day business don't need to be reflected as an important corporate activity. For example, if you own a sporting goods store, your day-to-day purchases or sales of inventory won't be reflected in your corporate minutes. Sales activity will certainly show up in your financial statements and tax returns. Documentation can take the form of a bill of sale, invoice, loan agreement, promissory note, mortgage, and so on. See Chapter 18 for further information.

What types of activities should be documented? Here are some examples:

- ✓ Purchasing or leasing automobiles or trucks
- ✓ Borrowing money or pledging corporate assets as security for a loan
- ✓ Selling of substantially all corporate assets
- ✓ Merging or dissolving the corporation
- ✓ Acquiring another business
- ✓ Loaning money
- ✓ Declaring a dividend or redeeming corporate stock
- ✓ Buying or leasing real estate

Documenting these types of transactions properly and timely provides you with an important tool in defending against efforts to deny tax deductions or impose personal liability on individual shareholders, officers, and directors.

Don't Fail to Deal with the Corporation at Arm's Length

It's common for shareholders, officers, and directors of small corporations to enter into a wide array of transactions with the corporation. For start-up businesses, corporate loans often come from these individuals. If the loans are truly intended to be repaid by the corporation, they should be documented with a corporate resolution, promissory note, and other loan documents. Interest rates and repayment provisions should be comparable to those the corporation would have been required to meet had the lender been a bank or other unrelated party.

Likewise, if the corporation is the lender and the borrower is a shareholder, officer, or director, the corporation must not offer this individual more favorable terms than a bank or unrelated lender. The temptation is great, but it must be avoided.

If loan terms are too favorable, adverse consequences may result for borrower and lender. For a corporate borrower, the loan could be disregarded and considered to be a contribution to the capital of the corporation. By treating a loan as equity, a lender won't be entitled to repayment with interest. Rather, any return of the money would come about as a dividend or return of capital. Dividends are taxable to the lender. If the loan is characterized as equity, S corporations may be considered to have an impermissible second class of stock, resulting in an unintended loss of S corporation status.

For an individual borrower, income tax may be due. The tax would be based on any loan amounts not repaid or on the difference between interest actually paid and the amount that would have been paid had the loan been at arm's length.

Similarly, buying or leasing assets from the corporation or selling or leasing them to the corporation can subject shareholders, officers, and directors to the same types of adverse consequences described earlier.

Suffice it to say that sweetheart deals between an individual shareholder, officer, or director and the corporation are subject to close scrutiny by the Internal Revenue Service, other shareholders, and creditors of the corporation.

Don't Neglect Your Corporate Taxes

Failure to plan for taxes is one of the primary causes of small business failure. This is a no-brainer. Yet, many individuals are surprised to learn that they may be personally responsible for unpaid corporate taxes at federal, state, and local levels. This applies to income taxes as well as payroll and other withholding taxes. The IRS and state tax officials sometimes aren't required to "pierce the corporate veil" in order to impose personal liability. Specific statutory authority allows federal and state officials to assess liability for certain unpaid taxes against individuals responsible for the corporation. Common targets are corporate presidents and treasurers, although directors and shareholders of small businesses may also be liable.

Don't Fail to File Required Reports

The state requires corporations to file a variety of reports with state agencies. The state requires franchise tax reports, annual reports, and similar reports if the corporation intends to continue doing business in the state. If reports aren't filed in a timely fashion, the corporate charter can be revoked, effectively dissolving the corporation.

If the corporate status is revoked, individual officers, directors, or shareholders may become personally liable for claims that otherwise would have been filed against the corporation.

Many states mail required annual report forms to a corporation's registered agent well in advance of the report due dates. Don't accidentally throw yours away or lose it in a pile of mail. The consequences can be extreme.

Don't Defraud Creditors and Shareholders

It's not nice to fool Mother Nature. It's also not a good idea to purposely attempt to fool your creditors or shareholders. Misrepresenting corporate financial status or misleading creditors or shareholders can allow a claim to be filed against the individual officer, director, or shareholder making the misrepresentation or the misleading statements.

You're required to exercise good faith in dealing with those the corporation does business with. If you owe your suppliers, vendors, landlords, and others money, they are your creditors. Don't allow them to do things for you on the basis of misrepresented or misleading facts. They won't be happy, and they do sue. Worse, they may stop doing business with you, and you may need them more than they need you. Word of mouth might also keep others from doing business with you, as well.

You're also required to use good faith in dealing with your shareholders. If you act purposely to misrepresent corporate financial status or to reduce the value of minority shareholder shares, expect to be sued in your individual capacity. While the corporation will be a party to any claim filed by creditors or shareholders, the officers or directors responsible for the misrepresentations or misleading actions can also expect to be a part of the fun.

Don't Engage in Criminal Conduct

If you don't already know this, you could be in trouble. There are thousands of criminal statutes on the books, both federal and state, and no one knows all of them. The good news is that officers, directors, and shareholders rarely go to jail for violations of laws that no one knows about. The bad news is that many officers, directors, or shareholders do go to jail each year because they engage in criminal activities.

Common criminal violations for which individuals have responsibility include lying (perjury), obstructing justice, dumping chemicals, killing or maiming people with products known to kill or maim, selling drugs, loan sharking, bilking people out of money, embezzling, filing false tax returns, or evading taxes.

Corporations pay fines; people go to jail.

Don't Fail to Maintain Adequate Insurance Coverage

Many lawyers believe that if the injury or harm is severe enough, some individual will always be personally liable regardless of the corporate form. This may be especially true if the corporation lacks adequate insurance coverage. Many court cases have imposed personal liability on officers, directors, and shareholders even though the corporation had done a good job of complying with corporate formalities. In almost every instance where personal liability is imposed, the corporation failed to maintain adequate insurance.

What is adequate insurance coverage? Like many things legal, you won't find a precise answer. Look at the facts and circumstances of a particular corporation to make this determination. Adequacy requires appropriate types of coverage (product liability, automobile) and amounts of coverage (the dollar amount that the insurance company will pay if you are found liable).

Imagine an automobile manufacturer that lacks product liability coverage. Plainly, any manufacturer of a product intended to be widely used by the public should be expected to have such coverage. The failure to do so could be used to disregard the corporate status and impose liability on responsible officers and directors. Assume further that our auto manufacturer has product liability insurance, but coverage is capped at $1,000 per claim, an unreasonable amount in light of the fact that an injury involving an automobile could result in hundreds of thousands of dollars of damage.

A corporation should have insurance coverage appropriate for the nature and type of its business. The amount of insurance should also be reflective of the types of injuries its products or services could cause.

Many corporations self-insure. To reduce the cost of insurance, these businesses retain monies to be used to pay liabilities generated by the corporation. Corporations that self-insure should maintain amounts adequate to meet the types of injuries its products or services might cause.

Chapter 25

Ten Common-sense Principles to Incorporate and Live Each Day By

ou were promised a bonus. This is it — simple rules to make your business life and family life a little better.

Know Your Personal Philosophy and Values

Many businesses spend lots of money putting together mission statements, value statements, and strategic plans. This is usually a wise investment of time and energy, especially if these documents are actually used to guide and shape business decisions.

Think about your personal philosophy, if you have one. Do you have certain expressed values that speak to who you are and how you intend to conduct your business? When you're pressed to make one of those really tough decisions — terminate an employee, choose a new piece of equipment over improved employee insurance coverage, buy a new business or sell all or part of your existing one, or close down your business — what are those philosophical anchors that help you make that decision?

Take the time to ask yourself these questions. Write down your life philosophy and values. Ask yourself how these things relate to the way you intend to conduct business. Knowing the answers to these questions will help you become successful — on your terms.

Get It in Writing

Business disputes often disintegrate into a issue of "he said, she said." Reliance on verbal assurances and agreements works much of the time, but predicting those times when such assurances and agreements fail to work is impossible. Your best safeguard is to get in the habit of putting things in writing. You don't need a formal legal contract in most instances. Rather, try a simple letter confirming a telephone conversation. If you don't have time for a letter, use the fax machine or e-mail — just keep a copy of the message.

Disagreements more often result from misunderstandings than fraud. When the message is verbal, it's more likely that people may assign different meanings to the same message. By sending a written confirmation or taking the additional time to reduce an agreement to writing, you minimize the risk of future disagreements. If the parties don't agree, it's always better to know this upfront than to learn it months and dollars down the road.

Similarly, use dated receipts, telephone message pads, and file memos to help recall conversations and exchanges of information or products. The small investment in time it takes to do these things could pay off big in the future.

Read the Entire Document When You Sign It

There's probably not a lawyer alive who hasn't had the opportunity to roast an opposing party and, in turn, witness his or her own client being roasted for the following:

Lawyer: "Can you identify this document for me?"

Witness: "It's an agreement to buy widgets from Acme, Inc."

Lawyer: "Is that your signature at the end of the agreement?"

Witness: "Yes." (It would be pretty awkward to say "No.")

Lawyer: "Is it your habit to read agreements before you sign them?"

Witness: "Yes." (Can you begin to see the noose tightening around the witness's neck?)

Of course, a paragraph in the agreement negates the witness's testimony, so you can imagine, the lawyer will want to draw this out as long as she can. She wants to see the witness squirm. She wants to make the witness look like an idiot.

The witness doesn't have a lot of options: either admit that he doesn't read legal documents or lie and say he does. Don't put yourself in this situation.

Business people are handed documents to review and approve every day. Documents come from all types of sources: employees, suppliers, vendors, landlords, bankers, and so on. More often than not, most of those documents probably get nothing more than a cursory glance, if that. A standard real estate contract, for example, has all of the provisions appearing to be on the front of the document. If you were to skip the back page, you'd miss the 25 paragraphs on the backside. Be smart — read the document!

If You Don't Understand, Ask Questions

How many times have you failed to ask a question because you thought it was a dumb one? How many times has the information you didn't obtain because you were too scared to ask come back to haunt you? Add these standard questions for your tool bag: Could you clarify that for me? Are you saying . . . ?

There is no such thing as a dumb question — there are, however, many dumb people who fail to ask important questions.

Be Consistent

Consistency is a virtue. People like to work, marry, and/or play golf with people known to be reliable and consistent. Consistency is dependable. You can count on it. It's not boring. Being consistent is a timesaver. People won't ask you for things (time off, more money) if they know the answer will be "No." This doesn't mean that you don't set up consistent policies and procedures that identify such things as time off and pay scales or wage increases.

If you are consistent, people know what to expect from you and what you expect from them. Being consistent means that you treat people in the same fashion. Don't terminate Martha for being late on a single occasion when Stan is late all of the time and is still around.

Consistency is good for morale. People who have a clear understanding of their individual roles and responsibilities will be happier.

Treat Others the Way You Would Like to Be Treated

Oh, yes, this is the Golden Rule you probably learned from your mother or elementary schoolteacher. In the course of a business day, how often do you take someone or something for granted? How often do you feel like someone else is taking you for granted? Most people are worthy of respect and dignity. Following the Golden Rule contributes to self-satisfaction and a high regard for self-worth. People who follow the Golden Rule are successful. Moreover, people who treat others with respect and dignity are often treated the same way by others.

For example, did you know that many sexual harassment and other similar claims could be avoided by simply creating an opportunity for people to be heard? This sounds like good common sense, right? Victims often want someone to talk to about what has happened and to be given an opportunity to be a part of any solution. Without such an outlet, lawsuits are often filed in frustration. Once in the legal system, things can get impersonal and spiral well beyond the expectations of any of the parties.

We are human. We make mistakes. Do we compound mistakes by trying to cover them up, or do we accept responsibility for our actions? Have you had the experience of someone coming up to you and saying, "I'm sorry, it was my fault. How can I make that up to you?" Refreshing, isn't it? Unfortunately, today's society wants to blame someone else. Too many people seek to avoid liability or responsibility by covering things up.

Some people have a knack for getting away with such behavior. Many more people have been caught in the act of covering things up, thereby compounding the original mistake. Don't be afraid to use common sense and do unto others. You know the drill.

Don't Try to Do It All

You have a business. You may also have a family, hobbies, and pets that take up bits of your time. How do you balance it all? Remember when computers were going to provide you with more leisure time? Has it happened?

Balance is important, and achieving it is a continual struggle. Realizing your personal strengths and weaknesses is an important component to achieving and maintaining balance.

Focus your time and energy on those things that are most important to you and your business. For example, are you better off drafting sale contracts or shareholder agreements, or does it make more sense to delegate these tasks to someone else? Don't be afraid to invest money in getting good professional advice when you need it. In the end, you'll save time and money, and you'll help maintain your balance and focus.

Anyone Can Be Sued at Any Time for Any Reason

Fortunately, this isn't really true. It just seems like it is. Popular media create this impression. Nonetheless, getting sued is never a pleasant experience. Even suing someone else can exact a physical, mental, and emotional toll — not to mention that litigation is also expensive. Using the common-sense tips described in this chapter will go a long way to keeping you out of court.

Sometimes, however, it may be the mark of a business's success or perceived success that a claim is filed against it. If someone thinks you're big with lots of money, you can become a target for a claim.

Court systems have safeguards that help reduce the impact of frivolous claims, but the system is far from foolproof. Good insurance can protect you from the types of liabilities usually associated with your business. More importantly, your insurance policy will cover the costs of defense by paying for your lawyer. Often, the cost of defending a claim far exceeds any potential liability from the claim.

Keep in mind, you have alternatives to going to court. For example, arbitration and mediation provide cost-effective and time-efficient options you should consider:

- In *mediation,* a neutral third person facilitates a discussion among the parties. While the goal is to help the parties reach agreement on all issues, sometimes the process serves to narrow the issues in dispute without resolving all issues. Mediation can be especially effective to promote and maintain ongoing business relationships such as those that might exist between a business owner and a key supplier or customer.

- *Arbitration* is a relatively informal process where the parties select one or more arbitrators. The arbitrator listens to both sides present their case. When all parties have provided testimony and evidence, the arbitrator makes a decision. The decision is usually binding on the parties in the same fashion as a decision by a judge or jury would be.

Organizations such as the American Arbitration Association can provide more information about these processes, as well as a list of qualified arbitrators and mediators in your area.

Principle Can Be Expensive

"I'm not going to let that so-and-so get away with this. I don't care how much it costs me." For some lawyers, this is music to their ears. For others, it's a sign that a client is about to make a bad decision and throw good money away.

When do you pull out all of your resources to pursue something you believe to be right? When do you let something go, even though you believe you are in the right? Can you let it go? What is just? What is fair? These are concepts with no clear definition.

Pursuit of principle can be expensive in more ways than one. If you go to court, you have legal fees and the uncertainty of how a judge or jury will rule. In court or out, you have losses caused by focus distracted away from business and family and time spent in battle. There can be intense physical and emotional toll caused by the wear and tear of the unresolved claim. This uncertainty and wear and tear can last for years.

Where do you draw the line? Here are some clues: What is the amount of measurable damage? Pride and honor may be real, but they have no dollar value. What will it cost to recover these damages? How long will it take to recover? If I'm successful, what are my chances of recovering money from this person? Remember, you can't get blood from a turnip. What are the chances that a judge or jury will actually agree with me?

Know When to Fold Them

Few things are more difficult than shutting the doors on your business. Like the aging athlete who hangs on for too long, many business owners can't see when their time is up. By waiting too long, opportunities to salvage or sell the business may be lost. Relationships with suppliers and customers may become irreparably damaged.

A good business plan will help you identify benchmarks by which you can measure the success of your business. It can also establish benchmarks that tell you that it's time to resort to other options.

Business failure is a frequent occurrence. Work with your professional team to help you look objectively at your business. If it's time, let it go. Success is often the end result of trial and error and many failures. Don't give up. Many entrepreneurs start up and close down multiple businesses until they get it right.

Appendix A

Sample Forms

· ·

*T*he sample forms here are just that — guidelines. For many small businesses, these samples will meet most of your start-up requirements. But know your state law before you file your articles because different states have different provisions. For example, some states may ask for specific language to be used. Some may require that you list a specific purpose of the business activities, while most states recognize a general business purpose clause. The bylaws are the rules of procedure for the corporation. Since the bylaws are the technical procedures, more complex structures will require legal advice. The minutes are important to show you are recording actions of the corporation. Use the sample minutes as a guideline to record your corporate activities. The section discussing minutes lists the types of activities to record.

Articles of Incorporation Sample

CERTIFICATE OF INCORPORATION OF

<Your Corporation Name, Inc.>

FIRST. The name of this corporation shall be:

<Your Corporation Name, Inc.>

SECOND. Its registered office in the State of <Your State of Incorporation> is to be located at <The Address of the Registered Office: Street Address, Suite Number> in the City of <city's name>, County of <County's Name>, <Zip Code>, and its registered agent at such address is <Name of the Registered Agent>.

THIRD. The purpose or purposes of the corporation shall be:

To engage in any lawful act or activity for which corporations may be organized under the General Corporation Law of <State of Incorporation>.

FOURTH. The total number of shares of stock which this corporation is authorized to issue is:

<number of shares> at <determine par value> par value.

FIFTH. The name and mailing address of the incorporator is as follows:

<name of the incorporator >

<street address of the incorporator >

<city, state, and zip code of the incorporator >

SIXTH. The Board of Directors shall have the power to adopt, amend, or repeal the bylaws.

IN WITNESS WHEREOF, The undersigned, being the incorporator hereinbefore named, has executed, signed, and acknowledged this certificate of incorporation this <date> of <month>, A.D. <year>.

_____

Jane Doe

Incorporator

Sample Bylaws

<u>BYLAWS</u>

OF

(a <State> corporation)

_____

<u>ARTICLE I</u>

<u>STOCKHOLDERS</u>

1. <u>CERTIFICATES REPRESENTING STOCK</u>. Certificates representing stock in the corporation shall be signed by, or in the name of, the corporation by the Chairperson or Vice-Chairperson of the Board of Directors, if any, or by the President or a Vice-President and by the Treasurer or an Assistant Treasurer or the Secretary or an Assistant Secretary of the corporation. Any or all the signatures on any such certificate may be a facsimile. In case any officer, transfer agent, or registrar who has signed or whose facsimile signature has been placed upon a certificate shall have ceased to be such officer, transfer agent, or registrar before such certificate is issued, it may be issued by the corporation with the same effect as if such person were such officer, transfer agent, or registrar at the date of issue.

Whenever the corporation shall be authorized to issue more than one class of stock or more than one series of any class of stock, and whenever the corporation shall issue any shares of its stock as partly paid stock, the certificates representing shares of any such class or series or of any such partly paid stock shall set forth thereon the statements prescribed by the General Corporation Law. Any restrictions on the transfer or registration of transfer of any shares of stock of any class or series shall be noted conspicuously on the certificate representing such shares.

The corporation may issue a new certificate of stock or uncertificated shares in place of any certificate theretofore issued by it, alleged to have been lost, stolen, or destroyed, and the Board of Directors may require the owner of the lost, stolen, or destroyed certificate, or such owner's legal representative, to give the corporation a bond sufficient to indemnify the corporation against any claim that may be made against it on account of the alleged loss, theft, or destruction of any such certificate or the issuance of any such new certificate or uncertificated shares.

2. UNCERTIFICATED SHARES. Subject to any conditions imposed by the General Corporation Law, the Board of Directors of the corporation may provide by resolution or resolutions that some or all of any or all classes or series of the stock of the corporation shall be uncertificated shares. Within a reasonable time after the issuance or transfer of any uncertificated shares, the corporation shall send to the registered owner thereof any written notice prescribed by the General Corporation Law.

3. FRACTIONAL SHARE INTERESTS. The corporation may, but shall not be required to, issue fractions of a share. If the corporation does not issue fractions of a share, it shall (1) arrange for the disposition of fractional interests by those entitled thereto, (2) pay in cash the fair value of fractions of a share as of the time when those entitled to receive such fractions are determined, or (3) issue scrip or warrants in registered form (either represented by a certificate or uncertificated) or bearer form (represented by a certificate) which shall entitle the holder to receive a full share upon the surrender of such scrip or warrants aggregating a full share. A certificate for a fractional share or an uncertificated fractional share shall, but scrip or warrants shall not unless otherwise provided therein, entitle the holder to exercise voting rights, to receive dividends thereon, and to participate in any of the assets of the corporation in the event of liquidation. The Board of Directors may cause scrip or warrants to be issued subject to the conditions that they shall become void if not exchanged for certificates representing the full shares or uncertificated full shares before a specified date, or subject to the conditions that the shares for which scrip or warrants are exchangeable may be sold by the corporation and the proceeds thereof distributed to the holders of scrip or warrants, or subject to any other conditions which the Board of Directors may impose.

4. STOCK TRANSFERS. Upon compliance with provisions restricting the transfer or registration of transfer of shares of stock, if any, transfers or registration of transfers of shares of stock of the corporation shall be made only on the stock ledger of the corporation by the registered holder thereof, or by the registered holder's attorney thereunto authorized by power of attorney duly executed and filed with the Secretary of the corporation or with a transfer agent or a registrar, if any, and, in the case of shares represented by certificates, on surrender of the certificate or certificates for such shares of stock properly endorsed and the payment of all taxes due thereon.

5. RECORD DATE FOR STOCKHOLDERS. In order that the corporation may determine the stockholders entitled to notice of or to vote at any meeting of stockholders or any adjournment thereof, the Board of Directors may fix a record date, which record date shall not precede the date upon which the resolution fixing the record date is adopted by the Board of Directors, and which record date shall not be more than sixty nor less than ten days before the date of such meeting. If no record date is fixed by the Board of Directors, the record date for determining stockholders entitled to notice of or to vote at a meeting of stockholders shall be at the close of business on the day next preceding the day on which notice is given, or, if notice is waived, at the close of business on the day next preceding the day on which the meeting is held. A determination of stockholders of record entitled to notice of or to vote at a meeting of stockholders shall apply to any adjournment of the meeting; provided, however, that the Board of Directors may fix a new record date for the adjourned meeting. In order that the corporation may determine the stockholders entitled to consent to corporate action in writing without a meeting, the Board of Directors may fix a record date, which record date shall not precede the date upon which the resolution fixing the record date is adopted by the Board of Directors, and which date shall not be more than ten days after the date upon which the resolution fixing the record date is adopted by the Board of Directors. If no record date has been fixed by the Board of Directors, the record date for determining the stockholders entitled to consent to corporate action in writing without a meeting, when no prior action by the Board of Directors is required by the General Corporation Law, shall be the first date on which a signed written consent setting forth the action taken or proposed to be taken is delivered to the corporation by delivery to its registered office in the State of Delaware, its principal place of business, or an officer or agent of the corporation having custody of the book in which proceedings of meetings of stockholders are recorded. Delivery made to the corporation's registered office shall be by hand or by certified or registered mail, return receipt requested. If no record date has been fixed by the Board of Directors and prior action by the Board of Directors is required by the General Corporation Law, the record date for determining stockholders entitled to consent to corporate action in writing without a meeting shall be at the close of business on the day on which the Board of Directors adopts the resolution taking such prior action. In order that

the corporation may determine the stockholders entitled to receive payment of any dividend or other distribution or allotment of any rights or the stockholders entitled to exercise any rights in respect of any change, conversion, or exchange of stock, or for the purpose of any other lawful action, the Board of Directors may fix a record date, which record date shall not precede the date upon which the resolution fixing the record date is adopted, and which record date shall be not more than sixty days prior to such action. If no record date is fixed, the record date for determining stockholders for any such purpose shall be at the close of business on the day on which the Board of Directors adopts the resolution relating thereto.

6. MEANING OF CERTAIN TERMS. As used herein in respect of the right to notice of a meeting of stockholders or a waiver thereof or to participate or vote thereat or to consent or dissent in writing in lieu of a meeting, as the case may be, the term "share" or "shares" or "share of stock" or "shares of stock" or "stockholder" or "stockholders" refers to an outstanding share or shares of stock and to a holder or holders of record of outstanding shares of stock when the corporation is authorized to issue only one class of shares of stock, and said reference is also intended to include any outstanding share or shares of stock and any holder or holders of record of outstanding shares of stock of any class upon which or upon whom the certificate of incorporation confers such rights where there are two or more classes or series of shares of stock or upon which or upon whom the General Corporation Law confers such rights notwithstanding that the certificate of incorporation may provide for more than one class or series of shares of stock, one or more of which are limited or denied such rights thereunder; provided, however, that no such right shall vest in the event of an increase or a decrease in the authorized number of shares of stock of any class or series which is otherwise denied voting rights under the provisions of the certificate of incorporation, except as any provision of law may otherwise require.

7. STOCKHOLDER MEETINGS.

- TIME. The annual meeting shall be held on the date and at the time fixed, from time to time, by the directors, provided, that the first annual meeting shall be held on a date within thirteen months after the organization of the corporation, and each successive annual meeting shall be held on a date within thirteen months after the date of the preceding annual meeting. A special meeting shall be held on the date and at the time fixed by the directors.

- PLACE. Annual meetings and special meetings shall be held at such place, within or without the State of Delaware, as the directors may, from time to time, fix. Whenever the directors shall fail to fix such place, the meeting shall be held at the registered office of the corporation in the State of Delaware.

- <u>CALL</u>. Annual meetings and special meetings may be called by the directors or by any officer instructed by the directors to call the meeting.

- <u>NOTICE</u> <u>OR</u> <u>WAIVER</u> <u>OF</u> <u>NOTICE</u>. Written notice of all meetings shall be given, stating the place if any, date, and hour of the meeting, the means of remote communication, if any, by which stockholders and proxyholders may be deemed to be present in person and vote at such meeting, and stating the place within the city or other municipality or community at which the list of stockholders of the corporation may be examined. The notice of an annual meeting shall state that the meeting is called for the election of directors and for the transaction of other business which may properly come before the meeting, and shall (if any other action which could be taken at a special meeting is to be taken at such annual meeting) state the purpose or purposes. The notice of a special meeting shall in all instances state the purpose or purposes for which the meeting is called. The notice of any meeting shall also include, or be accompanied by, any additional statements, information, or documents prescribed by the General Corporation Law. Except as otherwise provided by the General Corporation Law, a copy of the notice of any meeting shall be given, personally or by mail, not less than ten days nor more than sixty days before the date of the meeting, unless the lapse of the prescribed period of time shall have been waived, and directed to each stockholder at such stockholder's record address or at such other address which such stockholder may have furnished by request in writing to the Secretary of the corporation. Notice by mail shall be deemed to be given when deposited, with postage thereon prepaid, in the United States Mail. If a meeting is adjourned to another time, not more than thirty days hence, and/or to another place, and if an announcement of the adjourned time and/or place is made at the meeting, it shall not be necessary to give notice of the adjourned meeting unless the directors, after adjournment, fix a new record date for the adjourned meeting. Notice need not be given to any stockholder who submits a written waiver of notice signed by such stockholder before or after the time stated therein. Attendance of a stockholder at a meeting of stockholders shall constitute a waiver of notice of such meeting, except when the stockholder attends the meeting for the express purpose of objecting, at the beginning of the meeting, to the transaction of any business because the meeting is not lawfully called or convened. Neither the business to be transacted at, nor the purpose of, any regular or special meeting of the stockholders need be specified in any written waiver of notice or any waiver by electronic transmission.

- <u>STOCKHOLDER</u> <u>LIST</u>. The officer who has charge of the stock ledger of the corporation shall prepare and make, at least ten days before every meeting of stockholders, a complete list of the stockholders entitled to vote at the meeting, arranged in alphabetical order, and showing the address of each stockholder and the number of shares registered in the name of each stockholder. Such list shall be open to the examination of any stockholder, for any purpose germane to the meeting, for a period of at least ten days prior to the meeting: (i) one reasonably accessible electronic network, provided that the information required to gain access to this list is provided with notice of the meeting, (ii) during ordinary business hours, at the place of business of the corporation. If the meeting is to be held at a place, then the list shall also be produced and kept at the time and place of the meeting during the whole time thereof, and may be inspected by any stockholder who is present. If the meeting is to be held solely by means of remote communication, then the list shall also be given to the examination of any stockholder during the whole time of the meeting on a reasonably accessible electronic network, and the information required to access such list shall be provided with the notice of the meeting. The stock ledger shall be the only evidence as to who are the stockholders entitled to examine the stock ledger, the list required by this section or the books of the corporation, or to vote in person or by proxy at any meeting of stockholders.

- CONDUCT OF MEETING. Meetings of the stockholders shall be presided over by one of the following officers in the order of seniority and if present and acting - the Chairperson of the Board, if any, the Vice-Chairperson of the Board, if any, the President, a Vice-President, or, if none of the foregoing is in office and present and acting, by a chairperson to be chosen by the stockholders. The Secretary of the corporation, or in such Secretary's absence, an Assistant Secretary, shall act as secretary of every meeting, but if neither the Secretary nor an Assistant Secretary is present the chairperson of the meeting shall appoint a secretary of the meeting.

- PROXY REPRESENTATION. Every stockholder may authorize another person or persons to act for such stockholder by proxy in all matters in which a stockholder is entitled to participate, whether by waiving notice of any meeting, voting or participating at a meeting, or expressing consent or dissent without a meeting. Every proxy must be signed by the stockholder or by such stockholder's attorney-in-fact. No proxy shall be voted or acted upon after three years from its date unless such proxy provides for a longer period. A duly executed proxy shall be irrevocable if it states that it is irrevocable and if, and only as long as, it is coupled with an interest sufficient in law to support an irrevocable power. A proxy may be made irrevocable regardless of whether the interest with which it is coupled is an interest in the stock itself or an interest in the corporation generally.

- INSPECTORS. The directors, in advance of any meeting, may, but need not, appoint one or more inspectors of election to act at the meeting or any adjournment thereof. If an inspector or inspectors are not appointed, the person presiding at the meeting may, but need not, appoint one or more inspectors. In case any person who may be appointed as an inspector fails to appear or act, the vacancy may be filled by appointment made by the directors in advance of the meeting or at the meeting by the person presiding thereat. Each inspector, if any, before entering upon the discharge of duties of inspector, shall take and sign an oath faithfully to execute the duties of inspector at such meeting with strict impartiality and according to the best of such inspector's ability. The inspectors, if any, shall determine the number of shares of stock outstanding and the voting power of each, the shares of stock represented at the meeting, the existence of a quorum, the validity and effect of proxies, and shall receive votes, ballots, or consents, hear and determine all challenges and questions arising in connection with the right to vote, count and tabulate all votes, ballots, or consents, determine the result, and do such acts as are proper to conduct the election or vote with fairness to all stockholders. On request of the person presiding at the meeting, the inspector or inspectors, if any, shall make a report in writing of any challenge, question, or matter determined by such inspector or inspectors and execute a certificate of any fact found by such inspector or inspectors. Except as may otherwise be required by subsection (e) of Section 231 of the General Corporation Law, the provisions of that Section shall not apply to the corporation.

- QUORUM. The holders of a majority of the outstanding shares of stock shall constitute a quorum at a meeting of stockholders for the transaction of any business. The stockholders present may adjourn the meeting despite the absence of a quorum.

- VOTING. Each share of stock shall entitle the holder thereof to one vote. Directors shall be elected by a plurality of the votes of the shares present in person or represented by proxy at the meeting and entitled to vote on the election of directors. Any other action shall be authorized by a majority of the votes cast except where the General Corporation Law prescribes a different percentage of votes and/or a different exercise of voting power, and except as may be otherwise prescribed by the provisions of the certificate of incorporation and these Bylaws. If the certificate of incorporation so provides, in the election of directors, and for any other action, voting need not be by ballot.

8. STOCKHOLDER ACTION WITHOUT MEETINGS. Except as any provision of the General Corporation Law may otherwise require and unless otherwise provided in the Certificate of Incorporation, any action required by the General Corporation Law to be taken at any annual or special meeting of stockholders, or any action which may be taken at any annual or special meeting of stockholders, may be taken without a meeting, without prior notice and without a vote, if a consent in writing, setting forth the action so taken, shall be signed by the holders of outstanding stock having not less than the minimum number of votes that would be necessary to authorize or take such action at a meeting at which all shares entitled to vote thereon were present and voted. Prompt notice of the taking of the corporate action without a meeting by less than unanimous written consent shall be given to those stockholders who have not consented in writing. Action taken pursuant to this paragraph shall be subject to the provisions of Section 228 of the General Corporation Law.

ARTICLE II

DIRECTORS

1. FUNCTIONS AND DEFINITION. The business and affairs of the corporation shall be managed by or under the direction of the Board of Directors of the corporation. The Board of Directors shall have the authority to fix the compensation of the members thereof. The use of the phrase "whole board" herein refers to the total number of directors which the corporation would have if there were no vacancies.

2. QUALIFICATIONS AND NUMBER. A director need not be a stockholder, a citizen of the United States, or a resident of the State of Delaware. The initial Board of Directors shall consist of   persons. Thereafter the number of directors constituting the whole board shall be at least one. Subject to the foregoing limitation and except for the first Board of Directors, such number may be fixed from time to time by action of the stockholders or of the directors, or, if the number is not fixed, the number shall be   . The number of directors may be increased or decreased by action of the stockholders or of the directors.

3. ELECTION AND TERM. The first Board of Directors, unless the members thereof shall have been named in the certificate of incorporation, shall be elected by the incorporator or incorporators and shall hold office until the first annual meeting of stockholders and until their successors are elected and qualified or until their earlier resignation or removal. Any director may resign at any time upon notice given in writing or by electronic transmission to the corporation. Thereafter, directors who are elected at an annual meeting of stockholders, and directors who are elected in the interim to fill vacancies and newly created directorships, shall hold office until the next annual meeting of stockholders and until their successors are elected and qualified or until their earlier resignation or removal. Except as the General Corporation Law may otherwise require, in the interim between annual meetings of stockholders or special meetings of stockholders called for the election of directors and/or for the removal of one or more directors and for the filling of any vacancy in that connection, newly created directorships and any vacancies in the Board of Directors, including unfilled vacancies resulting from the removal of directors for cause or without cause, may be filled by the vote of a majority of the remaining directors then in office, although less than a quorum, or by the sole remaining director.

4. MEETINGS.

- TIME. Meetings shall be held at such time as the Board shall fix, except that the first meeting of a newly elected Board shall be held as soon after its election as the directors may conveniently assemble.

- PLACE. Meetings shall be held at such place within or without the State of Delaware as shall be fixed by the Board.

- CALL. No call shall be required for regular meetings for which the time and place have been fixed. Special meetings may be called by or at the direction of the Chairperson of the Board, if any, the Vice-Chairperson of the Board, if any, the President, or a majority of the directors in office.

- NOTICE OR ACTUAL OR CONSTRUCTIVE WAIVER. No notice shall be required for regular meetings for which the time and place have been fixed. Written, oral, or any other mode of notice of the time and place shall be given for special meetings in sufficient time for the convenient assembly of the directors thereat. Notice need not be given to any director or to any member of a committee of directors who submits a written waiver of notice signed by such director or member before or after the time stated therein. Attendance of any such person at a meeting shall constitute a waiver of notice of such meeting, except when such person attends a meeting for the express purpose of objecting, at the beginning of the meeting, to the transaction of any business because the meeting is not lawfully called or convened. Neither the business to be transacted at, nor the purpose of, any regular or special meeting of the directors need be specified in any written waiver of notice.

- QUORUM AND ACTION. A majority of the whole Board shall constitute a quorum except when a vacancy or vacancies prevents such majority, whereupon a majority of the directors in office shall constitute a quorum, provided, that such majority shall constitute at least one-third of the whole Board. A majority of the directors present, whether or not a quorum is present, may adjourn a meeting to another time and place. Except as herein otherwise provided, and except as otherwise provided by the General Corporation Law, the vote of the majority of the directors present at a meeting at which a quorum is present shall be the act of the Board. The quorum and voting provisions herein stated shall not be construed as conflicting with any provisions of the General Corporation Law and these Bylaws which govern a meeting of directors held to fill vacancies and newly created directorships in the Board or action of disinterested directors.

Any member or members of the Board of Directors or of any committee designated by the Board, may participate in a meeting of the Board, or any such committee, as the case may be, by means of conference telephone or other communications equipment by means of which all persons participating in the meeting can hear each other.

- CHAIRPERSON OF THE MEETING. The Chairperson of the Board, if any and if present and acting, shall preside at all meetings. Otherwise, the Vice-Chairperson of the Board, if any and if present and acting, or the President, if present and acting, or any other director chosen by the Board, shall preside.

5. <u>REMOVAL OF DIRECTORS</u>. Except as may otherwise be provided by the General Corporation Law, any director or the entire Board of Directors may be removed, with or without cause, by the holders of a majority of the shares then entitled to vote at an election of directors.

6. <u>COMMITTEES</u>. The Board of Directors may designate one or more committees, each committee to consist of one or more of the directors of the corporation. The Board may designate one or more directors as alternate members of any committee, who may replace any absent or disqualified member at any meeting of the committee. In the absence or disqualification of any member of any such committee or committees, the member or members thereof present at any meeting and not disqualified from voting, whether or not such member or members constitute a quorum, may unanimously appoint another member of the Board of Directors to act at the meeting in the place of any such absent or disqualified member. Any such committee, to the extent provided in the resolution of the Board, shall have and may exercise all the powers and authority of the Board of Directors in the management of the business and affairs of the corporation with the exception of any power or authority the delegation of which is prohibited by Section 141 of the General Corporation Law, and may authorize the seal of the corporation to be affixed to all papers which may require it.

7. <u>WRITTEN ACTION</u>. Any action required or permitted to be taken at any meeting of the Board of Directors or any committee thereof may be taken without a meeting if all members of the Board or committee, as the case may be, consent thereto in writing or by electronic transmission, and the writing or writings or electronic transmission or transmissions are filed with the minutes of proceedings of the Board or committee.

<u>ARTICLE III</u>

<u>OFFICERS</u>

The officers of the corporation shall consist of a President, a Secretary, a Treasurer, and, if deemed necessary, expedient, or desirable by the Board of Directors, a Chairperson of the Board, a Vice-Chairperson of the Board, an Executive Vice-President, one or more other Vice-Presidents, one or more Assistant Secretaries, one or more Assistant Treasurers, and such other officers with such titles as the resolution of the Board of Directors choosing them shall designate. Except as may otherwise be provided in the resolution of the Board of Directors choosing such officer, no officer other than the Chairperson or Vice-Chairperson of the Board, if any, need be a director. Any number of offices may be held by the same person, as the directors may determine.

Unless otherwise provided in the resolution choosing such officer, each officer shall be chosen for a term which shall continue until the meeting of the Board of Directors following the next annual meeting of stockholders and until such officer's successor shall have been chosen and qualified.

All officers of the corporation shall have such authority and perform such duties in the management and operation of the corporation as shall be prescribed in the resolutions of the Board of Directors designating and choosing such officers and prescribing their authority and duties, and shall have such additional authority and duties as are incident to their office except to the extent that such resolutions may be inconsistent therewith. The Secretary or an Assistant Secretary of the corporation shall record all of the proceedings of all meetings and actions in writing of stockholders, directors, and committees of directors, and shall exercise such additional authority and perform such additional duties as the Board shall assign to such Secretary or Assistant Secretary. Any officer may be removed, with or without cause, by the Board of Directors. Any vacancy in any office may be filled by the Board of Directors.

ARTICLE IV

CORPORATE SEAL

The corporate seal shall be in such form as the Board of Directors shall prescribe.

ARTICLE V

FISCAL YEAR

The fiscal year of the corporation shall be fixed, and shall be subject to change, by the Board of Directors.

ARTICLE VI

CONTROL OVER BYLAWS

Subject to the provisions of the certificate of incorporation and the provisions of the General Corporation Law, the power to amend, alter, or repeal these Bylaws and to adopt new Bylaws may be exercised by the Board of Directors or by the stockholders.

I HEREBY CERTIFY that the foregoing is a full, true, and correct copy of the Bylaws of _____ , a <State> corporation, as in effect on the date hereof.

Dated:

_____

Secretary of

(SEAL)

Organizational Minutes

Organizational minutes should reflect organizational activities of the corporation and the results of each annual meeting of directors and shareholders. Organizational minutes of directors may address the following:

- ✔ Approval of articles of incorporation and bylaws.

- ✔ Adoption of stock certificate to be used to evidence ownership of corporate shares.

- ✔ Approval of corporate seal, if one is to be used.

- ✔ Appointment of corporate officers.

- ✔ Authorization of the filing of an S corporation election form if that status is desired.

- ✔ Approval of Internal Revenue Code Section 1244 plan to issue small business corporation stock (optional).

- ✔ Issuance of shares (recite the names of the persons to receive shares, the number and class of shares to receive, and the consideration to be received in exchange for the shares and that when shares are issued and payment made, the shares will be fully paid and non-assessable).

- ✔ Designation of bank accounts and borrowing authority specifying the bank and the persons who have check writing and withdrawal authority.

- ✔ Approval and authority to execute any lease or purchase of office space or special equipment necessary for the business.

- ✔ Any other matters on the checklist that arise at the time of organization. If the directors aren't named in the articles, the incorporator should designate the initial directors in writing prior to the organizational minutes of the directors. This designation should also appear in the corporate minute book.

Sample Organizational Minutes Template
<Company Name>

Consent by Directors to Resolutions in Lieu of Organizational Meeting

<Date>

The undersigned, being all of the directors of **<Company Name>**, an <State of Incorporation> corporation, acting in accordance with the <State of Incorporation> Business Corporation Act, hereby consent

to the adoption of the following recitals and resolutions as if adopted at a duly called meeting of the board of directors of the corporation:

1. RESOLVED, that the bylaws attached hereto be and the same are hereby approved and adopted as the bylaws of the corporation.

   RESOLVED, that the specimen stock certificate attached hereto is approved as the stock certificate to be used by this corporation in conjunction with the issuance of its stock.

2. RESOLVED, that the corporate seal which is affixed to these resolutions be and the same is hereby approved as the official seal of the corporation.

3. RESOLVED, that the following persons are hereby appointed to serve in the offices which appear next to their names until their successors shall be duly appointed and shall qualify:

Name	Office
<Insert President's Name>	President
<Insert Vice-President's Name>	Vice-President
<Insert Secretary/Treasurer Name>	Secretary and Treasurer

4. RESOLVED, that this corporation shall issue against payment therefore <insert # of shares, type and par value of stock>, to each of <insert shareholder names> in exchange for the payment of <insert amounts of payment by shareholders, i.e., $1,000, etc.> by each, and that when payment is received, the shares shall be issued and shall be considered fully paid and non-assessable;

   FURTHER RESOLVED, that upon payment, <if applicable, insert allocation amounts of each director's payment> shall be allocated to the stated capital of the corporation and the remainder shall be allocated to the additional paid in capital of the corporation.

5. <Use only for S Corporation Designation, otherwise delete this section> RESOLVED, that this corporation elects to be treated as an S corporation, and in that regard shall cause the filing of an appropriate election on Internal Revenue Service *Form 2553.*

6. RESOLVED, that the president of the corporation is authorized to establish such depositary accounts for the corporation as she may deem necessary, acting on behalf of the corporation.

7. RESOLVED, that the actions of the officers and directors of this corporation in support of its incorporation are hereby approved, ratified, adopted, and confirmed.

8. RESOLVED, that the officers and directors of this corporation are authorized and directed to perform any and all acts and execute and deliver
any and all documents necessary to effectuate the foregoing resolutions.

_____

\<Insert Name\>

_____

\<Insert Name\>

_____

\<Insert Name\>

Being all of the Directors of the Corporation

Appendix B

Resources

● ●

Contacts for Your State of Incorporation

Alabama Secretary of State
Corporations Division
11 South Union Street, Suite 207
Montgomery, AL 36103-5616
Phone: 334-242-5324
www.sos.state.
al.us/business/
corporations.cfm

Alaska Department of Commerce & Economic Development
Division of Banking, Securities, and Corporations
State Office Building
P.O. Box 110808
Juneau, AK 99801-0808
Phone: 907-465-2530
Fax: 907-465-2549
www.dced.state.ak.us/bsc/
corps.htm

Arizona Corporation Commission
Tucson Corporations Division
400 West Congress
Tucson, AZ 85701-1347
Phone: 602-542-3135
Fax: 602-542-4990
www.cc.state.az.us/corp/
index.htm

Arkansas Corporations Division
Aegon Building
501 Woodlane, Suite 310
Little Rock, AR 72201
Phone: 501-682-3409 or 888-233-0325
www.sosweb.state.ar.us/
business.html

California Secretary of State
Corporations Unit and Branch Offices
1500 11th Street
Sacramento, CA 95814
Phone: 916-657-5448
www.ss.ca.gov/business/corp/
corporate.htm

Colorado Secretary of State
Corporations Office
1560 Broadway, Suite 200
Denver, CO 80202
Phone: 303-894-2251 or 303-894-2242
www.sos.state.co.us/pubs/
business/main.htm

Connecticut Secretary of State
Commercial Recording Division
30 Trinity Street
Hartford, CT 06106
Phone: 860-509-6001
Fax: 860-509-6068
www.sots.state.ct.us/
CommericalRecording/
CRDIndex.html

Delaware Secretary of State
Division of Corporations
401 Federal Street, Suite 4
Dover, DE 19901
Phone: 302-739-3073
Fax: 302-739-3812
www.state.de.us/corp/corp.htm

District of Columbia Department of Consumer and Regulatory Affairs
Corporations Division
941 North Capitol Street, N.E.,
Washington, DC 20002
Phone: 202-442-4400
Fax: 202-442-9445
www.dcra.org

Florida Secretary of State
Division of Corporations
P. O. Box 6327
Tallahassee, FL 32314
409 East Gaines Street
Tallahassee, FL 32399
Phone: 850-488-9000
www.dos.state.fl.us/doc/index.html

Georgia Secretary of State
Corporations Division
315 West Tower
2 Martin Luther King, Jr. Drive
Atlanta, GA 30334
Phone: 404-656-2817
Fax: 404-657-2248
www.sos.state.ga.us/corporations

Hawaii Department of Commerce and Consumer Affairs
Business Registration Division
1010 Richards Street
P.O. Box 40
Honolulu, HI 96813-2920
Phone: 808-586-2744
www.businessregistrations.com

Idaho Secretary of State
Corporations Division
700 West Jefferson,
Room 203
P.O. Box 83720
Boise, ID 83720-0080
Phone: 208-334-2300
Fax: 208-334-2282
www.idsos.state.id.us/

Illinois Secretary of State
Corporations Division
213 State Capitol
Springfield, IL 62706
Phone: 800-252-8980
www.sos.state.il.us/services/services_business.html

Indiana Secretary of State
Corporations Division
State House, Room 201
Indianapolis, IN 46204
Phone: 317-232-6576
Fax: 317-233-3283
www.state.in.us/sos/

Iowa Secretary of State
Business Services Division
1305 East Walnut
2nd Floor Hoover Building
Des Moines, IA 50319
Phone: 515-281-5204
www.sos.state.ia.us/business/services.html

Kansas Secretary of State
Corporations Division
120 S.W. 10th Avenue, Room 100
Topeka, KS 66612-1240
Phone: 785-296-4564
Fax: 785-296-4570
www.kssos.org/corpwelc.html

Kentucky Secretary of State
Corporations Division
700 Capital Avenue, Suite 152
State Capitol
Frankfort, KY 40601
Phone: 502-564-3490
Fax: 502-564-5687
www.sos.state.ky.us/

Louisiana Secretary of State
Commercial Division
P.O. Box 94125
Baton Rouge, LA 70804-9125
Phone: 225-925-4704
www.sec.state.la.us/omm/
comm-index.htm

Maine Secretary of State
Division of Corporations
101 State House Station
Augusta, ME 04333-0101
Phone: 207-287-4190
Fax: 207-287-5874
www.state.me.us/sos/cec/
corp/corp.htm

**Maryland State Department of
Assessments and Taxation**
Corporate Charter Division
301 West Preston Street
Baltimore, MD 21201
Phone: 410-767-1340
www.dat.state.md.us/
sdatweb/charter.html

**Massachusetts Secretary of the
Commonwealth**
Corporations Division
One Ashburton Place, 17th floor
Boston, MA 02108
Phone: 617-727-9640
www.state.ma.us/sec/cor/
coridx.htm

Michigan Department of Commerce
Corporation Division
6546 Mercantile Way
Lansing, MI 48911
P.O. Box 30054
Lansing, MI 48909
Phone: 517-241-6470
www.commerce.state.mi.us/
bcs/corp/

Minnesota Secretary of State
Business Services
180 State Office Building
St. Paul, MN 55155
Phone: 651-296-2803
Fax: 651-215-0683
www.sos.state.mn.us/business/
index.html

Mississippi Secretary of State
Corporate Division
202 North Congress Street, Suite 601
Jackson, MS 39201
P.O. Box 136
Jackson, MS 39205
Phone: 800-256-3494 or 601-359-1633
Fax: 601-359-1607
www.sos.state.ms.us/busserv/
corp/corporations.html

Missouri Secretary of State
Corporation Bureau
P.O. Box 778
Jefferson City, MO 65102-0778
Phone: 573-751-4153
www.mosl.sos.state.mo.us/
busser/soscor.html

Montana Secretary of State
Business Services Bureau
State Capitol, Room 225
P.O. Box 202801
Helena, MT 59620-2801
Phone: 406-444-3665
Fax: 406-444-3976
www.state.mt.us/sos/Business_
Services/business_services.
html

Nebraska Secretary of State
Room 1305, State Capitol
P.O. Box 94608
Lincoln, NE 68509-4608
Phone: 402-471-4079
Fax: 402-471-3666
www.nol.org/home/SOS/htm/
services.htm

Nevada Secretary of State
Commercial Recordings Division
101 North Carson Street, Suite 3
Carson City, NV 89701-4786
Phone: 775-684-5708
sos.state.nv.us/comm_rec/

New Hampshire Secretary of State
Corporate Division
State House, Room 204
Concord, NH 03301
Phone: 603-271-3244
www.state.nh.us/sos/corporate/
index.htm

New Jersey Secretary of State
Commercial Recording Division
30 Trinity Street
Hartford, CT 06106
Phone: 860-509-6002
Fax: 860-509-6068
www.sots.state.ct.us/

New Mexico Public Regulation Commission
P.E.R.A. Building
1120 Paseo de Peralta
P.O. Box 1269
Santa Fe, NM 87504
Phone: 505-827-4508
www.nmprc.state.nm.us/

New York Department of State
Division of Corporations
41 State Street
Albany, NY 12231-0001
Phone: 518-473-2492
Fax: 518-474-1418
www.dos.state.ny.us/corp/
corpwww.html

North Carolina Secretary of State
Corporations Division
P.O. Box 29622
Raleigh, NC 27626-0622
Phone: 919-807-2225
Fax: 919-807-2039
www.secretary.state.nc.us/
Corporations/

North Dakota Secretary of State
Business Information and Registration
600 East Boulevard Avenue, Dept. 108
Bismarck, ND 58505-0500
Phone: 701-328-4284 or toll free
800-352-0867 ext. 4284
Fax: 701-328-2992
www.state.nd.us/sec/

Ohio Secretary of State
Business Services Division
180 East Broad Street, 16th Floor
Columbus, OH 43215
Phone: 614-466-3910 or toll free
1-877-SOS-FILE
Fax: 614-466-3899
www.state.oh.us/sos/
busserinfo.html

Oklahoma Secretary of State
Business Filing Department
2300 North Lincoln Boulevard,
Room 101
Oklahoma City, OK 73105-4897
Phone: 405-522-4560
Fax: 405-521-3771
www.sos.state.ok.us/

Oregon Secretary of State
Corporation Division
Public Service Building
255 Capitol Street N.E., Suite 151
Salem, OR 97310-1327
Phone: 503-986-2200
www.sos.state.or.us/
corporation/corphp.htm

Pennsylvania Department of State
Corporation Bureau
P.O. Box 8722
Harrisburg, PA 17105-8722
Phone: 717-787-1057
www.dos.state.pa.us/corps/
corp.html

Rhode Island Secretary of State
Corporations Division
100 North Main Street, 1st Floor
Providence, RI 02903-1335
Phone: 401-222-3040
Fax: 401-222-1309
www.sec.state.ri.us/

South Carolina Secretary of State
Wade Hampton Office Building
Box 11350
Columbia, SC 29211
Phone: 803-734-2170 or 803-734-2155
www.scsos.com/

South Dakota Secretary of State
Corporate Division
Capitol Building
500 East Capitol Avenue, Suite 204
Pierre, SD 57501-5070
Phone: 605-773-4845
Fax: 605-773-4550
www.state.sd.us/sos/
sos.htm

Tennessee Secretary of State
Corporate Division
312 Eighth Avenue North
6th Floor, William R. Snodgrass Tower
Nashville, TN 37243
Phone: 615-741-2286
www.state.tn.us/sos/
service.htm

Texas Secretary of State
Corporations Division
P.O. Box 13697
Austin, TX 78711
1019 Brazos
Austin, TX 78701
Phone: 512-463-5555
www.sos.state.tx.us/corp/
index.shtml

Utah Department of Commerce
Division of Corporations and
Commercial Code
160 East 300 South
Salt Lake City, UT 84111
Phone: 801-530-4849 or 877-526-3994
www.commerce.state.ut.us/
corporat/corpcoc.htm

Vermont Secretary of State
Corporations Division
81 River Street, Drawer 09
Montpelier, VT 05609-1104
Phone: 802-828-2386
www.sec.state.vt.us/corps/
corpindex.htm

**Virginia State Corporation
Commission**
Office of the Clerk of Commission
P.O. Box 1197
Richmond, VA 23218
Phone: 804-371-9967
www.state.va.us/scc/

Washington Secretary of State
Corporations Division
801 Capitol Way South
P.O. Box 40234
Olympia, WA 98504-0234
Phone: 360-753-7115
www.secstate.wa.gov/corps/
default.htm

West Virginia Secretary of State
Corporations Division
Building 1, Suite 157-K
1900 Kanawha Boulevard East
Charleston, WV 25305-0770
Phone: 304-558-8000
Fax: 304-558-0900
www.state.wv.us/sos/corp/
default.htm

Wisconsin Department of Financial Institutions
Division of Corporate and Consumer
Services
Corporations Section,
3rd Floor
P.O. Box 7846
Madison, WI 53707-7846
Phone: 608-261-7577
Fax: 608-267-6813
www.wdfi.org/corporations/

Wyoming Secretary of State
Corporations Division
The Capitol
Cheyenne, WY 82002-0020
Phone: 307-777-5334
Fax: 307-777-5339
soswy.state.wy.us/corporat/
corporat.htm

The National Association of Secretaries of State (NASS)
www.nass.org

Additional Resources

ChamberBiz
1155 15th Street, Northwest, Suite 810
Washington, DC 20005
Phone: 888-948-1429
www.chamberbiz.com

The Company Corporation
2711 Centerville Road
Wilmington, DE 19808
Phone: 888-811-0111
www.incorporate.com

DIV2000
200 Pequot Avenue
Southport, CT 06490
www.div2000.com
E-mail: Admin@DIV2000.com

Find Law
1235 Pear Avenue #111
Mountain View, CA 94043
Phone: 650-210-1900
Fax: 650-940-4490
www.Findlaw.com

Inc.com
100 First Avenue, 4th Floor
Building #36
Charlestown, MA 02129
www.inc.com

The Legal Information Institute at Cornell University
www.law.cornell.edu

Martindale-Hubbel
www.lawyers.com

National Association for the Self-Employed
NASE Membership Services
P.O. Box 612067, DFW Airport
Dallas, TX 75261-2067
Phone: 800-232-6273
www.nase.org

National Association of Female Executives (NAFE)
P.O. Box 469031
Escondido, CA 92046-9925
Phone: 800-634-NAFE

National Association of Women Business Owners (NAWBO)
1411 K Street, N.W., Suite 1300
Washington, DC 20005
Phone: 800-556-2926
www.nawbo.org

National Black Business Council, Inc.
1100 Wayne Avenue, Suite 850
Silver Spring, MD 20910
Phone: 301-585-6222 or 888-264-6222
www.nbbc.org
E-mail: nbbc.admin@nbbc.org

National Business Association
P.O. Box 700728
Dallas, TX 75370
Phone: 800-456-0440 or 972-458-0900
Fax: 972-960-9149
www.nationalbusiness.org

National Federation of Independent Business
53 Century Boulevard, Suite 300
Nashville, TN 37214
Phone: 800-NFIB-NOW or
615-872-5300
www.nfib.com

nolo.com Law Center
1-800-728-3555
www.nolo.com
E-mail: cs@nolo.com

Online Women's Business Center
www.onlinewbc.org
E-mail: nafe@nafe.com

SCORE
409 Third Street, Southwest, 6th Floor
Washington, DC 20024
Phone: 202-205-6762 or 800-634-0245
Fax: 202-205-7636
www.score.org
E-mail: contact.score@sba.gov

Small Business School
P.O. Box 23100
New Orleans, LA 70183
Phone: 504-737-0089
www.SmallBusinessSchool.org

U.S. Chamber of Commerce
1615 H Street, N.W.
Washington, DC 20062-2000
Phone: 202-669-6000
www.Uschamber.org

U.S. Patent and Trademark Office
Crystal Plaza 3, Room 2C02
Washington, DC 20231
Phone: 800-786-9199
www.uspto.gov

U.S. Small Business Administration
www.sba.gov/sbdc

Appendix C

Glossary

. . . .

acquisition: Obtaining control of another corporation by purchasing all or a majority of its outstanding shares, or by purchasing its assets.

administrative dissolution: An involuntary dissolution of a corporation by an act of the Secretary of State or similar state authority, caused by the corporation's failure to comply with certain statutory requirements; especially the failure to file an annual report, to pay franchise taxes, or to maintain a valid registered agent.

advisory board of directors: An advisory board of directors are individuals appointed to advise an elected board of directors. This board isn't bound by the duties imposed upon elected board members, and the corporation isn't required to follow their recommendations.

agent: Anyone who is authorized to act on the behalf of another. A corporation acts only through its agents; therefore, it's important to define what actions an agent is authorized to perform.

agent for service of process: An agent, required to be appointed by a corporation, whose authority is generally limited to receiving process issued against the corporation. Also known as a registered agent or a resident agent.

amended certificate of authority: A document issued by a state to a foreign corporation evidencing that the corporation has amended its original certificate of authority.

amendment: An addition to, deletion from, or a change of existing provisions of the articles of incorporation of a domestic corporation.

annual meeting: A yearly meeting of shareholders at which directors are elected and other general business of the corporation is conducted.

annual report: A required annual filing in a state, usually listing directors, officers, and financial information. Also, an annual statement of business and affairs furnished by a corporation to its shareholders.

application for certificate of authority: The form filed in many states to qualify a corporation to transact business as a foreign corporation.

articles of incorporation: The document filed with the local secretary of state's office or corporation division. When filed with and approved by the secretary of state, the corporation comes into existence. Articles are a public record. Also known as the certificate of incorporation or corporate charter.

articles of organization: The title of the document filed in many states to register a limited liability company (LLC) with the state. Also known as articles of formation.

assumed name: A name other than the true name, under which a corporation or other business organization conducts business. Also referred to as a fictitious name, a trade name, or "doing business as" (d/b/a).

authorized shares: The maximum number of shares that a corporation may issue pursuant to its articles of incorporation.

basis: Basis is a tax and accounting term. With stock, basis is what you pay for stock and the fair market value of any property you contribute as payment for stock. Your gain or loss upon the sale or transfer of stock is measured against your basis in stock. If you sell for more than your basis, you have gain. If you sell for less, you have a loss.

board of directors: Board members are elected by shareholders to govern the business of the corporation. The board sets policy, appoints officers, and oversees the general operations of the corporation.

bond: A long-term debt secured by a mortgage on real property or a lien on other fixed assets.

business corporation act: A business corporation act is the collection of laws in each state that governs corporations.

business judgment rule: A court-based rule that can protect officers and directors from liability for their actions. Directors or officers can avoid liability if disinterested actions are taken in good faith with reasonable care. To use reasonable care, among other things, directors should take steps to make certain that they are kept informed about corporate matters.

buy and sell agreement: An arrangement whereby the surviving shareholders, or the corporation itself, agree to purchase the shares of a disabled, bankrupt, withdrawing, or deceased shareholder. This agreement provides for the orderly transition of shares by establishing a value for the shares to be purchased. Also known as stock purchase agreement.

bylaws: Bylaws are the internal regulations of a corporation that provide rules for the conduct of the corporation's business and affairs. In the event of a conflict between the state corporation law, articles of incorporation, and bylaws, the corporation law prevails over the articles, which prevail over the bylaws.

certificate of authority: The certificate of authority is the official document issued by a secretary of state to a foreign corporation that has successfully qualified to do business in that state.

certificate of good standing: A certificate issued by a state official as conclusive evidence that a corporation is in existence or authorized to transact business in the state. The certificate may set forth the corporation's name; that it is duly incorporated or authorized to transact business; that all fees, taxes, and penalties owed the state have been paid; that its most recent annual report has been filed; and, that articles of dissolution have not been filed. Also known as a certificate of existence or certificate of authorization.

certificate of incorporation: The title of the document filed in many states to create a corporation. Also known as the articles of incorporation or corporate charter.

close corporation: A corporation that elects in its articles of incorporation to be registered under the close corporation statutes of its state of incorporation. Some state close corporation statutes provide for a maximum number of shareholders. In addition, close corporation statutes may eliminate or limit the powers of the board of directors, prescribe preemptive rights to the shareholders, or relax the corporate formalities. Exact specifications vary by jurisdiction. Not all state statutes provide for a close corporation provision.

closely held corporation: Any corporation with shares that aren't traded on a public stock exchange. There are many more closely held corporations than close corporations.

common shares: A class of shares that has no special features and possesses no greater rights than any other shares.

consent resolutions: Any board or shareholder resolution signed and dated by the directors or shareholders of a corporation to authorize particular corporate action. Consent resolutions are often used for the convenience of directors and shareholders because they permit action to be authorized without requiring a formal meeting of directors or shareholders.

consolidation: The statutory combination of two or more corporations to create a new corporation.

constituent: A party to a transaction; a corporation involved in a merger, consolidation, or share exchange.

convertible security: A security that may be converted into another type of security.

corporate indicator: A word or an abbreviation of a word that must be included in a corporation's name to indicate that the named entity is a corporation. Valid corporate indicators include: incorporated, corporation, limited, company, inc., corp., ltd., and co. The list of acceptable corporate indicators will vary depending on where the corporation is registered.

corporate kit: A binder usually containing essential items for the routine maintenance and administration of a corporation or limited liability company. Corporate kits may include sample minutes and bylaws, stock certificates, a corporate seal, and stock ledger.

corporate opportunity: Corporate opportunity is a court-developed doctrine that precludes corporate directors, officers, and employees from taking personal advantage of certain business-related opportunities without first presenting the opportunity to the corporation to accept or reject. A director or officer who takes personal advantage of a business opportunity that the corporation could reasonably be expected to have an interest in could breach his or her duty to the corporation.

corporate seal: A corporate seal is a device made to either emboss or imprint certain company information onto documents. This information usually includes the company's name and date and state of formation. Corporate seals are often required when opening corporate or LLC bank accounts, distributing stock or membership certificates, or conducting other corporate business.

corporation: An artificial entity created under and governed by the laws of the state of incorporation.

corporation law: The statutory provisions of a state relating to domestic and foreign corporations.

cumulative voting: A procedure used for electing directors in which shareholders are entitled to multiply the number of votes they are entitled to cast by the number of directors for whom they are entitled to vote and cast the product for a single candidate or distribute the product among two or more candidates.

debenture: A long-term debt issued mainly to evidence an unsecured corporate debt.

debt: Debt is money or some other legal obligation owed to another. Commonly, debt results when you borrow money from another. With debt, the borrower and lender expect that the amounts borrowed will be repaid.

debt financing: A method of raising capital in which a corporation borrows money.

derivative action: A lawsuit by a shareholder on behalf of the corporation. It occurs whenever the corporation, acting through its board of directors or officers, fails to take action. Generally, a derivative action may only be filed after a demand has been made by the shareholders on the corporate board to take the proposed action, and the board refused to honor the demand. The lawsuit seeks to compel the corporation to take the required action.

derivative suit: A lawsuit brought by a shareholder on behalf of a corporation to protect the corporation from wrongs committed against it.

direct action: A lawsuit by a shareholder seeking to redress a wrong imposed on the shareholder filing the lawsuit. For example, if a corporation failed to pay a required dividend to a particular preferred shareholder, the preferred shareholder could file a direct action. A direct action involves harm to a particular shareholder. A derivative action generally involves harm to the corporation.

directors: The individuals who, acting as a group known as the board of directors, manage the business and affairs of a corporation.

dissenters right: A right granted to shareholders that entitles them to have their shares appraised and, in effect, purchased by the corporation if the corporation enters into certain transactions that the shareholders do not approve of.

dissolution/liquidation: Procedures by which a corporation ceases to engage in business. The process can be voluntary or involuntary. When in dissolution, all corporate activities must be focused on winding up the business and affairs of the corporation.

distribution: A transfer of money or other property made by a corporation to a shareholder in respect of the corporation's shares.

dividend: A distribution of corporate assets to its shareholders. Dividends generally are paid out of the corporation's net earnings and profits. The board of directors determines whether dividends are to be paid.

domain name: A unique identifier, similar to a telephone number, used to locate Web sites or e-mail addresses on the World Wide Web.

equity: Often described as funds provided by shareholders as payment for their stock. Equity capital is money and the value of property or services contributed to the capital of the corporation. Unlike debt, there is no legal obligation to repay the contributions.

equity financing: A method of raising capital in which a corporation sells shares of stock.

equity interest: An ownership interest; the interest of a shareholder as distinguished from that of a creditor.

fictitious name: A name other than the true name, under which a corporation or other business organization conducts business. Also referred to as an assumed name, a trade name, or "doing business as" (d/b/a).

fiduciary relationship: A relationship in which one party (the fiduciary) must act in good faith and with due regard to the best interests of the other party or parties.

foreign corporation: A term applied to a corporation doing business in a state other than its state of incorporation.

fractional share: Ownership in a corporation in an amount less than a full share.

franchise tax: A tax or fee usually levied annually upon a corporation, limited liability company, or similar business entity for the right to exist or do business in a particular state. Failure to pay the franchise tax or similar fees may result in the administrative dissolution of the company and forfeiture of the charter.

going public: The process by which a corporation first sells its shares to the public.

hostile takeover: A takeover that occurs without the approval of the target corporation's board of directors.

hybrid: In the context of this book, a hybrid is any interest in a corporation that has both debt and equity characteristics. For example, a debt might be convertible into shares of stock. The document creating the hybrid would specify the terms and conditions upon which the conversion could occur.

incorporation: The act of creating or organizing a corporation under the laws of a specific jurisdiction.

incorporator: The person or persons who sign the articles of incorporation prior to submitting the articles to the secretary of state or other appropriate office.

indemnification: A process by which corporate officers or directors may be reimbursed for expenses or liabilities incurred by virtue of being an officer or director.

involuntary dissolution: The termination of a corporation's legal existence pursuant to an administrative or judicial proceeding; dissolution forced upon a corporation rather than decided upon by the corporation.

judicial dissolution: Involuntary dissolution of a corporation by a court at the request of the state attorney general, a shareholder, or a creditor.

limited liability: One of the key benefits of incorporation; restricts the personal liability of corporate shareholders to the amount paid by the shareholders for their stock. To obtain this benefit, corporations must adhere to the organizational, maintenance, and compliance requirements prescribed by law.

limited liability company (LLC): A noncorporate form of business organization created as a separate legal entity under state statute. An LLC is governed in accordance with state law and the terms and conditions of an operating agreement. Owners of an LLC are referred to as members rather than shareholders. LLCs are generally able to provide the limited personal liability of corporations and the pass-through taxation of partnerships or S corporations.

limited partnership: A statutory form of partnership consisting of one or more general partners who manage the business and are liable for its debts, and one or more limited partners who invest in the business and have limited personal liability.

limited personal liability: The protection generally afforded a corporate shareholder, limited partner, or a member of a limited liability company from the debts of and claims against the company.

majority: More than 50 percent; commonly used as the percentage of votes required to approve certain corporate actions.

management: The board of directors and executive officers of a corporation, limited liability company, or similar business entity.

managers: The individuals who may be responsible for the maintenance, administration, and management of the affairs of a limited liability company (LLC). In some states, the managers serve a particular term and report to and serve at the discretion of the members. Specific duties of the managers may be detailed in the articles of organization or the operating agreement of the LLC. In some states, the members of an LLC may also serve as the managers.

members: The owner(s) of a limited liability company (LLC). Unless the articles of organization or operating agreement provide otherwise, management of an LLC is vested in the members in proportion to their ownership interest in the company.

membership certificates: Evidence of ownership of and membership in a limited liability company.

memorandum of action: A written summary of action taken or to be taken by directors. Memorializes actions taken by consent, rather than by a formal meeting.

merger: The statutory combination of two or more corporations in which one of the corporations survives and the other corporations cease to exist.

minority shareholder: A minority shareholder is any shareholder owning less than 50 percent of the issued and outstanding stock of the corporation.

minutes: The corporate minutes are the written record of transactions taken or authorized by the board of directors or shareholders. These are usually kept in the corporate minute book.

name registration: The filing of a document in a foreign state to protect the corporate name, often in anticipation of qualification in the state.

name reservation: A procedure that allows a corporation to obtain exclusive use of a corporate name for a specified period of time.

no par value shares: Shares for which the articles of incorporation don't fix a par value and that may be issued for any consideration determined by the board of directors.

not-for-profit corporation: A not-for-profit corporation is organized for some socially beneficial purpose, rather than for the direct monetary benefit of the directors or members. Not all not-for-profit corporations are tax exempt, and some make a profit. However, the profit isn't distributed to the members or directors. Also known as a non-profit corporation.

officers: Officers are appointed by the board of directors and are responsible for the day-to-day activities of the corporation. Common offices include president, secretary, and treasurer.

operating agreement: A contract among the members of a limited liability company governing the membership, management, operation, and distribution of income of the company.

organizational meetings: Meetings of incorporators or initial directors that are held after the filing of the articles of incorporation to complete the organization of the corporation.

organizer: The person(s) who perform the act of forming a limited liability company.

par value: A minimum price of a share below which the share cannot be issued, as designated in the articles of incorporation.

parent corporation: A corporation that owns a controlling interest in another corporation.

partnership: Any business association in which two or more persons agree to do business together. Various forms of partnership exist: a general partnership, a limited partnership, and a limited liability partnership.

pass through: In the context of corporations, pass through is a tax concept. It occurs in S corporations where tax attributes like income, gain, or loss are passed through to the shareholders and taxed at the shareholder level and not at the corporation level. Partnerships and limited liability companies also may enjoy pass-through taxation.

perpetual existence: Unlimited term of existence; characteristic of most business corporations.

piercing the corporate veil: A legal theory sometimes used to impose personal liability on shareholders, officers, and directors for corporate acts. This theory permits a court to disregard the separate identity of the corporation.

plurality: In general, a plurality is the largest of several numbers that may be less than a majority. It's important in the context of shareholder elections of directors. Directors typically are elected by a plurality vote.

pooling agreement: Any shareholder agreement where shareholders decide to pool their votes together on matters presented to the shareholders for decision. Most often, the pooling agreement will relate to the election of corporate directors.

preemptive rights: Preemptive rights, if they exist, protect the right of shareholders to maintain their proportionate interest in corporate stock. If preemptive rights exist, a corporation generally may not issue new shares of stock without first offering existing shareholders the opportunity to acquire that number of shares that would enable the shareholder to maintain his or her ownership interest. For example, you own 10 percent of the outstanding stock of ABC Corporation, and ABC proposes to issue an additional 100 shares of stock. If preemptive rights exist, you would have the right to purchase 10 additional shares, keeping your ownership interest at 10 percent. Like cumulative voting, preemptive rights exist automatically in some states unless you exclude them in the articles. In other states, preemptive rights don't apply at all unless you expressly include them in the articles.

preferred shares: A class of shares that entitles the holders to preferences over the holders of common shares, usually with regard to dividends and distributions of assets upon dissolution or liquidation.

pre-incorporation: The period of time prior to filing and approval of the articles is the pre-incorporation period. Individuals carrying out activities in support of the corporation during this time period are known as promoters. Promoters may be liable for all actions taken during the pre-incorporation period.

pro rata: Pro rata means proportionately. In the context of this book, S corporation shareholders receive a pro rata pass through of certain tax attributes such as income, gain, loss, deduction, or credit. If you own 10 percent of the stock of the S corporation, your pro rata share of these items would be 10 percent.

professional corporation: A corporation whose purposes are limited to professional services, such as those performed by doctors, dentists, and attorneys. A professional corporation is formed under special state laws that may stipulate exactly which professionals are required to incorporate under this status.

promissory note: A written promise to pay a specified sum within a stated amount of time at a stated amount of interest, if any.

promoter: One who generates interest and activity in and on behalf of a corporation before its formation. A promoter is usually personally liable for all pre-incorporation activities.

proxy: Shareholders may vote by proxy. A proxy is a written authorization signed by a shareholder authorizing another to vote his or her shares. Proxies are generally revocable.

qualification: The filing of required documents by a foreign corporation to secure a certificate of authority to conduct its business in a state other than the one in which it was incorporated. Limited liability companies or similar business entities may also conduct this process.

quorum: A quorum is that number of officers or directors who must be present at a meeting in order for action to be taken. Generally, a quorum is at least a majority of all directors or shareholders owning at least a majority of the outstanding shares. Quorum requirements can be raised or lowered (within limits). Corporate bylaws usually list the quorum requirements for a particular corporation.

record date: A date fixed by corporate bylaws or resolution of the corporate board that determines, for example, the shareholders who are eligible to vote or receive a dividend. You must be a shareholder as of the record date in order to vote at the relevant meeting or receive the relevant dividend.

redeemable shares: Shares subject to purchase by the corporation on terms set forth in the articles of incorporation.

registered agent: A person or entity designated to receive important tax and legal documents (also known as Service of Process) from the state on behalf of the corporation. The registered agent must be located and available at a legal address within the specified jurisdiction at all times. Failure to maintain a registered agent in the jurisdiction in which the corporation is registered may result in the administrative forfeiture of the corporate status. Also known as a resident agent.

registered office: This is the place where the registered agent may be found. If the address changes, a filing with the secretary of state's office or other appropriate state office is generally necessary.

reinstatement: Returning a corporation that has been administratively dissolved or has had its certificate of authority revoked, to good standing on a state's records.

resolution: A formal statement of any corporate board or shareholder decision. Resolutions describe the action or activity being approved and authorize particular officers or employees to carry out the activity. Resolutions are generally found in corporate meeting minutes or consent resolutions.

restated articles of incorporation: A document that combines all currently operative provisions of a corporation's articles of incorporation and amendments.

Revised Model Business Corporation Act (RMBCA): A model corporation statute created by the American Bar Association. Many states have adopted all or parts of the RMBCA as part of their state corporation law.

S corporation: A corporation granted a special tax status as specified under the Internal Revenue Code (IRC). The code is very explicit on how and when this election is made and the number of shareholders this type of corporation can have. Since this type of corporation pays no income tax, all gains and losses of the corporation pass through to the individual shareholders in proportion to their holdings.

scrip: A form used to represent the right to acquire fractional shares in lieu of issuing share certificates.

security: A contract between a business and an investor whereby the investor supplies money and experts to profit from his or her investment.

securities: Securities is a term broadly defined by state and federal securities laws. The term may include, among other things, notes, stock, voting trust certificates, pre-incorporation subscriptions, partnership interests, and limited liability company interests. Federal and state laws restrict both the offer and sale of securities.

securities laws: State and federal laws that govern the issuance, sale, and transfer of stocks and bonds. State securities laws are sometimes referred to as Blue Sky Laws.

service of process: The delivery of a legal or court document to a person who is thereby officially notified of some action or proceeding to which said person is commanded to respond within a stated period of time.

share: The unit into which the ownership interest in a corporation is divided.

share exchange: A statutory form of business combination in which some or all of the shares of one corporation are exchanged for some or all of the shares of another corporation and neither corporation ceases to exist.

shareholder/stockholder: Shareholders own the stock of a corporation, elect directors, and vote on important corporate matters as determined by the corporate statute, articles, or bylaws. In some states, the term, *stockholder* is used instead.

short-form merger: The statutory merger of a subsidiary into its parent corporation in which shareholder approval is not required.

sole proprietorship: An unincorporated business with a sole owner, in which the owner may be personally liable for business debts and claims against the business.

special meeting: A shareholder meeting called so that the shareholders may act on the specific matters stated in the notice of the meeting.

stock: Stock represents ownership of a corporation. Stock is commonly evidenced by the issuance of a certificate for the shares of stock, although many states don't require that a certificate actually be issued. Stock can have many characteristics: common, preferred, convertible, and so on. If the articles permit it, corporations may issue different types of stock, each containing different rights and preferences.

stock certificate: Evidence of ownership of shares in a corporation. May also be referred to as a share certificate.

stock purchase agreement/buy and sell agreement: A stock purchase or buy and sell agreement is any agreement between shareholders and the corporation relating to the ability of a shareholder to sell his or her shares of stock. These agreements often contain requirements for the corporation or other shareholders to buy another shareholder's stock in the event of that shareholder's death, disability, or retirement.

stockholders: Stockholders are the owners of a corporation based on their holdings. They own an interest in the corporation rather than specific corporate property. Also known as shareholders.

subscribers: Persons who agree under specific conditions to purchase shares in a corporation.

subscription: The agreement executed by a subscriber.

subsidiary: A corporation that is either wholly owned or controlled through ownership of a majority of its voting shares by another corporation or business entity.

supermajority: A requirement set forth in articles or bylaws requiring a vote greater than a simple majority in order to accomplish certain tasks. Common examples of circumstances using supermajority requirements include: article or bylaw amendments, decisions to merge or dissolve the corporation, or decisions that would require the expenditure of a large amount of money.

takeover: A merger, acquisition, or other change in the controlling interest of a corporation.

target: A corporation that is the focus of a takeover attempt.

tax-exempt organization: Any organization that is determined by the Internal Revenue Service (IRS) to be exempt from federal taxation of income. A tax-exempt may be required to operate exclusively for charitable, religious, literary, educational, or similar types of purposes.

trademark: A word or mark that distinctly indicates the source of a product or service, and that is legally reserved for the exclusive use of its owner.

treasury shares: Shares of a corporation reacquired by a corporation.

underwriter: A company that purchases shares of a corporation and arranges for their sale to the general public.

voluntary dissolution: Action by shareholders, incorporators, or initial directors to dissolve a corporation.

voting or pooling agreement: Any agreement by two or more shareholders to vote their shares in a particular manner; most often used in the election of directors.

voting rights: Rights of shareholders to vote their shares pursuant to provisions of statutes, the articles of incorporation, and the bylaws.

voting trust agreement: An arrangement among corporate shareholders that occurs when shareholders transfer their shares to a trustee in exchange for voting trust certificates. The trustee votes the shares as a block in the manner provided by the voting trust agreement. It's a means to preserve voting control of the corporation by the shareholders who are parties to the agreement.

watered shares: Shares that have been issued for a consideration less than the par or stated value of the shares.

winding up: The discharging of a corporation's liabilities and the distributing of its remaining assets to its shareholders in connection with its dissolution.

withdrawal: The statutory procedure whereby a foreign corporation obtains the consent of a state to terminate its authority to transact business there.

Index

• O •

Notes

Notes

Realize Your Dreams

For more than 100 years, The Company Corporation® has been helping entrepreneurs, professionals, and start-up business owners take control of their futures. Whatever your venture, we have the expertise you need to put your plans into action. From helping to file and maintain a legal corporation in all 50 states to registering a domain name and putting your company on the Internet, our specialized services make it easy and affordable for you to realize your dreams. Your success has been our business since 1899. **On-line: www.corporate.com/ifd or call: 1-888-811-0111.**

The Company Corporation®

Creating Successful Businesses Since 1899

The Company Corporation is an incorporation service company and does not offer legal or financial advice.

FOR DUMMIES®

A world of resources to help you grow

HOME, GARDEN & HOBBIES

Feng Shui
FOR DUMMIES

A Reference for the Rest of Us!

0-7645-5295-3

Gardening
FOR DUMMIES
2nd Edition

A Reference for the Rest of Us!

0-7645-5130-2

Guitar
FOR DUMMIES

A Reference for the Rest of Us!

0-7645-5106-X

Also available:

Auto Repair For Dummies
(0-7645-5089-6)

Chess For Dummies
(0-7645-5003-9)

Home Maintenance For
Dummies
(0-7645-5215-5)

Organizing For Dummies
(0-7645-5300-3)

Piano For Dummies
(0-7645-5105-1)

Poker For Dummies
(0-7645-5232-5)

Quilting For Dummies
(0-7645-5118-3)

Rock Guitar For Dummies
(0-7645-5356-9)

Roses For Dummies
(0-7645-5202-3)

Sewing For Dummies
(0-7645-5137-X)

FOOD & WINE

Cooking
FOR DUMMIES
2nd Edition

A Reference for the Rest of Us!

0-7645-5250-3

Cookies
FOR DUMMIES

A Reference for the Rest of Us!

0-7645-5390-9

Wine
FOR DUMMIES
2nd Edition

A Reference for the Rest of Us!

0-7645-5114-0

Also available:

Bartending For Dummies
(0-7645-5051-9)

Chinese Cooking For
Dummies
(0-7645-5247-3)

Christmas Cooking For
Dummies
(0-7645-5407-7)

Diabetes Cookbook For
Dummies
(0-7645-5230-9)

Grilling For Dummies
(0-7645-5076-4)

Low-Fat Cooking For
Dummies
(0-7645-5035-7)

Slow Cookers For Dummies
(0-7645-5240-6)

TRAVEL

Italy
FOR DUMMIES
2nd Edition

A Travel Guide for the Rest of Us!

0-7645-5453-0

Hawaii
FOR DUMMIES
2nd Edition

A Travel Guide for the Rest of Us!

0-7645-5438-7

Las Vegas
FOR DUMMIES
2nd Edition

A Travel Guide for the Rest of Us!

0-7645-5448-4

Also available:

America's National Parks For
Dummies
(0-7645-6204-5)

Caribbean For Dummies
(0-7645-5445-X)

Cruise Vacations For
Dummies 2003
(0-7645-5459-X)

Europe For Dummies
(0-7645-5456-5)

Ireland For Dummies
(0-7645-6199-5)

France For Dummies
(0-7645-6292-4)

London For Dummies
(0-7645-5416-6)

Mexico's Beach Resorts For
Dummies
(0-7645-6262-2)

Paris For Dummies
(0-7645-5494-8)

RV Vacations For Dummies
(0-7645-5443-3)

Walt Disney World & Orlando
For Dummies
(0-7645-5444-1)

Available wherever books are sold. Go to www.dummies.com or call 1-877-762-2974 to order direct.

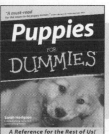

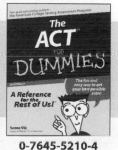

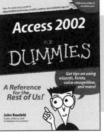